The Great All-American Wooden Toy Book

by Norman Marshall

Rodale Press, Emmaus, Pennsylvania

Printed in the United States of America on recycled paper, containing a high percentage of de-inked fiber.

Senior Editor: Ray Wolf
Produced by Scharff Associates, Ltd.
Editor: Lois Breiner
Writer: Bill Jones
Book Design: Jerry O'Brien
Cover Design: Jerry O'Brien
Cover Photo: Mitch Mandel

Photo Credits
Hands On magazine, Shopsmith, Inc.
Pages: 6, 20, 42, 60, 68, 82, 87, 88, 90, 93, 96, 110, 116, 121, 122, 142
Dayton Commercial Studio
Pages: 2, 8, 14, 28, 36, 44, 52, 72, 76, 102, 152, 159, 162, 172, 174, 177, 180, 183, 200, 204, 207
Illustration Credits
Hands On magazine, Shopsmith, Inc.
Pages: 3, 9, 21, 29, 31, 45, 50, 53, 69, 73, 117, 130, 133, 137, 143, 149, 156, 163, 170, 172, 174, 177, 180, 183, 191, 197

Library of Congress Cataloging-in-Publication Data

Marshall, Norm, 1932–1982.
    The great all-American wooden toy book.

    1. Wooden toy making.   I. Title.
TT174.5.W6M365   1986   745.592   86-15568
ISBN 0-87857-627-4   hardcover
ISBN 0-87857-628-2   paperback

    4   6   8   10   9   7   5   3   hardcover
    4   6   8   10   9   7   5   paperback

Contents

Foreword

Here's a book of woodworking plans that's bound to provide hours and hours of pleasure to woodworkers and children. The plans illustrated and explained within the covers of this book are more than just cut-and-dry how-to instructions for putting together wooden toys. The plans are actually directions for having fun—for both woodworkers and children.

Norman Marshall (1932-1982) led an active life as a naval aviator. Retiring from the Navy after 25 years with more than 5,000 hours of flying time, Norman sought to stay active in civilian life. Casting about for a hobby, he realized that he enjoyed designing things, and also enjoyed the nostalgic smell of fresh-sawn lumber. Because of his active imagination and his love of fun, Norman started designing toys in 1974 and continued to design and build toys until his death in 1982.

This book contains the designs of all the toys Norman had completed. They are the result of many hours of fun—the fun of study, the fun of design, the fun of woodworking, the fun of giving, and the fun of being appreciated. With this book, you'll share in all the fun Norman Marshall had.

Enjoy.

Bill Jones
March 1986

Preface: Making Toys

When I retired from the Navy after spending 25 years as a naval aviator, I looked around for a hobby. I wanted to do something with my life that was relaxing, useful, and fun. Remembering the nostalgic smell of freshly cut wood, I decided that woodworking would be a fun hobby, so I read some books on the topic. One book, *The Art of Making Wooden Toys* by Peter Stevenson, sparked my imagination and stirred my untapped training as an engineer. I knew that toy making was something that I wanted to do.

Stevenson talked about toy making in a way that interested me in the whole process of making toys. I started with the suggestions in his book and a few hand tools. Soon, though, I found hand tools too slow for what I wanted to do, so I purchased power tools to speed up the process. What I came up with is a hobby that suited me perfectly, hours of fun designing, machining, and building toys.

WOOD

The foundation for wooden toys is the wood itself. And there are many kinds, sizes, and types of wood available. Here's a short guide to help you in the selection of the wood best suited for the projects in this book.

For the uninitiated, wood comes in two basic varieties—hardwood and softwood. Hardwoods include oak, walnut, maple, and birch. They are good-looking woods, machine well, and hold finishes and stains nicely.

Softwoods include pine, fir, and cedar. As the name implies, these are softer in texture than hardwoods but have many of the same characteristics. The major difference is that their soft nature makes them easier to cut and sand.

One of the biggest differences between these two types of wood is the price; hardwoods are often two to four times more expensive than softwoods. This is where price makes a big difference in which type of wood you use for making toys.

Toy making is a lot of fun, and it's important that it stays that way. If you spend a lot of money on the wood, it makes the toy into more of a treasure, which takes away from some of its play value. I recommend you minimize your investment in wood for the toys in this book and select softwoods. You'll even find huge price differences between softwoods.

For instance, clear pine is often two to four times more expensive than #2 pine. Clear pine is fine to use and cheaper than many hardwoods, but #2 pine (also known as *construction grade*) is a better value because most of the parts used in toy making are small; as a result, knots can be worked around or hidden in glued-up stock.

Pine is readily available from any home center, lumberyard, or even some discount department stores. Ask your dealer for construction grade or #2 pine.

When looking through the wood selection at the lumberyard, keep the following in mind: Look for boards that are clear and free of knots. *Clear* means there is no bark on the edges or large sap pockets in the wood itself. Make sure the wood is straight and not cupped, bowed, or warped. Crooked wood is hard to work with and can throw measurements off during machining operations. However, because toy parts are small, you might want to go through a lumberyard's discount pile for some good values. Some of these boards can be cut into smaller, workable pieces.

The majority of projects in this book consist of small parts; therefore, I suggest you buy 1 × 4 stock to handle most of your needs.

A 1 × 4 is actually a 3/4"-thick × 3-1/2"-wide board; that's why I usually use increments of 3/4" for most of my projects. And, by gluing wood together, I can make 1-1/2", 2-1/4", and 3"-thick stock by gluing two, three, and four boards together.

Why glue up stock instead of buying thicker boards? I glue up stock to keep the color and grain pattern as consistent as possible throughout a project. The grain of thicker boards may vary because they're from another species of pine or from another tree. Sometimes this variation is considerable, so I always try to get most of the parts of a single toy from the same or similar boards.

If you decide to use hardwoods for these toys, opt for close-grained woods such as maple or birch. Open-grained woods such as oak or ash tend to collect dirt if not finished properly.

Also, some people are allergic to certain woods, including pine. If you make a toy for a child who has a lot of allergies, apply a finish that thoroughly seals the wood.

Wood from the lumberyard is usually already smooth on all four sides and ready to saw, cut, and drill. However, many of the parts in this book do not require wood that is 3/4" thick, but require stock that is 1/4" to 1/2" thick. To get wood from its normal 3/4" thickness to a smaller thickness you have to resaw the 3/4" stock.

Resawing stock can be done either on a table saw, bandsaw, or scroll saw although a bandsaw is the best for this function. To resaw stock, place a rip fence or guide board near the bandsaw blade; the distance is determined by how thick you want the stock. Secure the fence, then push the stock through holding it securely against the rip fence (use a fingerboard for an extra margin of safety). Make sure you push the stock with a pushstick to keep your hands safe.

When using a bandsaw to resaw stock, the saw blade leaves a rough surface. If your shop includes a thickness planer, plane the stock smooth. If you have a jointer, you can surface the stock. **CAUTION:** This is very dangerous. To safely surface stock on a jointer you must take the following precautions:

- Never surface stock less than 1/4" thick.
- Never surface stock less than 12" long.
- Never surface stock without the use of pushblocks.
- Never place your hands directly over the cutterhead (even with pushblocks).

Safe alternatives to surfacing stock are using a belt sander or a hand plane.

Another point about resawing stock: Some of the toy plans call for getting two 3/8"-thick pieces of stock by resawing a 3/4"-thick board. Due to the thickness of the saw blade, these two pieces of stock end up just under 3/8" thick. Actually, you'll get a good 3/8"-thick and 1/4"-thick board from a 3/4"-thick piece of stock. *Good* means that the thickness of the stock is a little thicker than the actual measurement by about 1/32". You can use stock less than or greater than 3/8" thick; simply adjust other measurements as you go.

Some lumberyards and home centers carry a variety of moldings suitable for toy making. Sometimes lumberyards will prepare quantities of special stock for a charge. Check different lumberyards to see if they will prepare stock or, if they can't, ask them where you could have it done.

If stock preparation seems involved to you, because all you really want to do is make a few toys, then here's a simpler method—use plywood. Many times I don't use plywood because I enjoy resawing and forming special lumber—it's a sort of therapy for me. But I understand the needs of others, too, and believe that there's no sacrifice of playability or compromise of quality when using plywood. Plywood is available in 1/4", 3/8", and 1/2" thicknesses, it doesn't warp, and it sands well. If you use plywood, buy quarter or half sheets of good cabinet grade plywood (specify *cabinet grade* or *A-B grade*). Obviously, using plywood is a good way to save time and still achieve great results.

Wood is available from more places than just lumberyards and home centers. You can find lots of different sizes of lumber in some of the most unsuspected places. For instance, if you have an old chest of drawers, look at the sides, bottoms, and backs of the drawers. Chances are these parts are made of a poplar, maple, or pine and varied in thickness. Take an old dresser or similar piece of furniture and salvage the lumber— it's a convenient source.

Another source of unusual lumber is in knickknacks found at flea markets and garage sales. Trays, spice racks, rolling pins (for the Model T tank truck, steamroller, or train tank car) are just a few of the items available. Look beyond the surface of the stock and imagine the rejuvenated bare wood as part of a new toy.

DOWELS

Besides using clear pine for these toys, my designs call for an extensive use of dowel rods for the axles, exhaust stacks, reinforcements, and many, many more parts. Typically available from lumberyards, home centers, and hardware stores, dowel rods are usually 3′ in length and come in a variety of diameters between 1/8″ and 1″.

I always keep a supply of dowels on hand for convenience. The sizes of dowel rods used in this book are 1/8″, 3/16″, 1/4″, 5/16″, 3/8″, 7/16″, 1/2″, 5/8″, and 3/4″. Keep at least two of each size on hand and, because 1/4″ dowels are used in almost every project, you should keep at least a half dozen on hand.

TOOLS

Toy making requires a few tools. Though it's not necessary to use a lot of power tools

when building these projects, they do make the job much easier. You can make these with hand saws, a power drill, a lathe, and a hand-held power jig saw.

If you're seriously interested in toy making, you need the right power tools. All the toys in this book have been built with a Shopsmith multipurpose tool and a bandsaw. The main functions used on the Shopsmith tool were the table saw, drill press, lathe, and disc sander. Of all the power tools available, a bandsaw and drill press are the most important, with a lathe, scroll saw, and disc sander close behind. When you add a table saw, belt sander, jointer, and planer, you've graduated to the major leagues. These tools make toy making a snap.

If you don't have all these tools, check with friends who have them and see about getting together to make some toys. Toy making is a great activity for any number of participants. Or check with local community centers—they often have facilities for part-time woodworkers.

Some of the special tools you'll need for making the toys in this book are hole saws (see Wheels). Hole saws are used throughout for making the wheels and miscellaneous parts. When drilling stock, brad-point bits are recommended for making the cleanest holes. If you're redrilling a hole to make it a larger diameter, use twist drill bits.

MATERIALS

At the end of every project there is a chart labeled Materials, which is actually a list of the materials required to build the project. Under the column heading Dimensions is a parenthetical note "finished dimensions in inches." This means the dimensions given are the *final* dimensions of each part. In some cases the parts must be made from larger pieces of stock or from several pieces of glued-up stock. Special conditions for making parts are noted in the written instructions. Be sure you always read through the entire plan first before buying or cutting any stock.

Each part in the materials list has measurements that are always given in the following order: thickness (how thick the stock is) × width (the measurement across the grain) × length (the distance with the grain). For round stock, dimensions are always listed as diameter × thickness or length (with no regard to grain direction). Grain direction is important for many of the projects, so be sure to keep them in mind when cutting stock to size.

Hardware and other items needed for the project are at the end of the materials list under Miscellaneous.

WHEELS

Wheels are the most important part of a toy. The wheels that I've designed for my toys are simple in design and execution. They're not truly realistic, which is fine for the child, but they do capture the realism necessary to add interest to the project for the builder. Here's a description of what it takes to produce these wheels.

Wheels in this book are made with hole saws. Hole saws are round, heavy steel cylinders with a saw edge on one end. They're powered by either a hand drill or a drill press. Hole saws work by cutting a circle in the wood until the saw cuts through to the other side. When the hole is completed, a wooden plug is left in the hole saw. Wheels are made from the plugs left from cutting holes in a piece of wood.

When using a 2"-diameter hole saw to create a 2" hole in a piece of wood, the plug that's left inside the hole saw is equal to 2" *minus* twice the thickness of the hole saw blade (remember, the blade is on both sides). Since the thickness of a hole saw blade is about 1/16", the diameter of the wooden plug inside the hole saw is about 1/8" less in diameter than the hole saw itself. So, when

2"-diameter wheels are called for in the plans, use a 2-1/8"-diameter hole saw to make the wheels.

Hole saws are used mostly by carpenters and plumbers for drilling large holes in joists and walls for pipes and wires during construction. I've used hole saws in this book between 3/4" diameter and 2-1/2" diameter in 1/8" increments. Instead of buying all hole saws at the same time, read through the plans for the toys you want to build and buy those saws first. Hole saws are commonly available at lumberyards, home centers, and hardware stores. Call ahead to make sure a store carries the size you want because many stores don't keep a large inventory of these tools.

There is a step-by-step process for making wooden wheels that leads to great results every time. Follow this procedure:

1. Prepare the stock. Whether the plans call for 3/4"- or 1/4"-thick stock, prepare it ahead of time. I prefer this option to making thick wheels and cutting them to size later; starting with the right stock takes less time and yields better-looking wheels. Because many of the projects in this book require the same wheels, prepare enough stock to make extra wheels for other toys.

Using a compass, lay out the wheels on the stock so you can maximize your materials. Allow 1/8" between the wheels for saw kerfs.

2. Make the "rim" kerf. As part of the design of the toys in this book, I've added a simple touch of realism to the designs by defining the rim and tire of each wheel. Form the rims using the hole saw called for in the plans, then cut the rim kerfs 1/8" deep. As you cut the rim kerfs, the 1/4" pilot drill on the hole saw creates a pilot hole in the stock for each wheel.

3. First, cut off the wheel. After forming the rim kerfs, you have a board with a series of

circles and pilot holes. Next, take the larger hole saw specified in the instructions and cut three-quarters of the way through the stock. After sawing all the wheels to this depth, flip the stock over and finish cutting out the wheels. If you were to try to cut out the wheels in one pass without flipping the stock over, the wheel plug would be stuck inside the hole saw. When you flip the stock over to complete the cut, most of the stock is sticking out of the saw.

4. Sand the wheels. Once the wheels have been cut out, they require sanding. Since the wheels already have a 1/4" hole in the center of them that was created by the hole saw, you can make a simple jig for sanding the wheels. Take a 1/4" × 3" carriage bolt and cut off the head with a hacksaw. Next, in the following order, place a nut, washer, wheel, washer, and nut, then tighten. Mount the bolt in a hand-held drill or a drill press and sand the wheels.

5. Redrill the axle hole. If the wheel you just made requires a larger axle hole than 1/4", now is the time to drill it. Use a twist drill bit of the appropriate size to drill out this hole. Do not attempt to drill a larger hole using a Forstner or brad-point bit—these require solid wood to make an effective hole.

An alternative to making wheels using hole saws is to cut them out of stock free hand with a coping saw, scroll saw, or bandsaw. The only thing you'll miss using this method is the rim kerf, but you can always draw that on if you desire.

If you're an adept lathe turner, it's possible to turn the wheels from solid stock on the lathe. When turning the wheels, mount them to a screw center for best results.

The easiest alternative to making wheels is to buy them already made. Many woodworking and craft supply houses and catalogs carry wheels.

GLUING AND CLAMPING

Gluing and clamping are important operations in any woodworking project. Because toys end up in the hands of children, special attention must be paid to these operations.

For all the projects in this book use aliphatic resin glue. This glue is cream-colored and better known by the brand names Franklin Titebond or Elmer's Carpenter's Glue. This glue sets up in about 20 minutes, requires only a half hour of clamping time, and fully cures in 24 hours. The most important advantages of aliphatic resin glue are that it's nontoxic (most important around children), water resistant, and can be easily sanded when fully cured.

Many types of clamps are available for the toy maker—C-clamps, bar clamps, parallel clamps, etc. When gluing up the projects in this book, remember the following tips:

- Preset your clamps *before* applying glue to any of the project surfaces. Presetting the clamps saves you time later when you need to be cleaning up excess glue.
- Do not apply excessive pressure while clamping. It not only damages the wood but also squeezes out too much of the glue and starves the joint. Apply steady, firm pressure.
- Use cawls to protect the wood when gluing. Cawls are pieces of scrap wood that go between the clamp and the wood to prevent the clamp from damaging the surface of the wood.
- Even though the clamping time for aliphatic resin glue is relatively short (see manufacturer's instructions), allow stock that's to be turned on a lathe to remain clamped for 24 hours. If you plan ahead, this is easily worked into the schedule, and it provides an extra margin of safety.
- Make sure you always have enough clamps to do the job. Inadequately and

unevenly clamped joints can be weak and give out after a while.

Applying glue is a critical part of any woodworking project, and there are a few things that you can do to make the process go smoothly.

- Make sure all the parts you're going to glue are clean and free of dust.
- Apply glue to project parts evenly. Don't apply an excessive amount, but don't be stingy, either.
- Apply glue to any end grain first, then to the remaining pieces. After gluing all the parts, go back and apply glue to the end grain again. End grain absorbs more glue due to the capillary action of wood cells.
- After clamping the parts together, clean up glue "squeeze out" with a wet rag. A wet rag raises the grain a little, but it's by far the most effective way to clean up excess glue. Rinse the rag often.

Sometimes gluing and clamping don't provide an adequate bond between two surfaces. In this case it's necessary to reinforce a bond with something that will hold the parts together securely. Examples of reinforcements are nails (brads), screws, and wooden dowels.

Many of the plans in this book call for dowel reinforcements. When dowels are used, glue and clamp the parts together and allow the glue to dry. Once the glue has cured, drill the appropriate size dowel hole through the parts and glue a dowel into the hole. Leave a little of the dowel exposed and sand it flush with the surface after the glue dries.

If you wish, you can skip the dowel reinforcement and use flathead wood screws instead. Brass screws add an extra flair to the toy.

The only place that brads are called for is on the truck assemblies of the train cars.

Here the wheel covers require a brad to secure the fragile assembly.

MASS PRODUCTION

Mass production is a term that carries a negative connotation for woodworkers. The love of one-of-a-kind projects is probably the biggest drawing card of handmade wooden objects. But in the field of toy making, making more than one toy at a time means providing that much more fun for more children—and that's the name of the game.

The majority of time producing any woodworking project is spent preparing the stock and setting up the machine to make a cut or drill a hole. It takes very little time to make extra parts once everything is set up, so mass production of toys (making two or twenty) really makes good use of your time. But mass production doesn't mean sacrificing the quality or charm of wooden toys—it's genuinely a case where more is better. (It's also a good way to use up a lot of otherwise useless scraps of wood in the scrap bin.)

When you think about it, going to a store and buying four Model T's, two bulldozers, and three trains (or even five boxcars) would seem foolish and extravagant; but constructing all of those toys would make you a hero.

If you don't want to make more than one of a model, check all the parts in the materials lists of similar toys (Model T's, trains, etc.). Even if you make just one of each toy, many parts are interchangeable with other toys. Planning and building similar models at the same time is also a way to maximize your time in the shop.

PATTERNS AND TEMPLATES

Many plans in this book require odd-shaped parts that can't be made using straight cuts on a table saw. Making these parts requires drawing the outline of the contours on the stock, then cutting or sanding the block of wood to shape. Odd pieces are drawn in the plans either with 1/2"-square grids or with detailed measurements, and there are several ways to get the pattern of your piece from the plans to the wood itself.

One way is to carefully transfer all the points and lines from the plans to the stock. If you transfer a pattern this way, make sure you use a sharp pencil and a good straightedge for the straight parts and a french curve for the curved sections. If the pattern is laid out on a grid, draw the grid first on the stock, then transfer the lines.

Another way to transfer patterns is to draw them onto shirt cardboard or old file folders and cut them out. These cutout patterns are called *templates*. They'll save you hours of work when you're building more toys.

The only problem with cardboard templates is that they wear out after a while. If you want more permanent templates use scraps of plastic laminate (Formica), pieces of tempered hardboard (Masonite), or plywood. A power scroll saw is the best tool for cutting these hard materials, and a 1/4" hole is drilled into each template so it can be hung up on a nail in your shop.

Locating holes on a piece of stock is very important since other parts of the toy may have matching holes. Use extra care when locating holes on your stock by using a sharp pencil and marking an "X" at the *center* of the hole. When using templates, locate holes with a 1/32"-diameter hole on the template material (for cardboard, that's a tack hole; for hard materials, use a slightly larger hole). Then, when you use the template, locate the holes with a sharp pencil or a pushpin.

If you want to make a toy larger or smaller than designated in the plans, you'll need to make the templates in proportion. Lay out the changed patterns in the same way as explained previously. If the plan you're using calls for a grid, simply make the grid squares larger or smaller in proportion to your new size. For instance, the plans in this book call for 1/2" squares, so use 3/4", 3/8", or 1" squares—whatever the new size of your toy calls for—just make sure all parts go up or down in proportion.

FINISHES

Many folks like to paint toys, and there's nothing wrong with that. However, painting a toy can keep it from reaching a child's hands an extra day or two. Almost all the toys I make have no finish on them at all. But for the toy maker who wants to go that extra mile, here are some tips to keep in mind when finishing toys.

- Always use nontoxic paints on toys. *Nontoxic* means that the paints include no heavy metals such as lead, cadmium, or selenium in the ingredients. Old paints are the culprits—buy new, safe paints just to be sure.
- If you want a natural finish, use Behlen's Salad Bowl Finish or a polyurethane. Danish oils aren't nontoxic for 30 days and tung oils are never nontoxic.
- When painting a model, use oil primer on the parts first for best results. Also, paint parts prior to assembly, but be careful not to get any paint on future gluing surfaces.

Whether you paint a project or not, decorate the toy with decals made from colored contact paper. Contact paper is available from hardware and department stores. For lettering, use self-stick letters available from office supply stores. They're easy to apply and add a lot of interest to your toys.

Norm Marshall
1932-1982

Acknowledgements

No book is the result of any one person, and this book is no exception. We're deeply indebted to the many individuals who helped in making this book a reality.

Most of all, thanks goes to Caryl Marshall for her desire to see the plans for Norman's toys shared with thousands of woodworkers throughout the world.

A special thanks goes to Gary Triftshouser for the many, many hours spent transcribing Norm Marshall's drawings into detailed plans for this publication.

Many thanks also go to Dan Gabriel for his professionalism in the photography that did justice to the designs in this book. And thanks to Rhonda Day for her efforts in coordinating materials that appeared in *Hands On* magazine.

Bill Jones

The Great All-American Wooden Toy Book

MODEL T CAR

The Model T car, or "Tin Lizzy," was Henry Ford's answer to a truly affordable automobile for the American family. Manufactured by the millions, Model T's became a common sight on the streets and highways of America for many years.

Building one of these cars is a lot of fun; making more than one doubles the pleasure. Remember that Henry Ford was the first to capitalize on the idea of the assembly line, and this toy is ideal for mass production. You might want to get together with some of your woodworking friends and set up an assembly line for this toy. Many woodworkers have made this particular toy by the dozens to give away at Christmas. So get your shop "tooled up" and begin your assembly.

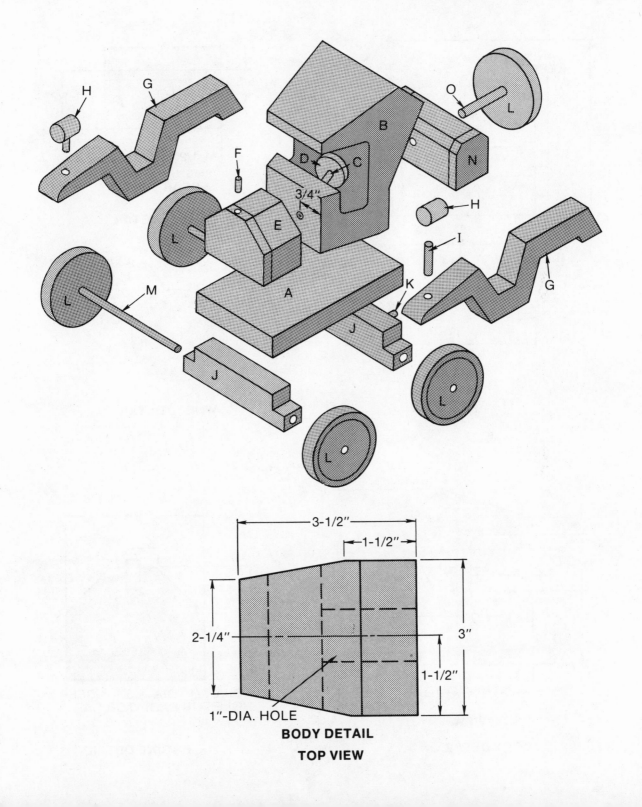

3/4"

2-1/4"

3-1/2"

1-1/2"

3"

1-1/2"

1"-DIA. HOLE

BODY DETAIL

TOP VIEW

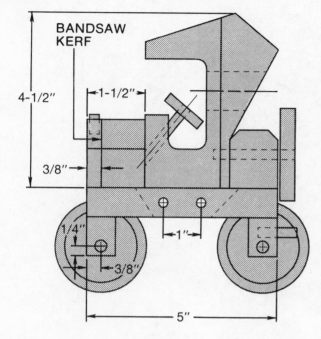

BANDSAW KERF

4-1/2"

1-1/2"

3/8"

1/4"

1"

3/8"

5"

SIDE VIEW

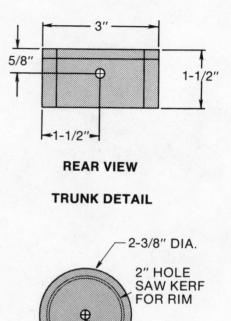

3"

5/8"

1-1/2"

1-1/2"

REAR VIEW

TRUNK DETAIL

2-3/8" DIA.

2" HOLE SAW KERF FOR RIM

1/4" DIA.

WHEEL DETAIL

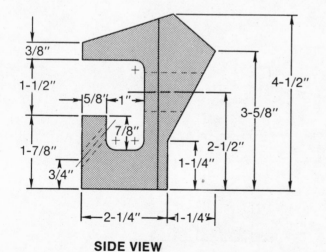

3/8"

1-1/2"

5/8"   1"

7/8"

1-7/8"

3/4"

4-1/2"

3-5/8"

2-1/2"

1-1/4"

2-1/4"   1-1/4"

SIDE VIEW

BODY DETAIL

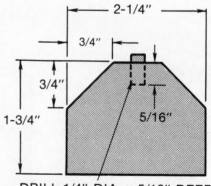

2-1/4"

3/4"

3/4"

1-3/4"

5/16"

DRILL 1/4"-DIA. × 5/16"-DEEP HOLE FOR RADIATOR CAP.

ENGINE DETAIL

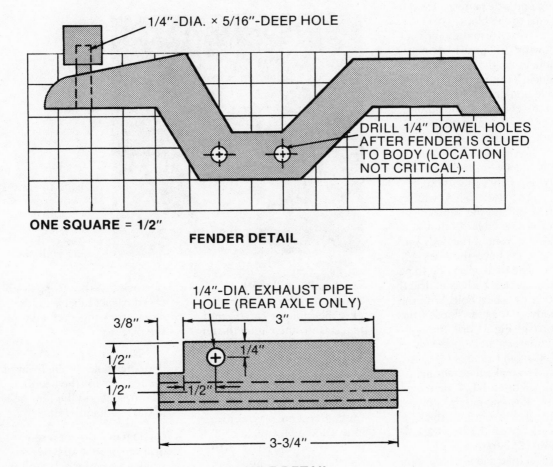

1/4"-DIA. × 5/16"-DEEP HOLE

DRILL 1/4" DOWEL HOLES AFTER FENDER IS GLUED TO BODY (LOCATION NOT CRITICAL).

ONE SQUARE = 1/2"

FENDER DETAIL

1/4"-DIA. EXHAUST PIPE HOLE (REAR AXLE ONLY)

3/8"   3"

1/2"   1/4"

1/2"   1/2"

3-3/4"

AXLE DETAIL

PROCEDURE

1. BASE ASSEMBLY

Cut the stock for the base (A) to length and width. If you're making a lot of these cars, rip long boards to 3" wide; then cut them to 5" lengths.

Next, cut stock to length and width to form the 3/4" × 1" × 3-3/4" axle holders (J). Clamp the axle stock securely to a drill press table and drill the 5/16"-diameter axle holes where indicated in the plans.

After the holes have been drilled, lay out and cut the notches on the ends of the holders. Since these pieces are small, use only a coping saw, scroll saw, or bandsaw to cut the notches. Drill the 1/4" exhaust pipe hole in the rear axle; then glue the exhaust pipe (K) into place. Glue and clamp the axle holders to the base; then set the base assembly aside.

2. BODY

The complicated shape of the body (B) is really simple to make—it's just a matter of compound cutting (cutting on two surfaces).

Glue up four pieces of 1 × 4 stock to form a 3"-wide block (the glue lines run vertically); then cut the stock to yield a 3" × 3-1/2" × 4-1/2" block. (You may want to make more than one block at this time for other Model T projects—just glue up longer boards and allow for one block per every 4-3/4" of length.) Transfer the top and side patterns from the plans to the block.

Next, form the rear window by drilling a 1"-diameter hole through the back of the block. Turn the block on its side and drill three 3/8" holes in the corners of the cutout. The location of these holes is indicated by the small crosses on the side detail drawing. Use a bandsaw or scroll saw to cut out the entire side contour.

To get the 2-1/4" width on the front, tilt the bandsaw or scroll saw table 10° and, keeping the front of the body on the table, bevel the sides.

The final operation to perform on the body is to drill the steering wheel hole. With the body on the rear slope of the top (see Fig. 1), drill the 1/4"-diameter steering wheel hole 3/4" from the edge.

To make the steering wheel, use a 1-1/4"-diameter hole saw and cut the steering wheel (D) from 1/4"-thick stock. Insert the steering column (C) into the steering wheel hole and glue the steering wheel to the column. Set the body aside.

3. ENGINE

Glue up and clamp three pieces of 3/4" × 1-3/4" × 10" stock to form the block for the engine (E). The extra stock is for the other Model T's but, more importantly, for safe handling of the stock during machining. After getting the stock to the proper thickness and width, chamfer the top edges with a bandsaw, scroll saw, or power sander. Cut the engine(s) to length; then form the 1/16"-deep radiator line with a bandsaw blade.

Fig. 1. To drill the steering column hole, turn the body upside down and let it rest on the rear slope of the roof.

Finally, drill the 1/4"-diameter radiator hole and glue the radiator cap (F) into place. Glue and clamp the engine to the base; then glue the body in place.

4. TRUNK

The trunk (N) is formed in much the same way as the engine. Glue up a couple of pieces of 3/4" × 1-1/4" × 10"-long stock and chamfer the edges. Create the trunk "straps" like you did the engine radiator line by making a 1/16"-deep saw kerf with a bandsaw or scroll saw. Glue and clamp the trunk to the base. Sand the front and back of the car assembly flush.

5. FENDERS

Make up a cardboard template for the fenders; then transfer the fender outline (G) onto a piece of stock. Cut out the fenders using a scroll saw or bandsaw.

NOTE: You can pad-saw the fenders by putting two pieces

of stock together using double-faced carpet tape. With the stock stuck together, cut out the pieces.

Next, drill the 1/4"-diameter holes in the front of the fenders for the headlamp columns (I) and the 1/4" holes in the headlamps (H).

CAUTION: Do not attempt to drill the headlamp holes on small pieces of stock. Drill the holes in a longer piece of dowel; then cut the headlamps to length.

Attach the fenders to the car assembly with glue and clamps. When the glue is completely dry, drill two 1/4"-diameter reinforcement holes on each side of the car. Glue the reinforcement dowels into place and sand them flush.

6. WHEELS

Make up 3/8"-thick stock for the wheels (L). Make up a lot of stock to make extra wheels for use on other Model T's. Use a 1-7/8"-diameter hole saw to create the "rim" on the wheels. Next, cut out the wheels using a 2-1/2"-diameter hole saw. Make at least five wheels for this model. (The other models use the identical wheel, so make extras and set them aside.)

Cut the axles (M) to length and glue the wheels in place. Drill a 1/4"-diameter × 1-3/4"-deep hole through the trunk and into the body. Glue the spare tire holder (O) into place and add the spare tire.

MATERIALS

Part	Description	Pieces	Dimensions
			(finished dimensions in inches)
A	Base	1	3/4 × 3 × 5
B	Body	1	3 × 3-1/2 × 4-1/2
C	Steering column	1	1/4 dia. × 1-3/4
D	Steering wheel	1	1-1/8 dia. × 1/4
E	Engine	1	2-1/4 × 1-3/4 × 1-1/2
F	Radiator cap	1	1/4 dia. × 1/2
G	Fenders	2	3/4 × 2 × 7-1/4
H	Headlamps	2	5/8 dia. × 5/8
I	Headlamp columns	2	1/4 dia. × 1
J	Axle holders	2	3/4 × 1 × 3-3/4
K	Exhaust pipe	1	1/4 dia. × 1
L	Wheels	5	2-3/8 dia. × 3/8
M	Axles	2	1/4 dia. × 4-1/2
N	Trunk	1	1-1/2 × 1-1/4 × 3
O	Spare tire holder	1	1/4 dia. × 2-1/4
P	Reinforcement pins (not shown)	4	1/4 dia. × 1-1/2

MODEL T TRUCK

After Henry Ford began building the affordable American car, he started working on variations of the idea. One of the most popular versions of the Model T was the pickup truck—a vehicle the farmer could use to replace the horse-drawn wagon.

This version of the pickup truck uses many of the features and measurements of the sedan. And, if you look at the tank truck, you'll see a lot of things in common with this pickup. If you haven't already made the sedan or tank truck, check out these plans and make extra parts for them while you're making the pickup.

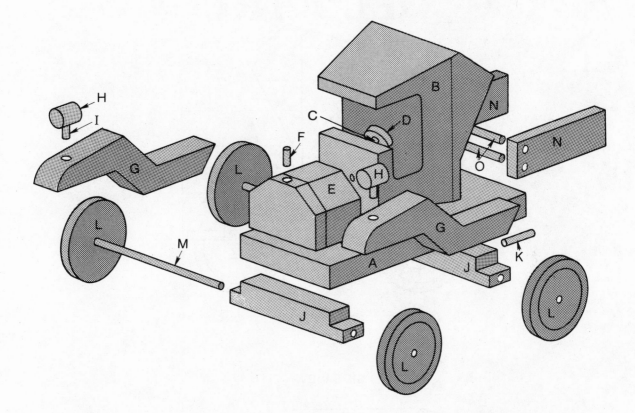

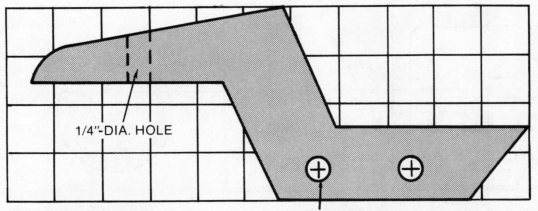

1/4"-DIA. HOLE

DRILL 1/4"-DIA. DOWEL HOLES AFTER
FENDER IS GLUED TO THE BODY.

ONE SQUARE = 1/2"

FENDER DETAIL

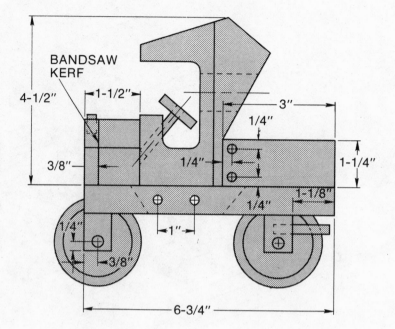

SIDE VIEW

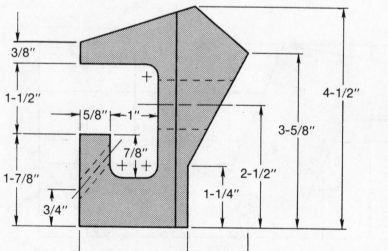

SIDE VIEW

BODY DETAIL

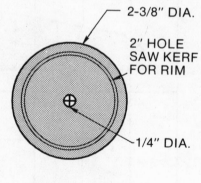

WHEEL DETAIL

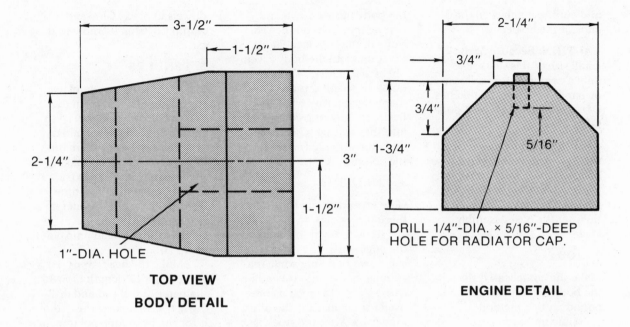

1"-DIA. HOLE

TOP VIEW

BODY DETAIL

DRILL 1/4"-DIA. × 5/16"-DEEP
HOLE FOR RADIATOR CAP.

ENGINE DETAIL

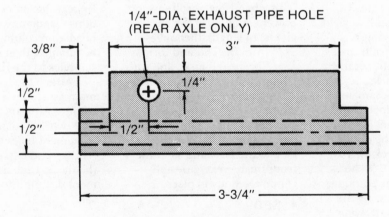

1/4"-DIA. EXHAUST PIPE HOLE
(REAR AXLE ONLY)

AXLE DETAIL

PROCEDURE

1. BASE ASSEMBLY

Cut the stock for the base (A) to length and width. If you're making several of these trucks, rip long boards to 3" wide; then cut them to 6-3/4" lengths. The base stock is the same width for all three models, but lengths on each model vary.

Next, cut stock to length and width to form the 3/4" × 1" × 3-3/4" axle holders (J). Clamp the axle holder stock securely to a drill press table and drill the 5/16"-diameter axle holes where indicated in the plans. After the holes have been drilled, lay out and cut the notches on the ends of the holders.

CAUTION: Because of the small size of this stock, use only a coping saw, scroll saw, or bandsaw to cut the notches. DO NOT attempt this cut on a table saw.

After the notches are cut, drill the 1/4"-diameter exhaust pipe hole and glue the exhaust pipe (K) in place. Glue and clamp the axle holders to the base; then set the base assembly aside.

2. BODY

Make the complicated shape of the body (B) using a compound cutting method.

Glue up four pieces of 1 × 4 stock to form a 3"-thick block, and orient the block so the glue lines run vertically. Cut the stock to length to yield a 3"-wide × 3-1/2"-long × 4-1/2"-tall block; then transfer the top and side patterns from the plans to the block.

Next, drill a 1"-diameter hole through the block from the back for the back window (this only needs to be drilled 2" deep). Turn the block on its side and drill three 3/8" holes in the corners of the cutout as indicated in the plans by the little crosses on the drawing detail. Cut out all the side contours with a bandsaw or scroll saw.

To get the 2-1/4" width on the front, tilt the bandsaw or scroll saw table 10° and, keeping the front of the body on the table, bevel the sides.

The 1/4"-diameter steering wheel hole is drilled by turning the body upside down and resting the block on the rear slope of the roof (see Fig. 1).

Complete the body assembly by using a 1-1/4"-diameter hole saw to cut out the 1-1/8"-diameter steering wheel (D). Insert the steering column (C) into the steering wheel hole and glue the steering wheel to the column. Set the body aside.

3. ENGINE

Glue up and clamp together three pieces of 3/4" × 1-3/4" × 10" stock to form the block for the engine (E). The extra stock is for safe handling while machining, but it's not wasted because the extra stock can be used for engines for the other Model T's. After the stock is the proper thickness and width, chamfer the top edges with a bandsaw, scroll saw, or power sander. Cut the engine(s) to length; then measure 3/8" from the end and form a 1/16"-deep "radiator" line with a bandsaw or scroll saw blade.

Finally, drill the 1/4"-diameter radiator hole and glue the radiator cap (F) into place. Glue and clamp the engine to the base and sand the front flush. Next, glue and clamp the body in place.

4. BED

The easiest way to form the bed (O, P) is to prepare a 3/4" × 1-1/4" × 10" piece of stock. (The extra length is for safe handling when resawing later.) Next, locate and drill the two dowel holes for the bed front (O); then resaw the stock to form 1/4"-thick pieces. Cut the sides to length; then glue the dowels in place. Glue and clamp the bed assembly to the base.

5. FENDERS

Make a cardboard template for the fenders (G) from the plans. Transfer the pattern to the stock; then use a bandsaw or scroll saw to cut them out. If you're planning on making the tank truck, make extra fenders for that at this time. Next, drill the 1/4"-diameter holes in the front of the fenders for the headlamp columns (I).

Make the headlamps (H) by taking a 12" length of 5/8"-diameter dowel rod and drilling a 1/4" hole near the end of it for the headlamp column. Once you've drilled the hole, cut the headlamp to length. Repeat this process for the other headlamp. Glue the headlamp columns to the headlamps; then glue these assemblies to the fenders.

Attach the fenders to the main assembly with glue and clamps. After the glue dries, drill two 1/4"-diameter reinforcement holes through the fenders and into each side of the truck. Glue the reinforcement dowels into place and sand flush.

6. WHEELS

Prepare 3/8"-thick stock for the wheels (L); then use a 1-7/8"-diameter hole saw to create the "rims." Next, cut out the wheels using a 2-1/2"-diameter hole saw; then sand.

Cut the axles (M) to length; then glue the wheels and axles to the truck.

MATERIALS

Part	Description	Pieces	Dimensions
			(finished dimensions in inches)
A	Base	1	3/4 × 3 × 6-3/4
B	Body	1	3 × 3-1/2 × 4-1/2
C	Steering column	1	1/4 dia. × 1-3/4
D	Steering wheel	1	1-1/8 dia. × 1/4
E	Engine	1	2-1/4 × 1-3/4 × 1-1/2
F	Radiator cap	1	1/4 dia. × 1/2
G	Fenders	2	3/4 × 2 × 5-1/4
H	Headlamps	2	5/8 dia. × 5/8
I	Headlamp columns	2	1/4 dia. × 1
J	Axle holders	2	3/4 × 1 × 3-3/4
K	Exhaust pipe	1	1/4 dia. × 1-1/2
L	Wheels	5	2-3/8 dia. × 3/8
M	Axles	2	1/4 dia. × 4-1/2
N	Sides	2	1/4 × 1-1/4 × 3
O	Bed front	2	1/4 dia. × 3
P	Reinforcement pins (not shown)	4	1/4 dia. × 1-1/2

MODEL T TANK TRUCK

Model T's were used in a variety of ways. Henry Ford had created the universal chassis on which America could power herself.

Taking a lesson from Ford himself, the designer created yet another variation of the Model T. The plans for a tank truck are very similar to the truck in the previous project. Besides the tank on the back, the only other changes are in the body and the length of the base.

While you're building this tank truck, think of other designs that could utilize this chassis. By using this basic assembly, you can create your own designs like a stake truck, a moving van, or even a wrecker. The ideas are as endless as your imagination.

But do remember that the easiest way to make variations on this truck is to have spare parts on hand—especially wheels, engines, and fenders. While making this model, make lots of extra parts—you won't regret it.

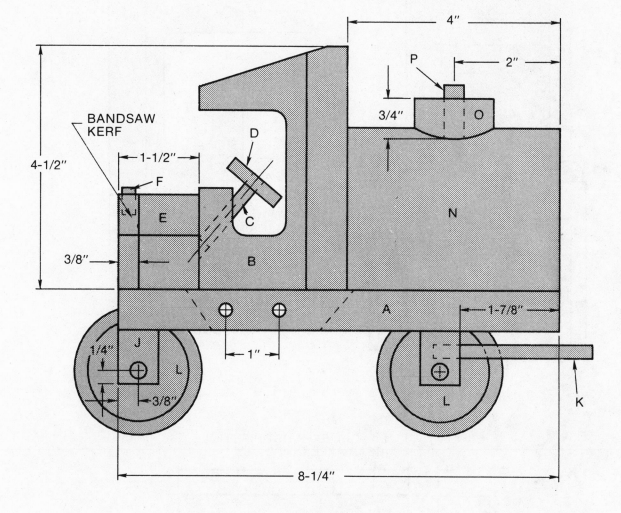

BANDSAW KERF

4-1/2"

4"

2"

P

3/4"

O

D

1-1/2"

F

E

C

B

N

3/8"

A

1-7/8"

J

1/4"

L

1"

L

3/8"

K

8-1/4"

SIDE VIEW

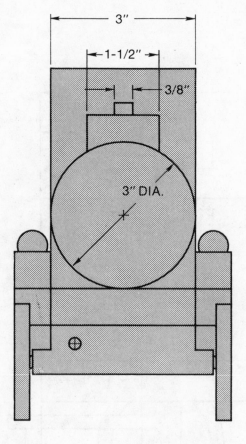

REAR VIEW

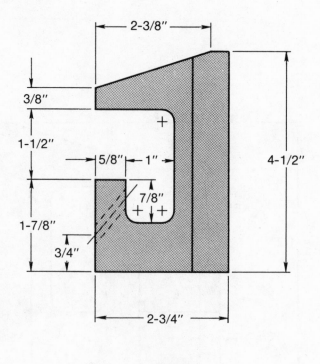

SIDE VIEW

BODY DETAIL

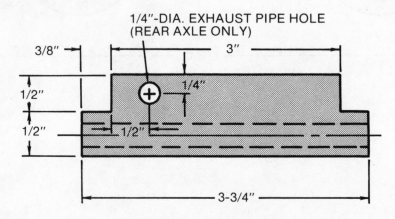

1/4"-DIA. EXHAUST PIPE HOLE
(REAR AXLE ONLY)

AXLE DETAIL

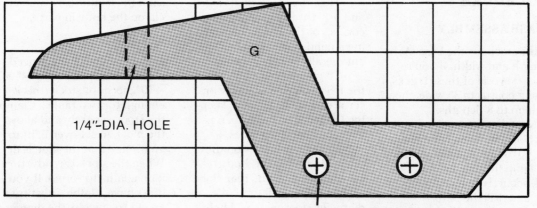

1/4"-DIA. HOLE

ONE SQUARE = 1/2"

DRILL 1/4"-DIA. DOWEL HOLES AFTER
FENDER IS GLUED TO THE BODY.

FENDER DETAIL

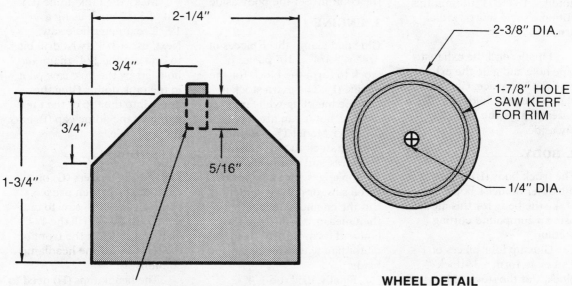

2-1/4"

3/4"

3/4"

1-3/4"

5/16"

DRILL 1/4"-DIA. × 5/16"-DEEP
HOLE FOR RADIATOR CAP.

ENGINE DETAIL

2-3/8" DIA.

1-7/8" HOLE
SAW KERF
FOR RIM

1/4" DIA.

WHEEL DETAIL

PROCEDURE

1. BASE ASSEMBLY

Cut the stock for the base (A) to length and width. If you're making several of these trucks, rip long boards to 3" wide, then cut them to 8" lengths.

Next, cut the stock to length and width to form the 3/4" × 1" × 3-3/4" axle holders (J). Clamp the axle holder stock securely to a drill press table and drill the 5/16"-diameter axle holes where indicated in the plans. After the holes have been drilled, lay out and cut the notches on the ends of the holders.

CAUTION: Because of the small size of stock, use only a coping saw, scroll saw, or bandsaw for cutting the notches. DO NOT attempt this cut on a table saw or radial arm saw.

Finally, drill the exhaust pipe hole and glue the exhaust pipe (K) into place. Glue and clamp the axle holders to the base; then set the base assembly aside.

2. BODY

The truck body (B) is similar to the other Model T bodies. Make the body for this model using a compound cutting method.

Glue up four pieces of 1 × 4 stock to form a 3"-thick block. Cut the stock to length to yield a 3" × 2-3/4" × 4-1/2" block. Transfer the top and side patterns from the plans to the block.

Turn the block on its side and drill three 3/8" holes in the corners of the cutout. Now, using a bandsaw or scroll saw, cut out all the side contours.

To get the 2-1/4" width on the front, tilt the bandsaw or scroll saw table 10° and, keeping the front of the body on the table, bevel the sides.

Unlike the bodies on the other Model T's, this body cannot be set on the rear slope of the roof to drill the 1/4"-diameter steering wheel hole. Instead, clamp the stock securely and estimate the location and angle of the hole; it's not critical. Finally, using a 1-1/4"-diameter hole saw, cut out the steering wheel (D). Insert the steering column (C) into the steering wheel hole and glue the steering wheel to the column. Set the body aside.

3. ENGINE

Glue and clamp three pieces of 3/4" × 1-3/4" × 10" pieces of stock to form the block for the engine (E). The extra stock is for safe handling while machining, but it can also be used for other Model T's. After getting the stock to the proper thickness and width, chamfer the top edges with a bandsaw, scroll saw, or power sander. Cut the engine(s) to length; then measure 3/8" from the end and form a 1/16"-deep radiator line with a bandsaw blade.

Finally, drill the 1/4"-diameter × 3/8"-deep radiator hole and glue the radiator cap (F) into place. Glue and clamp the engine to the base and

sand the front flush. Glue and clamp the body in place.

4. TANK

For the tank (N), you'll need to glue up four pieces of 3/4" × 3" × 10" pieces of stock (this is enough for two tanks). Clamp the stock securely and allow the block to set overnight to guarantee that the glue is dry. When the stock is ready, turn it on a lathe to round. If you don't have a lathe, substitute an old rolling pin; the diameter doesn't have to be exact.

Next, flatten one side of the tank about 1/4". Set the tank on a drill press table and drill the 1-1/2" hole in the top for the tank dome. Use a spade bit or Forstner bit to form this hole. Glue and clamp the tank to the base.

Make the tank dome (O) out of 3/4" stock using a 1-5/8"-diameter hole saw. Next, use a 3/8" twist drill bit to drill out the 1/4"-diameter hole left by the hole saw pilot in the tank dome. Glue the dome into the top of the tank and glue the dome cap (P) into the 3/8" hole.

5. FENDERS

Lay out the fenders (G) on a piece of stock; then use a bandsaw or scroll saw to cut them out. Next, drill the 1/4"-diameter holes in the front of the fenders for the headlamp columns (I).

The headlamps (H) need to be drilled for the headlamp columns (I). Drill the column holes in the headlamp stock before you cut the headlamps to final dimension; this assures safe handling of the stock while drilling. After drilling the holes, cut the headlamps to length. Glue the headlamp columns to the headlamps; then glue these assemblies to the fenders.

Attach the fenders to the main assembly with glue and clamp them securely. After the glue dries, drill two 1/4"-diameter reinforcement holes through the fenders and into each side of the truck. Glue the reinforcement dowels into place and sand flush.

6. WHEELS

Prepare 3/8"-thick stock for the wheels (L); then use a 1-7/8"-diameter hole saw to create the "rims." Next, cut out the wheels using a 2-1/2"-diameter hole saw. Make extra wheels for other Model T's while you're at it.

Cut the axles (M) to length, then glue the wheels and axles to the truck.

Your Model T tank truck is now complete and ready to go to work. Paint the truck anyway you wish and consider using an old gas company logo on the side of the tank like "Pure," "Shell," or even the Texaco star.

MATERIALS

Part	Description	Pieces	Dimensions
			(finished dimensions in inches)
A	Base	1	3/4 × 3 × 8-1/4
B	Body	1	3 × 2-3/4 × 4-1/2
C	Steering column	1	1/4 dia. × 1-3/4
D	Steering wheel	1	1-1/8 dia. × 1/4
E	Engine	1	2-1/4 × 1-3/4 × 1-1/2
F	Radiator cap	1	1/4 dia. × 1/2
G	Fenders	2	3/4 × 2 × 5-1/4
H	Headlamps (not shown)	2	5/8 dia. × 5/8
I	Headlamp columns (not shown)	2	1/4 dia. × 1
J	Axle holders	2	3/4 × 1 × 3-3/4
K	Exhaust pipe	1	1/4 dia. × 3
L	Wheels	5	2-3/8 dia. × 3/8
M	Axles (not shown)	2	1/4 dia. × 4-1/2
N	Tank	1	3 dia. × 4
O	Tank dome	1	1-1/2 dia. × 3/4
P	Tank dome cap	1	3/8 dia. × 1

BULLDOZER

Little contractors will enjoy preparing building sites on the carpet or in the sandbox with their own bulldozer. And the life-like caterpillar tracks and two-position blade (which locks into place with the exhaust stack) add an interest for both you and the child.

To construct this project, you need basic woodworking skills. Also, be sure to read through all the instructions for tips on making the chassis, tracks, and blade. After you've finished the bulldozer, make the low-boy trailer so you'll be able to move this piece of equipment from one site to another.

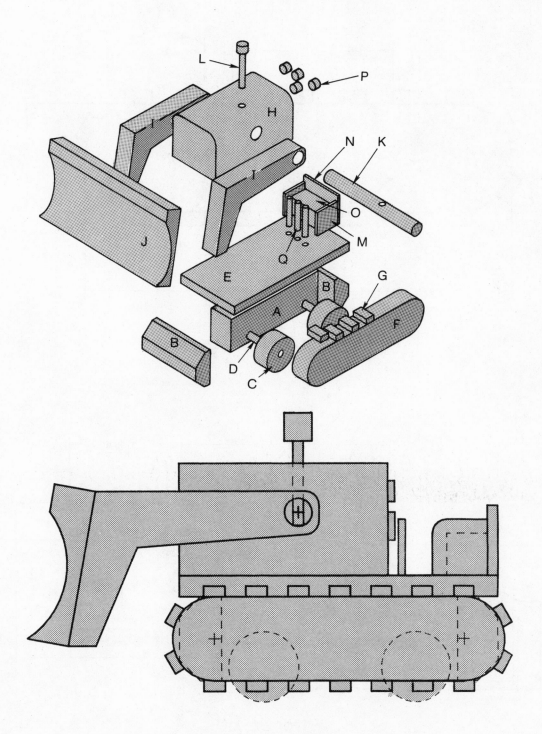

SIDE VIEW

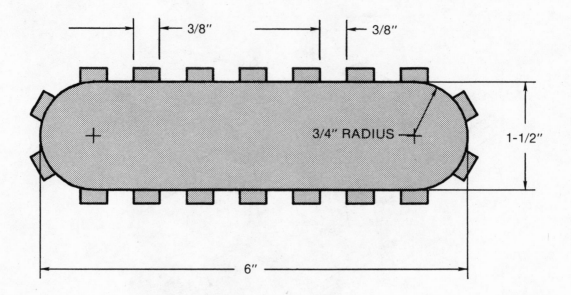

3/8"   3/8"

3/4" RADIUS

1-1/2"

6"

TRACK DETAIL

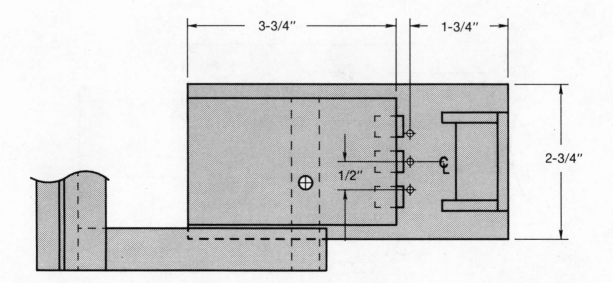

3-3/4"   1-3/4"

2-3/4"

1/2"

**TOP DETAIL
(ABOVE PLATFORM)**

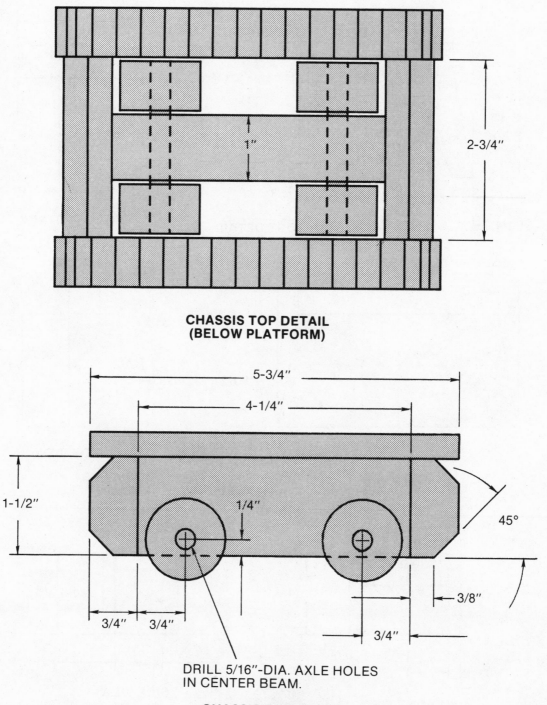

**CHASSIS TOP DETAIL
(BELOW PLATFORM)**

CHASSIS SIDE DETAIL

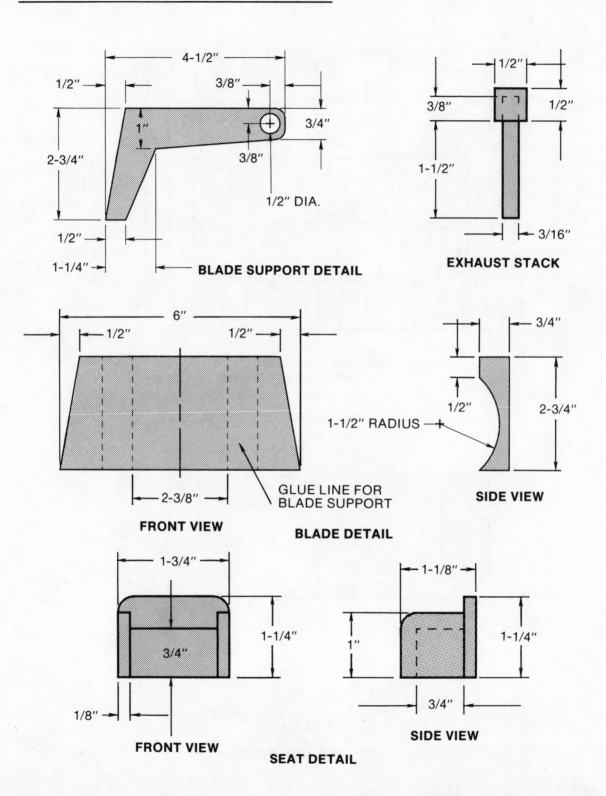

BLADE SUPPORT DETAIL

EXHAUST STACK

FRONT VIEW

BLADE DETAIL

SIDE VIEW

SEAT DETAIL

FRONT VIEW

SIDE VIEW

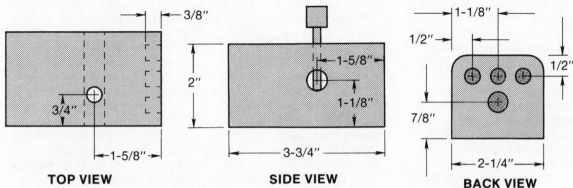

TOP VIEW   **SIDE VIEW**   **BACK VIEW**

ENGINE DETAIL

PROCEDURE

1. CHASSIS

The first step in constructing the bulldozer is to build the chassis. Begin by cutting the chassis center beam (A) to the final dimensions and drilling the two 5/16"-diameter axle holes where indicated in the plans.

Next, prepare the end beams (B) by chamfering a long piece of stock then cutting the parts to length—this will make handling the stock safer if you're using power tools. Make the end beams as close to 2-3/4" long as possible since this dimension determines the wheel clearance. Assemble the wheels (C) and axles (D) to the center beam with glue. Finally, glue and clamp the end beams to the center; then set the entire assembly aside.

2. TRACKS

To make the tracks, use a power sander or scroll saw to round the ends of the track blocks (F). Next, prepare a 3/16" × 3/8" × 36" piece of stock for making the track lugs (G). Cut the 36 lugs to length. Then, starting with the top and bottom center lugs, glue and clamp the lugs onto the track block two at a time. Use a spare lug as a spacer as you go.

When you get to the ends of the track blocks, you'll need to make the end lugs slightly concave to fit flush on the blocks. To do this, wrap sandpaper around a piece of closet pole or large dowel and sand the inside faces of the remaining lugs. Glue and clamp the end lugs in place and space them evenly to make up for any variations in the size of the track blocks. Once the glue has thoroughly dried, sand the sides of the track assemblies flush and set aside.

3. ENGINE

Make the engine (H) by gluing up three pieces of 3/4" stock and sanding it so the block is square; then round the top side edges. Next, locate the holes you'll need to drill—one on top, one through the side, and four in the rear. Note that the hole through the top must be in direct line with the hole through the side.

After drilling the holes, sand the blade axle (K) and insert it through the side of the engine. Using the exhaust stack hole as a guide, drill a 3/16"-diameter hole through the blade axle. Remove the blade axle and, with a twist drill bit, redrill the hole in it to 1/4" diameter so a child will not have to precisely line up the axle hole with the engine hole to engage the lock. Finally, glue the gauges in place and set the engine aside for assembly later.

4. BLADE ASSEMBLY

The concave curve on the blade (J) looks difficult to make, but it's simple. There are three recommended methods for making the curve. First, you could use a coving procedure on a table saw. Although this is probably the most dangerous method, it can be done if all safety rules listed in your table saw owner's manual are followed and all other safety procedures are followed. When coving the blade, work with a piece of stock at least 18" long and always use a push block. The second method of coving a blade is to use a bandsaw. With this method, cut the stock to length, then hold it on edge to cut the curve. After cutting the cove, angle the sides. Since bandsaws leave a rough surface, you'll need to do a little sanding after using this method.

The easiest and safest way to cove a blade for this bulldozer (and the road grader) is to use the roller end of a belt sander or a 2"-diameter or larger drum sander. You'll be surprised how fast coarse or medium sandpaper cuts pine. After making the blade, cut it to length and angle the sides.

Next, make the blade supports (I). For added strength, make sure the grain goes diagonally. Drill the blade axle holes in the supports; then glue and clamp the supports to the blade. If you wish, reinforce the blade support with dowel pins.

5. SEAT ASSEMBLY

To make the seat, cut out all the seat parts (M,N,O) and contour them according to the plans. Glue and clamp the sides to the seat (O) and sand the back side flush. Then glue

on the back and sand it flush with the sides.

6. EXHAUST STACK

You can make two types of exhaust stacks. The first is like the one in the photo—it's made from a 3/8"-diameter dowel with a 3/16"-diameter dowel through the middle of it. The second type, shown in the plans, is easier to make. This "can" type exhaust stack is made by drilling a 3/16" hole in 1/2" dowel stock. Next, cut the 1/2" dowel and 3/16" dowel to length and glue and clamp them together.

7. CHASSIS ASSEMBLY

Cut the chassis platform (E) to final dimension and drill holes for the control levers (Q) as indicated in the plans. Glue and clamp the seat assembly to the platform, then set the platform assembly aside.

Glue and clamp the track block assemblies to the end beams. Dry-clamp these assemblies first to make sure the wheels roll freely. After the glue has dried, glue and clamp the platform to the chassis assembly. Glue the control levers (Q) in place.

8. ENGINE/BLADE ASSEMBLY

Attach the blade assembly to

the engine by first inserting the blade axle (K) through the hole in the side of the engine. Next, dry-assemble the blade supports to the axle and turn the axle so the hole in it lines up with the exhaust stack hole. Lock the blade axle in place by inserting the exhaust stack; then, set the engine and blade assembly on a flat surface to put the blade in the up position (that is, the bottom of the blade is level with the bottom of the engine). With the blade and engine in this position, glue the blade supports to the blade axle. After the glue has dried, glue and clamp the engine/blade assembly to the chassis.

9. FINISHING TOUCHES

After the glue has dried, thoroughly sand the project with medium or fine sandpaper. Make sure there are no sharp edges—especially on the blade.

If you want to paint this toy, prime it with an oil-based primer and spray the entire toy with yellow paint. After the paint has dried, paint the tracks, exhaust stack, levers, and seat black.

MATERIALS

Part	Description	Pieces	Dimensions
			(finished dimensions in inches)
A	Chassis center beam	1	1-1/2 × 1 × 4-1/4
B	Chassis end beams	2	3/4 × 1-1/2 × 2-3/4
C	Wheels	4	1-1/4 dia. × 3/4
D	Axles	2	1/4 dia. × 2-5/8
E	Chassis platform	1	3/8 × 2-3/4 × 5-3/4
F	Track blocks	2	3/4 × 1-1/2 × 6
G	Track lugs	36	3/16 × 3/8 × 3/4
H	Engine	1	2-1/4 × 2 × 3-3/4
I	Blade supports	2	3/4 × 2-3/4 × 4-1/2
J	Blade	1	3/4 × 2-3/4 × 6
K	Blade axle	1	1/2 dia. × 3-7/8
L	Exhaust stack	1	1/2 dia. × 1/2
		1	3/16 dia. × 1-7/8
M	Seat sides	2	1/8 × 1 × 1
N	Seat back	1	1/8 × 1-1/4 × 1-3/4
O	Seat	1	3/4 × 3/4 × 1-1/2
P	Dashboard gauges	1	1/2 dia. × 1/2
		3	3/8 dia. × 1/2
Q	Control levers	3	1/8 dia. × 1-1/4

CONSTRUCTION NOTES

1. For safe handling, parts B,G,J, and L are cut to final length after all other woodworking operations have been performed on them.

2. Wheels are made using a 1-3/8"-diameter hole saw.

ROAD GRADER

After the bulldozer has cleared a building site, the road grader comes in for the final leveling—just before the final smoothing with the steamroller. This plan for building a road grader has all the right ingredients: simple woodworking, realism, and a lot of playability.

The design features a movable blade that can be positioned straight across or moved to the right or left. Another feature is the optional open-sided engine compartment with the engine visible. Build this engine or just fill in the space with a block of wood.

To get this toy from site to site, build a heavy equipment transporter for it just like the one used for the bulldozer. Follow the plans for the low-boy trailer, but make the trailer floor just a few inches longer.

Read through all the instructions here first to find the sequence for constructing this road grader. And, as with all the toys in this book—enjoy.

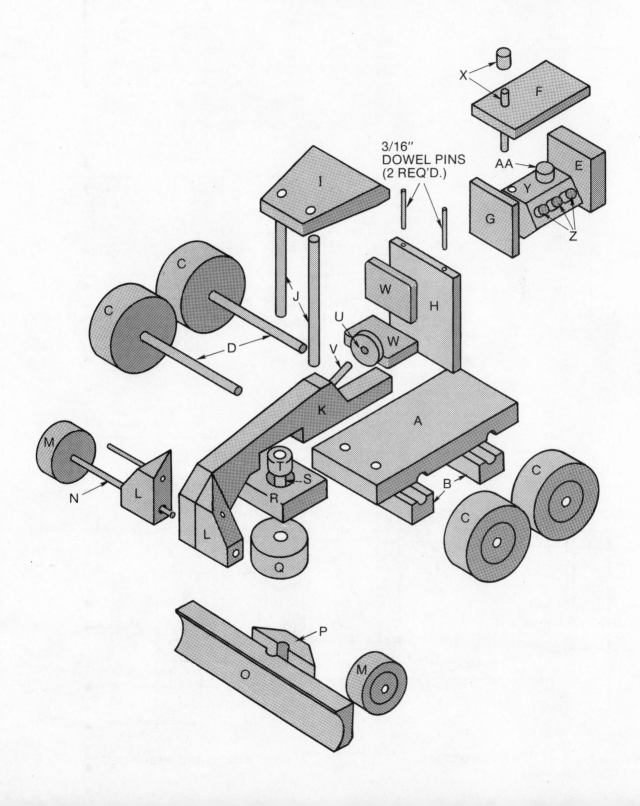

3/16"
DOWEL PINS
(2 REQ'D.)

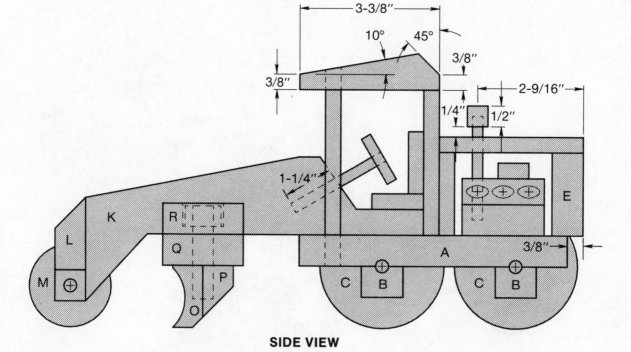

SIDE VIEW

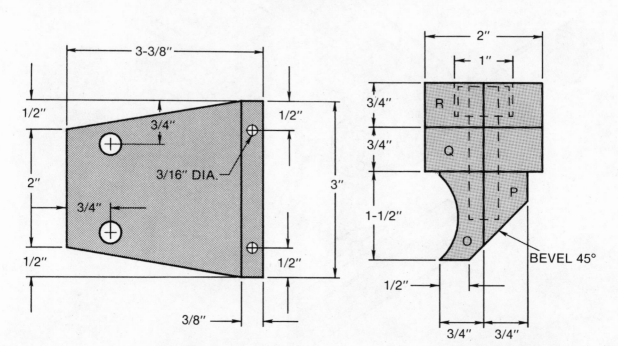

ROOF DETAIL

BLADE ASSEMBLY DETAIL

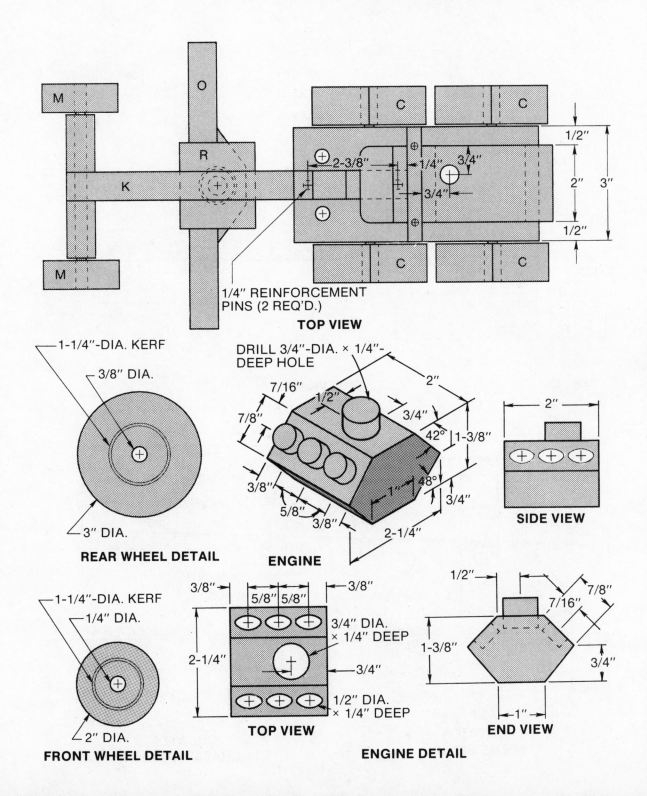

1/4" REINFORCEMENT
PINS (2 REQ'D.)

TOP VIEW

1-1/4"-DIA. KERF

3/8" DIA.

3" DIA.

REAR WHEEL DETAIL

DRILL 3/4"-DIA. × 1/4"-
DEEP HOLE

7/16"

7/8"

3/8"

5/8"

3/8"

2"

3/4"

42°

1-3/8"

1"

48°

3/4"

2-1/4"

ENGINE

2"

SIDE VIEW

1-1/4"-DIA. KERF

1/4" DIA.

2" DIA.

FRONT WHEEL DETAIL

3/8"

5/8" 5/8"

3/8"

2-1/4"

3/4" DIA.
× 1/4" DEEP

3/4"

1/2" DIA.
× 1/4" DEEP

TOP VIEW

1/2"

7/8"

7/16"

1-3/8"

3/4"

1"

END VIEW

ENGINE DETAIL

2-3/8"

1/4"

3/4"

3/4"

1/2"

2"

3"

1/2"

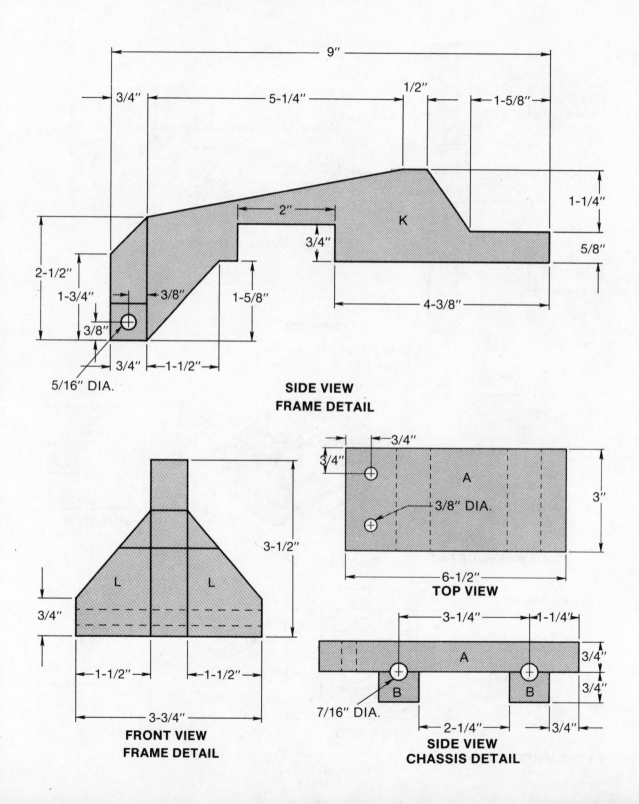

**SIDE VIEW
FRAME DETAIL**

TOP VIEW

**FRONT VIEW
FRAME DETAIL**

**SIDE VIEW
CHASSIS DETAIL**

PROCEDURE

1. BASE

Begin by taking the base (A) and gluing the rear axle holders (B) in place. Clamp the stock securely and allow the assembly to set overnight to make sure the glue is thoroughly dry. After the glue has dried, drill the 7/16"-diameter axle holes, then set the base assembly aside.

2. WHEELS

To make the rear wheels (C), laminate three pieces of 3/4" stock together to form a 2-1/4 × 3-1/2" × 8" piece of stock. Clamp the stock securely and allow the glue to dry thoroughly as for the base assembly. Once the glue has dried, use a bandsaw or scroll saw to cut out two 3"-diameter wheels. Next, resaw these 2-1/4"-thick blanks to form the 1-1/8"-thick wheels. Next, take the wheels and, using a 1-1/4"-diameter hole saw, cut a 1/4"-deep saw kerf in each one to form the boundary between the tire and the rim. Drill out the 1/4" holes created by the hole saw to a 3/8" diameter with a 3/8" twist drill bit.

Form the smaller front wheels (M) with a 2-1/8" hole saw. The rims for these wheels are created with a 1-1/4" hole saw.

NOTE: To save time later, use a 2-1/8"-diameter hole saw to cut out the blade pivot ring (Q); a 1"-diameter hole saw to cut out the blade pivot pinlock (T); and a 1-3/8" hole saw to cut out the steering wheel (U).

Sand all these parts and set aside.

3. ENGINE

Building the engine takes a little time, but it really adds a lot of interest to the model. The engine consists of a simple block of wood measuring 1-3/8" × 2-1/4" × 2", but start with a block at least 12" long for safe handling while machining.

Begin by constructing the block (Y). Set up a table saw to cut the necessary bevels on a 12"-long piece of glued-up stock. After cutting the bevels, drill 1/2"-diameter holes for the pistons (Z) according to the plans. Next, drill a 3/4"-diameter hole in the top of the engine for the air cleaner (AA). Glue the pistons and air cleaner into place, then set the engine aside.

4. ENGINE COMPARTMENT

Glue and clamp the engine hood (F) to the engine radiator (E) and the engine hood support (G). If you made the simple engine block in the last section, glue it into place at this time. Note that the engine hood should overhang the wood block about 1/8" on each side. Finally, round the top and side edges of the hood.

Set the assembly aside.

5. CAB

Begin construction of the cab by cutting the contours on the roof (I). First, tilt the bandsaw table 45° and cut the rear bevel. Then, reset the table to 10°

and cut the front bevel. If you do not have a bandsaw, use a belt sander or hand plane.

After beveling the top of the roof, mark the front edge 1/2" in from the sides and draw a line from the front edge back to the peak (see plans). Cut along these lines to complete the top contour of the roof.

Now place the roof flat on the base with the front edge of the roof flush with the front of the base, then set the engine compartment on the base against the rear of the roof. The engine compartment radiator should overhang the base by approximately 3/8". If it doesn't, cut or sand the front edge of the roof so that the engine compartment overhangs the proper amount.

Once the roof is the proper size, mark the position of the 3/8"-diameter cab front supports. Set the front edge even with the front of the base and drill the holes in both parts at the same time. To secure the stock, use masking tape or double-sided carpet tape between the two parts. Drill two 1/8"-diameter holes located 3/16" from the back edge of the roof. These holes will act as pilot holes for doweling later.

Begin assembly by first gluing the engine and engine hood assembly (E,F,G) to the base. Clamp these assemblies securely. Once the glue has cured, glue the cab rear panel (H) to the engine compartment and base. Now insert the two cab forward supports (J) into place and attach the cab roof (I). Using the pilot holes in the rear of the cab roof, drill holes for 3/16" dowels through the roof and cab rear panel. Glue the dowels in place. Since the dowels at the front and rear of the cab roof will protrude, sand them flush once the glue has dried.

6. FRAME

Transfer the design for the frame (K) to the stock and cut out with a bandsaw or scroll saw. Next, take the front axle supports (L) and cut the front profile of these pieces. Glue and clamp the axle supports to the frame. After the glue has dried, drill the 5/16"-diameter axle hole as indicated. At the same time, drill a 1/4"-diameter hole somewhere above the axle hole for a reinforcing dowel pin; then, drill the 1/4"-diameter steering column hole.

Finally, tilt the bandsaw table 45° and cut the front bevel on the axle supports.

7. BLADE

The blade (O) is made by one of two methods. The first method is to cove the stock using the table saw, a procedure described in many woodworking books. If you elect to cove the blade using the table saw, be careful to follow all of the manufacturer's safety instructions. When coving stock for the road grader, start with a piece at least 18" long. Cut the stock to length after you've completed the cove.

Another method, one that's much safer, is to use the spindle end of either a hand-held or stationary belt sander. Use coarse sandpaper for this operation and, as in the previous method, begin with stock that's longer than required and cut it to length when the coving has been completed.

Next, take the blade back support (P) and cut bevels on each side of it. Glue the back support to the blade.

NOTE: The bottom of the blade and the back support are still square to provide a firm support for drilling.

After the glue has dried, glue and clamp the blade pivot ring (Q) to the blade assembly. Once the glue has dried, drill the 1/2"-diameter hole for the blade pivot pin (S) as shown in the plans.

Complete the blade assembly by cutting or power sanding the bevel on the back of the blade and blade support.

8. SWIVEL ASSEMBLY

The blade on this road grader swivels from side to side. To make the blade swivel, take the blade retaining block (R) and, using a 1" drill bit, drill a hole in the center of the block to a depth of 1/2". Next, drill a 1/2"-diameter hole through the remainder of the stock. Once you've drilled the two holes, take the blade pivot pinlock (T) you made in step 2 and drill out the 1/4" pilot hole to 1/2". Glue the blade pivot pin (S) into the pivot pinlock (T).

Insert the pivot pin assembly (S,T) through the blade retaining block (R), then glue and clamp part R to the frame (K). Be careful not to get any glue in the pivot recess. Once the glue has dried, glue the blade pivot pin (S) into the blade assembly.

9. ASSEMBLY

Begin assembly by gluing the steering column (V) into the frame; then glue the steering wheel (U) to the column. Now glue and clamp the frame to the base. After the glue has dried, drill through the base and frame as indicated for dowel reinforcement. Glue the seat (W) in place and glue the wheels to the axles.

To make the exhaust stack (X), drill a 1/4"-diameter hole in the engine hood and into the engine block; then glue the stack into place.

10. FINISHING TOUCHES

If you want to paint this toy, use equipment yellow on the body and inside the wheels. Use black on the wheels, engine, seat, blade, steering wheel, and exhaust stack.

MATERIALS

Part	Description	Pieces	Dimensions
			(finished dimensions in inches)
A	Base	1	3/4 × 3 × 6-1/2
B	Rear axle holders	2	3/4 × 1 × 3
C	Rear wheels	4	3 dia. × 1-1/8
D	Rear axles	2	3/8 dia. × 5-3/8
E	Engine radiator	1	3/4 × 2 × 2
F	Engine hood	1	3/8 × 2 × 3-1/2
G	Engine hood support	1	3/8 × 2 × 2
H	Cab rear panel	1	3/8 × 3 × 3-1/2
I	Cab roof	1	3/4 × 3 × 3-3/8
J	Cab front supports	2	3/8 dia. × 4-7/8
K	Frame	1	3/4 × 3-1/2 × 9
L	Front axle supports	2	3/4 × 1-1/2 × 2-1/2
M	Front wheels	2	2 dia. × 3/4
N	Front axle	1	1/4 dia. × 5-3/8
O	Blade	1	3/4 × 1-1/2 × 7-1/2
P	Blade back support	1	3/4 × 1-1/2 × 3
Q	Blade pivot ring	1	2 dia. × 3/4
R	Blade retaining block	1	3/4 × 2 × 2-1/4
S	Blade pivot pin	1	1/2 dia. × 2-1/4
T	Blade pivot pinlock	1	7/8 dia. × 1/2
U	Steering wheel	1	1-1/4 dia. × 1/4
V	Steering column	1	1/4 dia. × 2-1/2
W	Seat	1	3/8 × 1-1/2 × 2
		1	3/8 × 1-1/4 × 2
X	Exhaust stack	1	1/2 dia. × 1/2
		1	1/4 dia. × 2-1/2
Y	Engine block	1	1-3/8 × 2-1/4 × 2
Z	Pistons	6	1/2 dia. × 1/2
AA	Carburetor air cleaner	1	3/4 dia. × 5/8

STEAMROLLER

No construction site would be complete without a steamroller to smooth out the ground after all the leveling and grading have been finished. The powerful steamroller fascinates children by the way it can easily flatten anything in its path. And grown-ups are amazed by the power this mighty machine can exert.

To round out the construction toys, the steamroller makes a perfect companion to the road grader and the bulldozer. Any child can have fun with this toy on the carpet or in the sandbox.

As with the other toys, read all the instructions first before making any cuts. When you finish this toy, you could make a low-boy trailer for it, too—just like the one you can make for the bulldozer.

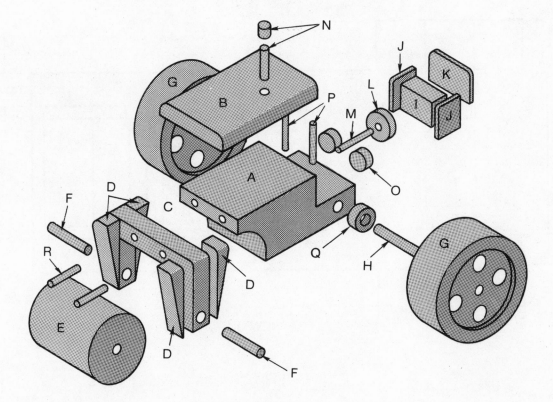

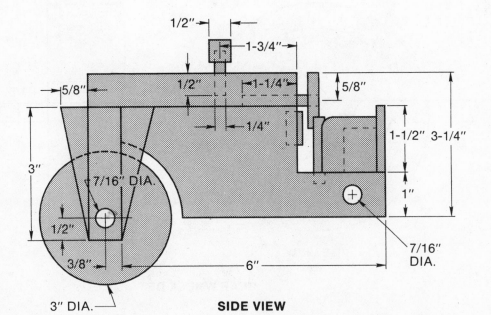

SIDE VIEW

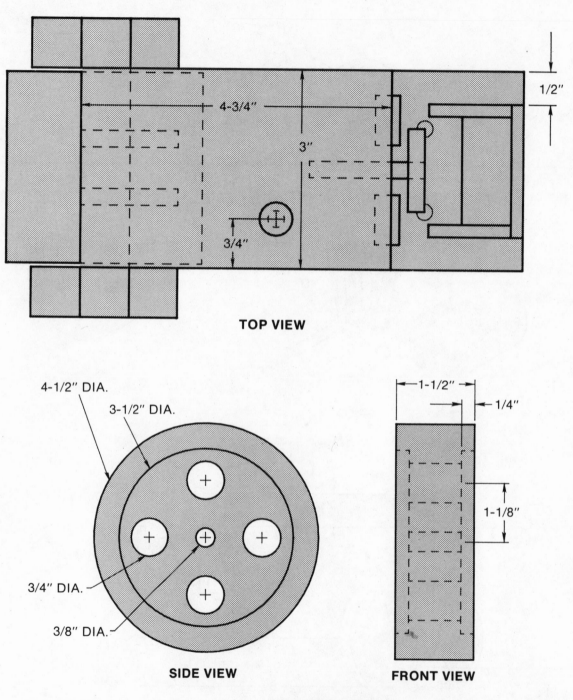

TOP VIEW

1/2"

4-3/4"

3"

3/4"

4-1/2" DIA.

3-1/2" DIA.

3/4" DIA.

3/8" DIA.

SIDE VIEW

1-1/2"

1/4"

1-1/8"

FRONT VIEW

REAR WHEEL DETAIL

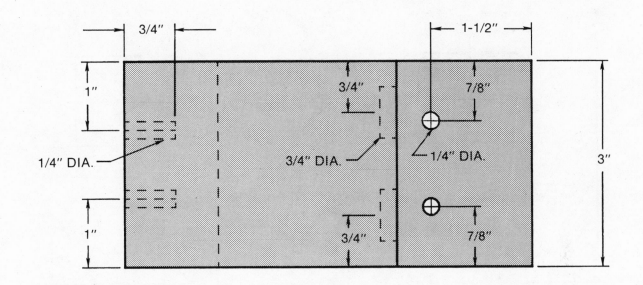

TOP VIEW

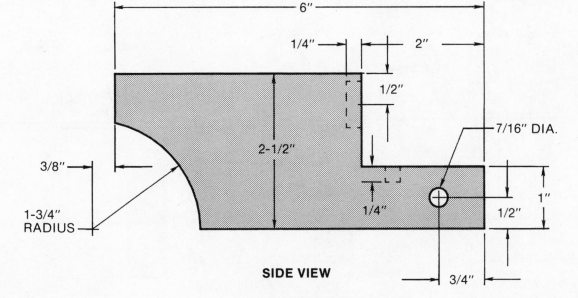

SIDE VIEW

CHASSIS DETAIL

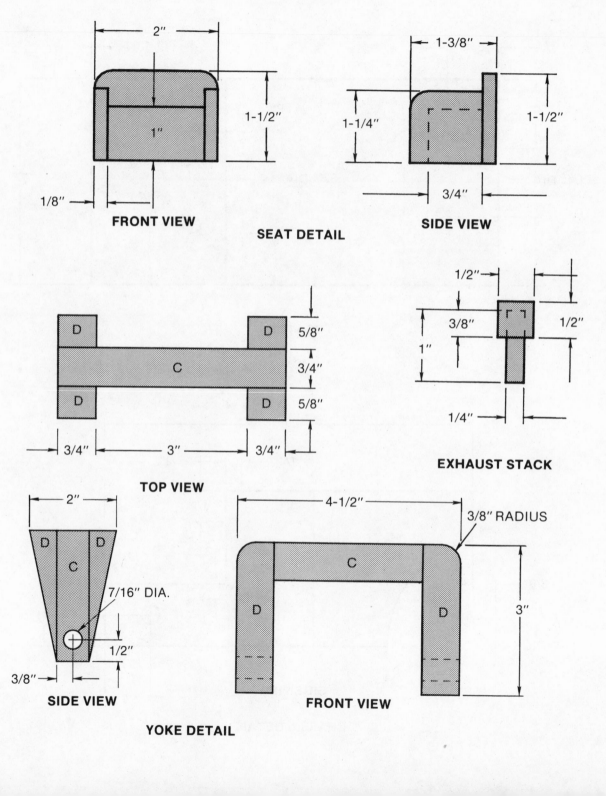

2″

1-3/8″

1″

1-1/2″

1-1/4″

1-1/2″

1/8″

3/4″

FRONT VIEW

SIDE VIEW

SEAT DETAIL

D   D

5/8″

C

3/4″

D   D

5/8″

3/4″   3″   3/4″

TOP VIEW

1/2″

3/8″

1/2″

1″

1/4″

EXHAUST STACK

2″

D   D

C

7/16″ DIA.

1/2″

3/8″

SIDE VIEW

4-1/2″

3/8″ RADIUS

C

D   D

3″

FRONT VIEW

YOKE DETAIL

PROCEDURE

1. STOCK PREPARATION

This project requires some lathe work, so it's important to prepare turning stock ahead of time. Read through the steps on making the roller (E) and rear wheels (G). Then prepare the stock according to the method you prefer. The only other stock you'll need to prepare is the chassis, which requires gluing and clamping together four pieces of 3/4" stock. Cut the rest of the pieces to size according to the list of materials.

2. CHASSIS

Once the glued stock for the chassis (A) has dried, sand the block square, then use a bandsaw or scroll saw to cut out the contour in the back for the seat and control levers.

Before cutting out the front curved section, drill the 1/4"-deep holes for the gauges. Drilling them now is easier, since there's plenty of stock to support the front end as you drill. Notice, though, that the steering wheel column hole has to be drilled after the front yoke is in place.

The round concavity in the front for the roller is a little tricky to do, but not difficult. Place a 3/4" piece of stock on the front of the chassis to mark the location of the cut. Next, place the point of a compass even with the bottom of the chassis (see Fig. 1). Draw a 1-3/4"-radius arc on the chassis. Cut out the recessed area using a bandsaw or scroll saw;

then sand the area smooth with a drum sander.

Complete the chassis by drilling a 7/16"-diameter hole for the rear wheel axle as indicated in the drawings.

3. ROLLER YOKE

The roller yoke assembly has five parts for appearance as well as strength. Begin construction of the yoke by drilling a 7/16"-diameter hole through the piece of 3/4" × 3" × 4-1/2" roller yoke (C) stock. Now use the bandsaw or scroll saw to cut out the yoke profile. As you can see, the arms of the yoke are weak at this point because of grain direction, so be careful handling the piece once it's cut out.

Glue and clamp the roller yoke (C) to the front of the chassis flush with the top. After the glue has dried, drill two 1/4"-diameter holes through the yoke and into the chassis; then glue in two dowel pins for reinforcement. Allow the dowels to protrude about 1/16"; then sand flush when the glue has dried.

Cut out the roller yoke supports (D) using a bandsaw or scroll saw; then glue and clamp them to the roller yoke. After the glue has dried, round the top edges of the yoke with a sander or rasp.

4. ENGINE COVER

The engine cover (B) fits over the top of the chassis and gives

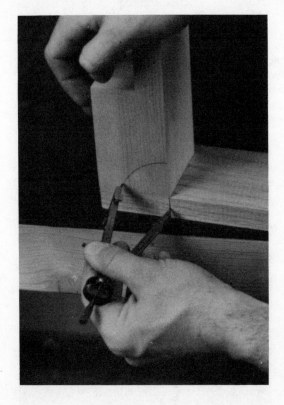

Fig. 1. Locate the radius for the roller by placing the chassis on a piece of 3/4" scrap.

it a finished look. If you didn't cut the engine cover to size in step 1, do so now. Drill the 1/2"-deep hole for the exhaust stack as shown in the plans. Then round the top edges of the cover using a belt or disc sander, and sand the top of the chassis assembly so it's flat and even. Glue and clamp the cover to the chassis.

After the glue has thoroughly dried, drill the 1/4"-diameter steering column hole in the chassis. (It's important that the glue is dry since the steering column hole is so near the glue line.)

5. REAR WHEELS

The rear wheels (G) are made from two pieces of laminated stock that's been glued and clamped for at least 24 hours. After the glue has completely dried, cut out the rear wheels with a bandsaw or scroll saw.

Now, if you have a lathe, mount one of the wheels on a screw center and make a 1/4"-deep recess with a parting tool

and roundnose chisel (see Fig. 2). Mark the center of the wheel while it is spinning.

Turn the wheel around, remount it, then cut the recess on the other side. Repeat this process for the other wheel. After you've finished cutting the recesses, sand the wheels while they are still on the lathe.

Drill the 3/4"-diameter holes where indicated in the plans. To guarantee against any splintering when drilling these holes, drill them part way through from one side until the bit just penetrates the other side. Stop drilling, then turn the wheel over and complete the hole.

Because of the recess cut into the wheels, they must clear the rear of the chassis, so two spacers (Q) must be made. Make these 1"-diameter pieces with a 1-1/8"-diameter hole saw. After cutting the 1"-diameter blanks, enlarge the hole from 1/4" to 3/8" diameter. Using a twist drill bit, expand the holes in the spacers.

CAUTION: The spacers must be clamped securely while drilling. Do not attempt to hold the spacers by hand when drilling.

6. ROLLER

The roller (E) is made from four pieces of glued-up stock. When cutting the stock for this part, make the pieces at least 3" long. (Longer stock would be better since you can always use round stock to make more steamrollers or the other toys in this book.) After the turning stock has been clamped for at least 24 hours, turn it on a lathe to 2-7/8" diameter.

If you don't have a lathe, try cutting an old rolling pin to length. If the hole diameter of a rolling pin is different than 7/16", adjust the hole in the yoke (C) and the diameter of the roller pins (F) accordingly.

7. STEERING WHEEL

The steering wheel (L) is made like most wheels in this book— with a hole saw. Use a 1-3/8" hole saw to make the 1-1/4"-diameter steering wheel out of 1/4"-thick stock. Again, make extras and set them aside for other toys. Glue the steering wheel to the steering column (M) and glue the assembly into the chassis/cover assembly. Then glue the control levers (P) in place.

8. SEAT

The seat (I,J,K) can be made from either 3/16"- or 1/8"-thick stock. Cut the sides (J) and back (K) out of 3/16"-thick stock. Next, cut the seat (I) to size and glue and clamp the seat together. After the glue

Fig. 2. The recesses on the rear wheels (G) are made by mounting the wheel blanks to a lathe and using a parting tool and roundnose chisel to turn the profile.

has dried, sand the seat and glue and clamp it in place on the chassis.

9. FINISHING TOUCHES

Finishing up the construction of this toy is simple. Make the parts for the exhaust stack and glue and clamp these parts together. Once this assembly has dried, glue and clamp it into the engine cover.

Finally, glue the front roller into place with the two pins (F). Glue the rear wheels in place, but don't forget to put the spacers on both sides between the chassis and the wheels. After gluing the wheels and roller, wait 15 minutes, then test them to make sure they're not glued in place.

MATERIALS

Part	Description	Pieces	Dimensions
			(finished dimensions in inches)
A	Chassis	1	3 × 2-1/2 × 6
B	Engine cover	1	3/4 × 3 × 4-3/4
C	Roller yoke	1	3/4 × 3 × 4-1/2
D	Roller yoke supports	4	3/4 × 5/8 × 3
E	Roller	1	3 dia. × 2-7/8
F	Roller pins	2	3/8 dia. × 2
G	Rear wheels	2	4-1/2 dia. × 1-1/2
H	Rear wheel axle	1	3/8 dia. × 5-5/8
I	Seat	1	3/4 × 1 × 1-5/8
J	Seat sides	2	1/8 × 1-1/4 × 1-1/4
K	Seat back	1	1/8 × 1-1/2 × 2
L	Steering wheel	1	1-1/4 dia. × 1/4
M	Steering column	1	1/4 dia. × 1-3/4
N	Exhaust stack	1	1/4 dia. × 1
		1	1/2 dia. × 1/2
O	Gauges	2	3/4 × 3/8
P	Control levers	2	1/4 dia. × 1-1/2
Q	Wheel spacers	2	1 dia. × 3/8
R	Dowel pins	2	1/4 dia. × 1-1/2

CONSTRUCTION NOTES

1. Parts (E) and (G) must be glued and clamped at least 24 hours before turning.

2. Use a 1-1/8"-diameter hole saw to make part (Q), and a 1-3/8"-diameter hole saw to make part (L).

CRANE

Every construction site needs a crane to move materials. Here's a simple-to-build crane that looks more complicated to make and operate than it actually is. When it's completed, this toy has a cab that rotates 360°, a boom that raises and lowers, and a hook that goes up and down on a cable. The boom and crank handles lock into place to add even more realism.

NOTE: You can build the "tracked look" wheel arrangement in these plans, or you can use the chassis plans from the bulldozer project.

You can adapt this design to some of the other toys in this book. For instance, instead of making a chassis assembly for this crane, design your own flatbed car for the Santa Fe train. Or make one of the trucks longer and mount the crane on the bed.

Before you begin make sure you have the S-hook, washers, screw eyes, and string on hand.

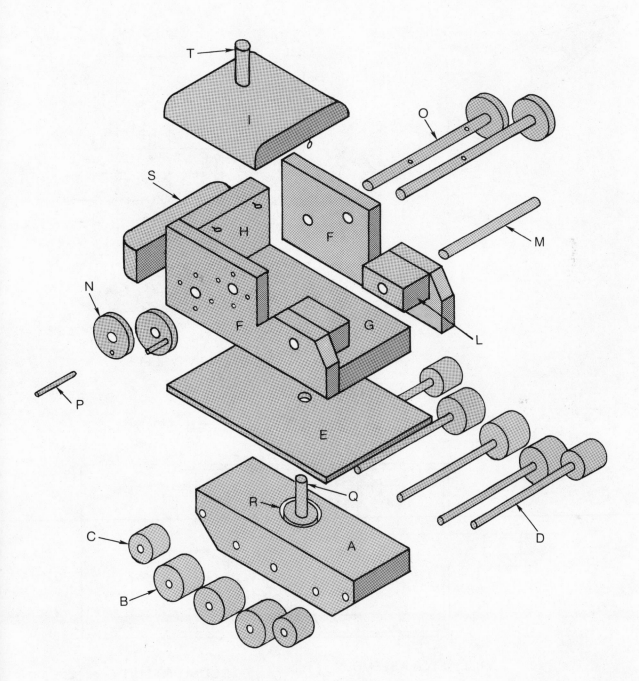

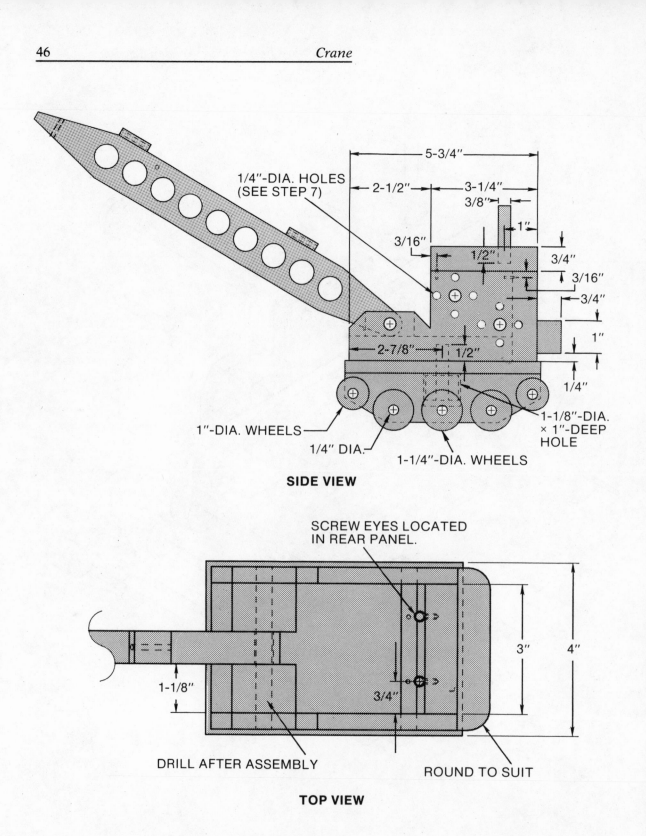

1/4"-DIA. HOLES (SEE STEP 7)

5-3/4"

2-1/2"

3-1/4"

3/8"

1"

3/16"

1/2"

3/4"

3/16"

3/4"

2-7/8"

1/2"

1"

1/4"

1-1/8"-DIA. × 1"-DEEP HOLE

1"-DIA. WHEELS

1/4" DIA.

1-1/4"-DIA. WHEELS

SIDE VIEW

SCREW EYES LOCATED IN REAR PANEL.

3"

4"

1-1/8"

3/4"

DRILL AFTER ASSEMBLY

ROUND TO SUIT

TOP VIEW

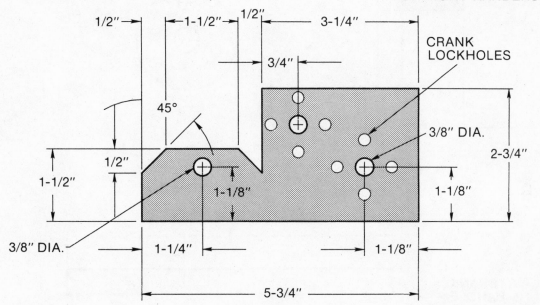

NOTE: PLACE ON LEFT
SIDE FOR LEFT-HANDERS
AND ON RIGHT SIDE
FOR RIGHT-HANDERS.

CRANK
LOCKHOLES

3/8" DIA.

3/8" DIA.

CAB SIDE DETAIL

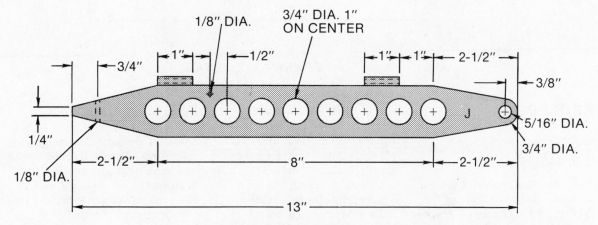

1/8" DIA.

3/4" DIA. 1"
ON CENTER

3/8"

5/16" DIA.

3/4" DIA.

1/8" DIA.

BOOM DETAIL

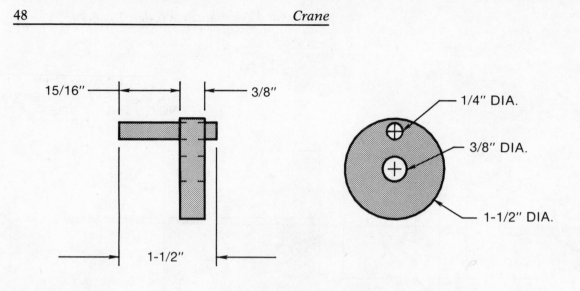

15/16" 3/8"

1/4" DIA.

3/8" DIA.

1-1/2" DIA.

1-1/2"

CRANK WHEEL DETAIL

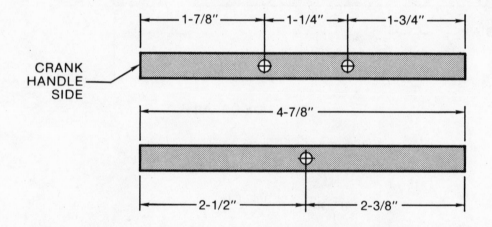

1-7/8" 1-1/4" 1-3/4"

CRANK HANDLE SIDE

4-7/8"

2-1/2" 2-3/8"

CRANK AXLE DETAIL

PROCEDURE

1. CHASSIS

Start by gluing up stock for the chassis. Use three pieces of 3/4" stock to get a 2-1/4"-thick block. Once the glue dries, square up the block using a belt or disc sander—don't attempt to join or plane the stock square with a power jointer or planer because this stock is too small to handle safely.

After the block has been squared, locate and drill the 5/16"-diameter axle holes. Next, drill the pivot pin lock-hole using a 1-1/4"-diameter spade bit or Forstner bit. If you're using the bulldozer chassis, the hole will be bigger than the width of the center beam; but that's no problem, because the pivot pin will still clear the tracks and wheels.

Once you've drilled all the holes, chamfer the ends of the chassis 30°, then sand the chassis smooth—be careful to keep the top edges sharp and square. Set the chassis aside and go on to the next step.

2. WHEELS

Cut out the six main wheels (B). They are 1-1/4" in diameter and can be made with a 1-3/8"-diameter hole saw. Next, cut out the four secondary wheels (C) and the cab pivot pinlock (R) using a 1-1/8"-diameter hole saw. The hole saw leaves a rough edge on the wheels, so sand them smooth once you've finished cutting them out.

When making the main wheels, also make the blanks for the boom and hook crank wheels (N). These blanks are 1-1/2" in diameter and are made with a 1-5/8"-diameter hole saw. Make two of the blanks out of 3/4" stock and resaw them to a 3/8" thickness, or just make four wheels out of 3/8" stock. Set the crank wheels aside for further machining later.

3. CAB

To make the cab, first transfer the pattern for the sides (F) to a piece of 3/4"-thick stock. Carefully locate all angles and holes, except the crank lockholes; these will be located and drilled later. Next, drill all the holes; then, using a bandsaw or scroll saw, cut out the contours on the sides. Then, with a bandsaw or scroll saw, resaw the sides to a 3/8" thickness.

An alternative to cutting out and resawing stock for the sides is to make the sides out of 3/8" stock. When doing this,

cut out the parts first; then stick them together with carpet tape and drill the holes—this will keep the holes in alignment.

After you've finished with the drilling and cutting operations on the sides, drill a 3/8"-diameter × 1/2"-deep hole in the top of the cab roof (I) for the exhaust stack (T). Next, drill a 3/8"-diameter × 1/2"-deep cab pivot pin (Q) hole where indicated in the cab floor (G).

Next, locate and install two screw eyes in the cab rear panel (H) where indicated in the drawings. Since these hooks are located close to the top of the panel, you'll need to make starter holes to prevent the stock from splitting.

You're now ready to assemble the cab. Start the assembly by gluing and clamping the sides (F) to the floor (G) and rear panel (H). After the glue dries, sand the back of the assembly flush. Next, round the counterweight (S) and glue and clamp this into place. While the glue is drying, round the roof (I) and install the screw eye in it as indicated in the plans. Set the roof aside for assembly later.

The final step in constructing the cab is to glue and clamp the boom anchor supports (L) in place. After the glue dries, drill the 3/8" boom anchor pin holes using the holes already drilled in the sides as guides.

4. CRANK ASSEMBLIES

Take the crank wheels you've already made and, if they're

3/4" stock, resaw them into equal parts. Sand the wheels, then redrill the 1/4"-diameter holes to a 3/8" diameter. (The larger hole is necessary for the 3/8"-diameter axles.) To properly center the drilling operation, use a twist drill bit. Next, drill the 1/4" handle holes in two of the wheels; then, set all of the wheels aside.

For the locking crank system to work, the axles must slide back and forth. Since they slide, the holes for the boom and hook cables are not placed in the centers of the axles. Place the holes according to the plans; then drill them using a V-block, or tilt the table. (See Fig. 1.)

Dry-assemble the crank wheels to the axles and locate the crank locking holes on the cab sides. Put the holes on the right side for a right-handed child and on the left for a left-hander. Remove the crank assemblies and drill the holes in the cab sides.

Assemble the crank assemblies with glue. The boom axle goes in the bottom rear position and the hook axle goes in the top front position.

5. CRANE BOOM

After cutting the crane boom (J) stock to length, locate all the holes and contours. Next, drill the 3/4"-diameter "lightening" holes, the 7/16"-diameter anchor pin hole, and the 1/8"-diameter cable run holes located in the front of the boom and in the cable guides (K). Round the boom contours on a disc or belt sander. After finishing all the contouring of the boom, glue and clamp the cable guides into place.

Sand the boom and slide it into position between the boom anchor supports located on the cab. Check the fit. If it's too tight, sand the boom. After achieving a good fit, secure the boom in place by gluing the anchor pin (M) into position.

6. ASSEMBLY

Glue the cab pivot pin (Q) into the bottom of the cab floor. Then, drill a 7/16"-diameter hole in the center of the platform (E). Next, using a 3/8" twist drill, enlarge the 1/4"-diameter hole of the cab pivot pinlock (R) to 3/8" diameter. Glue the lock to the pin.

Place the cab assembly on the platform (E) with the pivot pin (Q) through the hole in the platform. Glue the cab pivot pinlock assembly through the

cab floor and into the cab floor. The platform is still loose at this point but attached to the cab assembly by the pivot pinlock.

After the glue has dried, carefully spread more glue on the top of the chassis. Be careful not to get any in the lockhole. Attach the platform to the chassis and clamp in position.

Finally, assemble the wheels (B,C) and axles (D) to the chassis with glue.

7. HOOK AND BOOM ASSEMBLY

Begin stringing the crane boom by cutting a 30" length of nylon cord. Slightly singe both ends of the cord with a match to prevent it from becoming unraveled. Next, thread one end of the line through one of the holes in the back crank axles. Bring up the

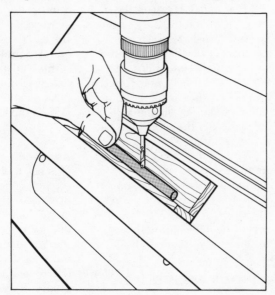

Fig. 1. When drilling the holes in the axles, use a V-block or some other piece of wood to back up the stock.

line through the screw eye above it in the rear panel, then take it straight out the front and through the 1/8" hole in the side of the boom. After you thread the line through the boom, lead it back down to the cab, through the other screw eye in the rear panel, and through the other hole in the back axle. Hold the boom level and pinch the cord where it comes out of the axle. Now raise the boom and tie a knot where you're pinching it. Trim the cord and singe the knot with a match.

For the hook assembly, cut a length of string about 3' long and slightly singe both ends to prevent unraveling. Tie one end around two or three 1/2" flat washers. Thread the other end through the hole in the end of the boom and down through the two cable guides. Set the roof on the cab and run the cord through the screw eye on the roof and down through the front crank axle. Tie a knot in the end of the cord and singe the knot. If everything works satisfactorily, glue and clamp the roof in place.

Finally, take an S-hook and crimp one end of it around the washers. The S-hook will pick up a lot of items, so experiment with it. Attach a magnetic message hook for the refrigerator to the hook cable, or even a little toy bucket. Whatever you and your young construction helper decide, you'll surely agree that this toy is a great deal of fun.

MATERIALS

Part	Description	Pieces	Dimensions
			(finished dimensions in inches)
A	Chassis	1	1-1/2 × 2-1/4 × 6
B	Main wheels	6	1-1/4 dia. × 3/4
C	Secondary wheels	4	1 dia. × 3/4
D	Wheel axles	5	1/4 dia. × 4
E	Platform	1	1/4 × 4 × 6
F	Cab sides	2	3/8 × 2-3/4 × 5-3/4
G	Cab floor	1	3/4 × 3 × 5
H	Cab rear panel	1	3/4 × 3 × 2-3/4
I	Cab roof	1	3/4 × 3-1/4 × 3-3/4
J	Crane boom (not shown)	1	3/4 × 1-1/2 × 13
K	Crane hook cable guides (not shown)	2	1/4 × 3/4 × 1
L	Boom anchor supports	2	3/4 × 1-1/8 × 1-1/2
M	Boom anchor pin	1	3/8 dia. × 3-3/4
N	Hook and boom crank wheels	4	1-1/2 dia. × 3/8
O	Crank wheel axles	2	3/8 × 4-7/8
P	Crank handles	2	1/4 dia. × 1-1/2
Q	Cab pivot pin	1	3/8 dia. × 1-1/2
R	Cab pivot pinlock	1	1 dia. × 3/4
S	Counterweight	1	3/4 × 1 × 3-3/4
T	Exhaust stack	1	3/8 dia. × 1-3/4

MISCELLANEOUS
1/4" screw eyes (3)
#16 or #18 twisted nylon string (7')
Medium S-hook
1/2" washers (2 or 3)

CONSTRUCTION NOTES

1. For safe handling, cut part K to size after drilling the 1/8"-diameter hole.

2. The wheels (B,C,N,R) are made using 1-5/8"-, 1-3/8"-, and 1-1/8"-diameter hole saws.

TRACTOR CAB

Trucks move America. They haul everything from raw materials to finished goods in flatbeds and tankers. Two types of trucks provide the power to pull these trailers—the tractor cab and cab-over-engine, which follows this project.

Most of the parts of this truck are interchangeable with the parts for the cab-over-engine truck, so it's easy to build both at the same time. Also, the trailers that follow can be hauled by either style of cab. The main differences between the trucks are the sizes of the chassis and engines.

The design of this truck is simple and straightforward, with a sense of realism. And, by making the base of the truck a little longer, you can make a variety of intermediate trucks.

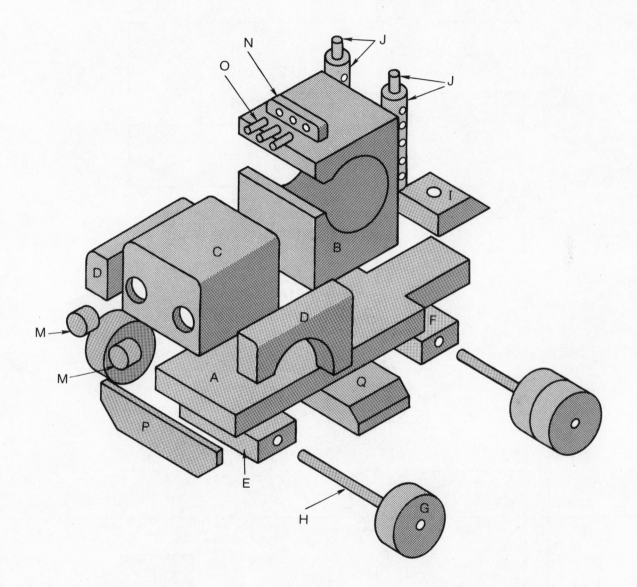

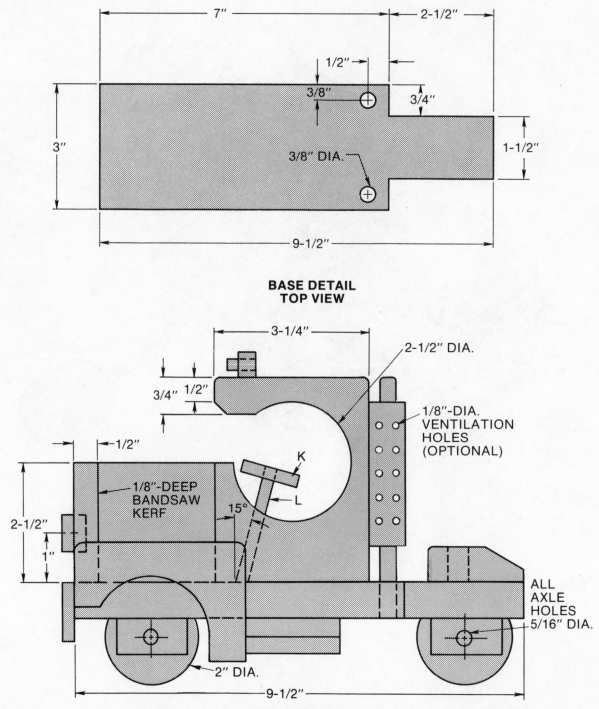

**BASE DETAIL
TOP VIEW**

SIDE VIEW

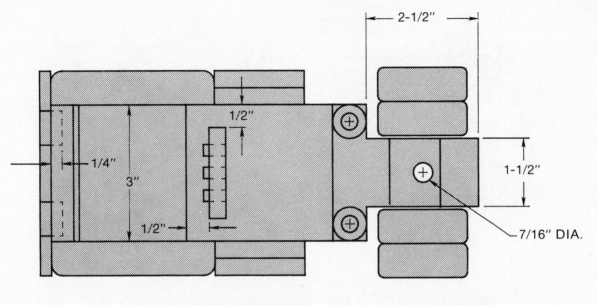

TOP VIEW

2-1/2"

1-1/2"

7/16" DIA.

1/2"

1/4"

3"

1/2"

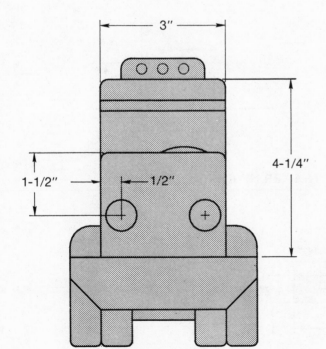

FRONT VIEW

3"

4-1/4"

1-1/2"

1/2"

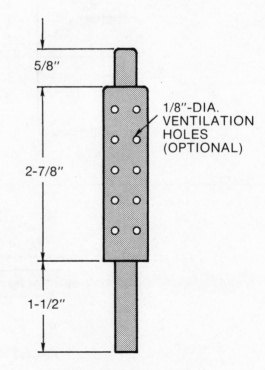

EXHAUST STACK DETAIL

5/8"

2-7/8"

1-1/2"

1/8"-DIA. VENTILATION HOLES (OPTIONAL)

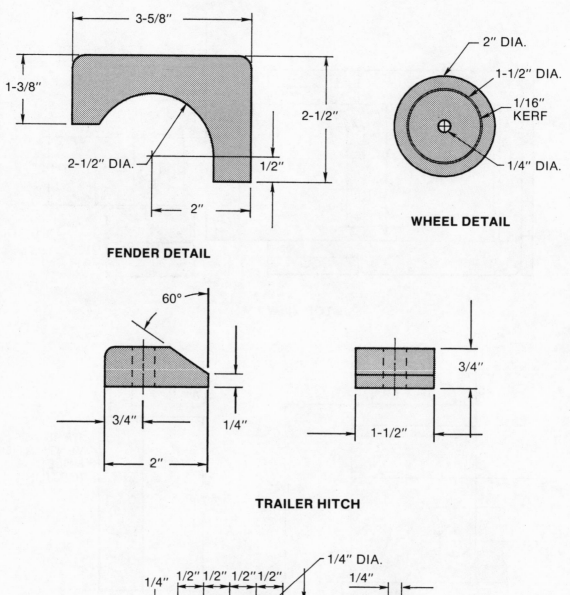

3-5/8''

1-3/8''

2-1/2''

2-1/2'' DIA.

1/2''

2''

FENDER DETAIL

2'' DIA.

1-1/2'' DIA.

1/16'' KERF

1/4'' DIA.

WHEEL DETAIL

60°

3/4''

1/4''

2''

3/4''

1-1/2''

TRAILER HITCH

1/4'' DIA.

1/4''

1/2'' 1/2'' 1/2'' 1/2''

1/2''

2''

FRONT VIEW

1/4''

3/8''

SIDE VIEW

LIGHT BLOCK DETAIL

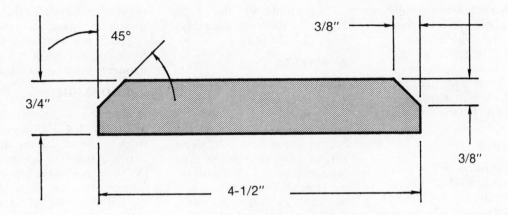

STEP DETAIL

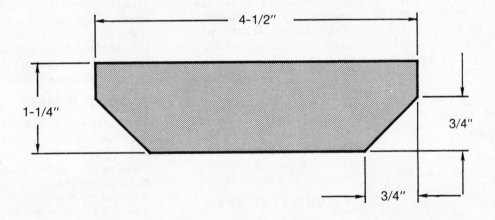

FRONT BUMPER DETAIL

PROCEDURE

1. BASE

Cut the base (A) to shape as shown. If you're making a longer truck for a customized design, continue to use the same wheel cutout configuration at the rear of the base.

After cutting out the rear wheel notches, drill the 3/8"-diameter exhaust stack holes as indicated. Finish the base assembly by drilling the 5/16"-diameter axle holes through the axle holders (E, F), then gluing and clamping them to the base.

2. CAB

Glue and clamp together four pieces of 3/4" × 3-1/4" × 4-1/4" stock to form the cab block (B). After the glue dries, sand the block square and transfer the cab pattern to it. Cut out the cab using a band-saw, scroll saw, or coping saw.

NOTE: Most hole saws will not cut through the 3"-thick stock.

Drill a 1/4"-diameter hole for the steering column (L);

then insert the steering column into the hole, but don't glue it in place yet. (The steering wheel will be added later.) Finally, glue and clamp the cab to the chassis and check the steering column to make sure it still turns. Set the assembly aside.

3. ENGINE

Glue four pieces of 3/4" stock to form a 3" × 2-1/2" × 3" block for the engine (C). Sand the block square after the glue dries; then round off the edges according to the plans.

Using a bandsaw or scroll saw, form the outline of the grill by making a 1/8"-deep saw kerf 1/2" from the front of the engine. Next, drill the 3/4"-diameter holes for the headlights; then glue the lights in place. Finally, glue and clamp the engine to the chassis. After the glue dries, power-sand the sides of the truck flush.

4. FENDERS

Cut the stock for the fenders (D) to size. Then use a 2-1/2"-diameter hole saw and cut the circular profile as shown. Round off the top and front outside edges.

NOTE: There is a right and left fender, and they are not interchangeable. Be sure to mark the edges you're going to round.

Glue and clamp the fenders to the truck assembly flush with the front.

5. WHEELS

Make the wheels (G) with a 2-1/8"-diameter hole saw. Before you cut them out of the stock, use a 1-1/2"-diameter hole saw to make a 1/16"-deep kerf to define the rim and tire. Next, cut out the wheels using the larger hole saw; then mount them on an arbor and sand them. Assemble the wheels and axles (H) to the truck assembly with glue.

While the hole saw is set up, cut out the 1-1/4"-diameter steering wheel (K) from 1/4" stock with a 1-3/8"-diameter hole saw. Sand the steering wheel and glue it in place.

6. TRAILER HITCH

Cut the trailer hitch (I) to size according to the list of materials. Drill the 7/16"-diameter hole as indicated in the plans; then power-sand the bevel on the top. Glue and clamp the hitch to the truck assembly.

7. EXHAUST STACKS

The exhaust stacks (J) are composed of two parts—a 3/4" dowel and a 3/8" dowel. First, drill a 3/8" hole through the length of the 3/4" dowel. To do this, make sure the 3/4" dowel is securely clamped to the drill press table. Next, glue the 3/8" dowels into place. For a realistic touch, add ventilation holes by drilling a series of 1/8"-diameter holes on each stack.

8. ROOF LIGHTS

Drill three 1/4"-diameter holes in a 1/2" × 3/4" × 2" piece of stock as shown. Cut the stock in two to form the light holders (N). (Save one of the holders for another truck.) Next, glue the 1/4"-diameter lights (O) into place; then glue and clamp the light block assembly to the roof.

9. STEP

Make the step (Q) according to the drawings. Cut 3/4" stock to width, then crosscut it to length. Chamfer the ends and sand the piece. Glue and clamp the step to the truck assembly.

10. FRONT BUMPER

The easiest way to make the front bumper (P) is to form a 3/4" × 1-1/4" × 4-1/2" block of stock with the proper profile. Next, cut the block into 1/4"-thick pieces. (Save extra bumpers for other trucks.) Glue the bumper in place.

Your tractor truck is now complete and ready for a trailer. Roll on to the trailer section and build the kind of trailer (or trailers) you want.

MATERIALS

Part	Description	Pieces	Dimensions
			(finished dimensions in inches)
A	Base	1	3/4 × 3 × 9-1/2
B	Cab	1	3 × 3-1/4 × 4-1/4
C	Engine	1	3 × 2-1/2 × 3
D	Fenders	2	3/4 × 2-1/2 × 3-5/8
E	Front axle holder	1	3/4 × 1-1/2 × 3
F	Rear axle holder	1	3/4 × 1-1/2 × 1-1/2
G	Wheels	6	2 dia. × 3/4
H	Axles	2	1/4 dia. × 4-5/8
I	Trailer hitch	1	3/4 × 1-1/2 × 2
J	Exhaust stacks	2	3/4 dia. × 3
		2	3/8 dia. × 5-1/4
K	Steering wheel	1	1-1/4 dia. × 1/4
L	Steering column	1	1/4 dia. × 2-1/2
M	Headlights	2	3/4 dia. × 1/2
N	Roof light holder	1	3/8 × 1/2 × 2
O	Roof lights	3	1/4 dia. × 1/2
P	Front bumper	1	1/4 × 1-1/4 × 4-1/2
Q	Step	1	3/4 × 2 × 4-1/2

CONSTRUCTION NOTES

1. There are two fenders (D), left and right. Double-check the position of the fender on the chassis before rounding.

2. The radiator on the engine (C) is formed by a thin saw kerf.

CAB-OVER-ENGINE

As with the tractor cab, this cab-over-engine truck
can haul any of the toy trailer projects featured in
this book. Or, you can make several intermediate size
trucks. For example, you can lengthen the base to accommodate the crane. Also, you can devise your own
hi-cube or dump truck. The design possibilities are
endless.

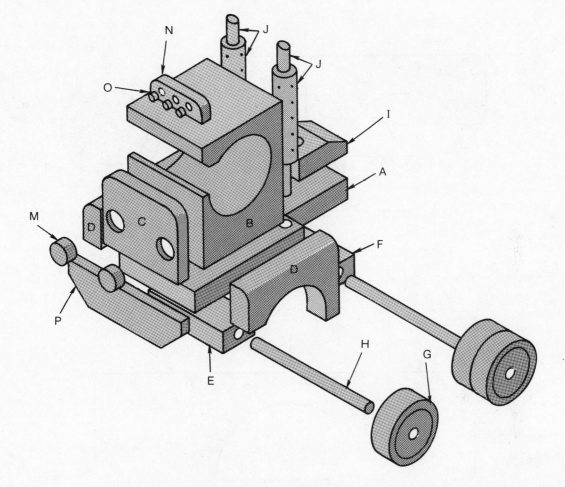

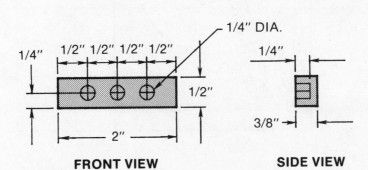

1/4" DIA.

1/4"

1/2" 1/2" 1/2" 1/2"

1/2"

2"

FRONT VIEW

1/4"

3/8"

SIDE VIEW

LIGHT BLOCK DETAIL

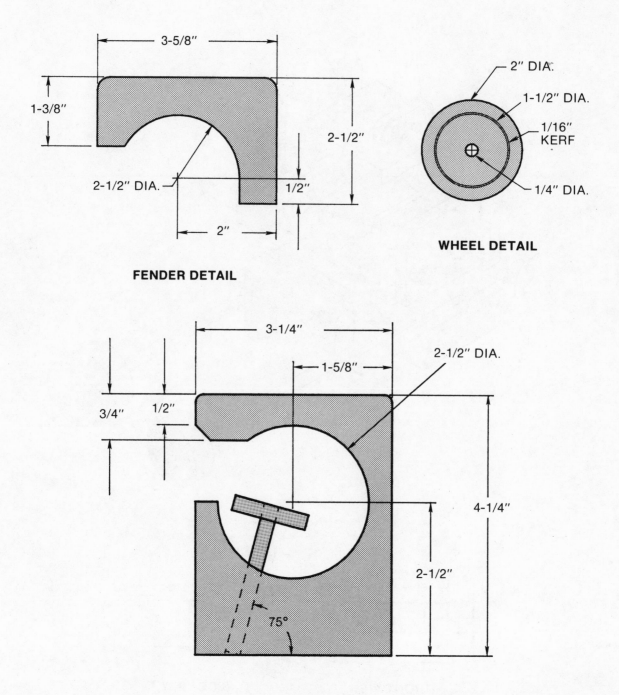

3-5/8"

1-3/8"

2-1/2"

2-1/2" DIA.

1/2"

2"

FENDER DETAIL

2" DIA.

1-1/2" DIA.

1/16" KERF

1/4" DIA.

WHEEL DETAIL

3-1/4"

1-5/8"

2-1/2" DIA.

3/4"   1/2"

4-1/4"

2-1/2"

75°

SIDE VIEW

CAB DETAIL

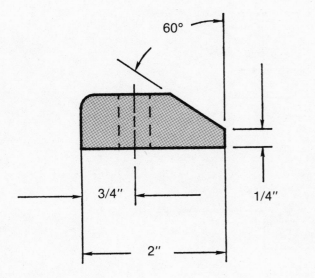

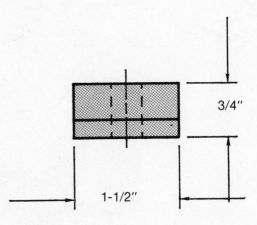

TRAILER HITCH

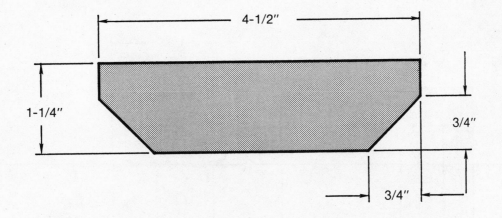

FRONT BUMPER DETAIL

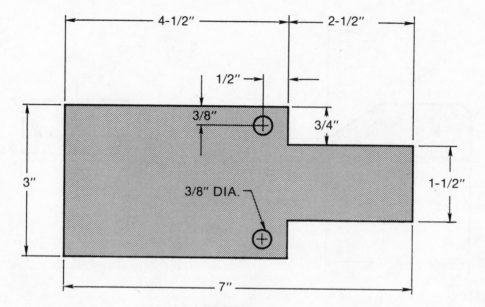

4-1/2"

2-1/2"

1/2"

3/8"

3/4"

3"

3/8" DIA.

1-1/2"

7"

TOP VIEW

BASE DETAIL

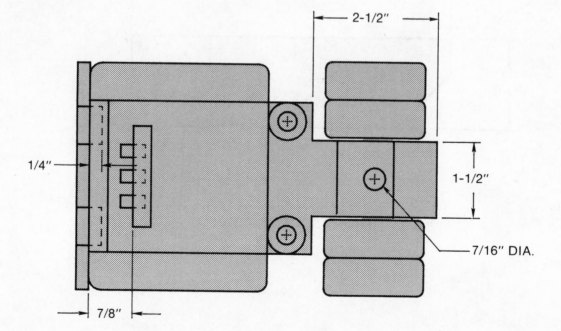

2-1/2"

1/4"

1-1/2"

7/16" DIA.

7/8"

TOP VIEW

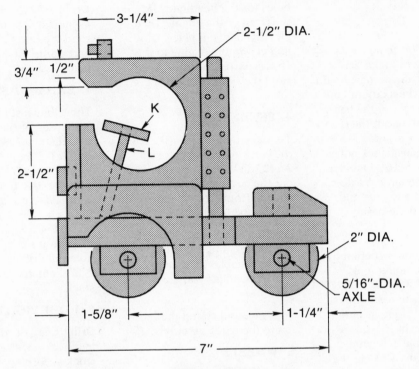

SIDE VIEW

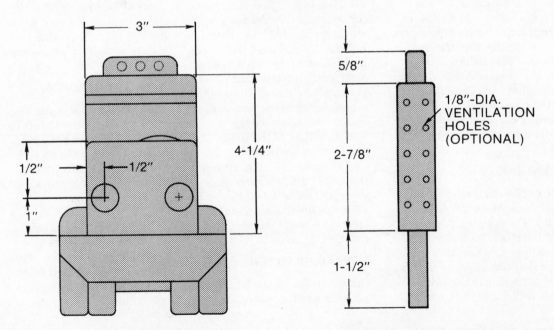

FRONT VIEW   **EXHAUST STACK DETAIL**

PROCEDURE

1. BASE

Cut the base (A) to shape as shown. If you're making a longer truck, all you have to do is make the wheel cutout consistent at the rear of the base.

After cutting out the rear wheel notches, drill the 3/8"-diameter exhaust stack holes. Next, drill the 5/16"-diameter axle holes through the axle holders (E, F), and glue and clamp these to the base.

2. CAB

Begin cab (B) construction by gluing and clamping four pieces of 3/4" × 3-1/4" × 4-1/4" stock together to form the basic cab block. After the glue dries, sand the block square and transfer the cab pattern to it from the plans. Cut out the cab using a bandsaw, scroll saw, or coping saw. Drill a 1/4"-diameter hole for the steering column and insert the column in the hole, but don't glue it in place (the steering wheel will be added later). Finally, glue and clamp the cab to the chassis and check the steering column to make sure it still turns. Set assembly aside.

3. ENGINE

The engine (C) is made from 3/8" stock. Make the piece out of a 3/4"-thick piece; then resaw the stock, reserving the extra engine for another truck. Round off the edges of the engine according to the plans. Next, drill the 3/4"-diameter

holes for the headlights (M) in the front of the engine; then glue the lights in place. Glue and clamp the engine to the chassis. After the glue dries, sand the sides of the truck flush.

4. FENDERS

To make the fenders (D), cut the stock to size, then use a 2-1/2"-diameter hole saw and cut the circular profile as shown. Round off the top and front outside edges.

NOTE: There is a right and left fender, and they are not interchangeable. Be sure to mark the edges you are going to round.

Glue and clamp the fenders to the truck assembly.

5. WHEELS

Make the wheels (G) with a 2-1/8"-diameter hole saw. Before you cut them out of the stock, use a 1-1/2"-diameter hole saw to make a 1/16"-deep kerf to define the rim and tire. Next, cut out the wheels using the larger hole saw. Mount the wheels on an arbor and sand them; then assemble the wheels and axles (H) to the truck assembly with glue.

While you're at it, cut out the 1-1/4"-diameter steering wheel (K) using a 1-3/8"-diameter hole saw. Sand the steering wheel, then glue it to the steering column.

6. TRAILER HITCH

Cut the trailer hitch (I) to size according to the materials list.

Drill the 7/16"-diameter hole as indicated in the plans; then sand the bevel on the top. Glue and clamp the hitch to the truck assembly.

7. EXHAUST STACKS

The exhaust stacks (J) are composed of two parts—a 3/4" dowel and a 3/8" dowel. First, drill a 3/8" hole through the length of the 3/4" dowel. Be sure the 3/4" dowel is securely clamped to the drill press table. Next, glue the 3/8" dowel into place. For a realistic touch, you may want to add ventilation holes by drilling a series of 1/8"-diameter holes on each stack.

8. ROOF LIGHTS

Drill three 1/4"-diameter holes in a 1/2" × 3/4" × 2" piece of stock according to the plans. Cut the stock in two to form the roof light holder (N). Glue the 1/4"-diameter roof lights (O) into place; then glue and clamp the light block assembly to the roof.

9. FRONT BUMPER

The easiest way to make the front bumper (P) is to form a block of stock with the proper profile, then cut the block into 1/4"-thick pieces. Save extra bumpers for other trucks. Glue the bumper in place.

Your cab-over-engine truck is now complete and ready for a trailer. Roll on to the trailer section and build the kind of trailer or trailers you require.

MATERIALS

Part	Description	Pieces	Dimensions
			(finished dimensions in inches)
A	Base	1	3/4 × 3 × 7
B	Cab	1	3 × 3-1/4 × 4-1/4
C	Engine	1	3/8 × 2-1/2 × 3
D	Fenders	2	3/4 × 2-1/2 × 3-5/8
E	Front axle holder	1	3/4 × 1-1/2 × 3
F	Rear axle holder	1	3/4 × 1-1/2 × 1-1/2
G	Wheels	6	2 dia. × 3/4
H	Axles	2	1/4 dia. × 4-5/8
I	Trailer hitch	1	3/4 × 1-1/2 × 2
J	Exhaust stacks	2	3/4 dia. × 3
		2	3/8 dia. × 5-1/4
K	Steering wheel (not shown)	1	1-1/4 dia. × 1/4
L	Steering column (not shown)	1	1/4 dia. × 2-1/2
M	Headlights	2	3/4 dia. × 1/2
N	Roof light holder	1	3/8 × 1/2 × 2
O	Roof lights	3	1/4 dia. × 1/2
P	Front bumper	1	1/4 × 1-1/4 × 4-1/2

CONSTRUCTION NOTE

1. There are two fenders (D), left and right. Double-check the position of the fender on the chassis before rounding.

LOW-BOY TRAILER

The primary purpose of the low-boy trailer is to haul steamrollers, bulldozers, cranes, and road graders from one building site to another. These trailers are an integral part of any construction company—including yours.

The trailer is easy to build and is suitable for the bulldozer and crane. You'll need a longer trailer for the steamroller or road grader; just build a longer bed. When making one of these trailers, take time to build some extras.

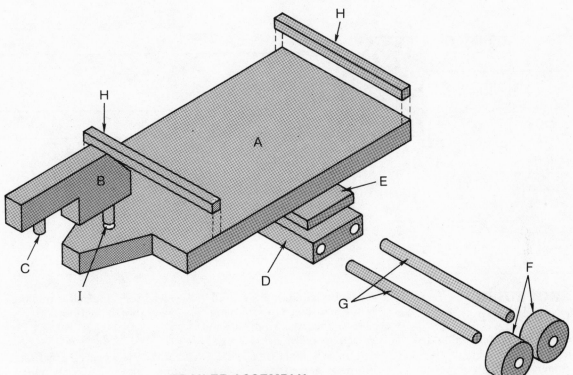

TRAILER ASSEMBLY

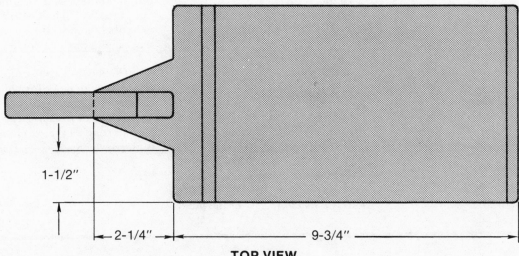

1-1/2"

2-1/4"

9-3/4"

TOP VIEW

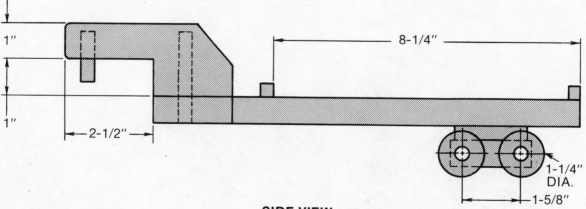

SIDE VIEW

PROCEDURE

1. PREPARATION

Cut all the parts listed under materials. For a longer trailer, change the length of part A— all other parts remain the same. As with all the projects in this book, be sure to make extra parts.

2. FLOOR

Lay out the front contour of the trailer floor (A) on the stock. Using a bandsaw or scroll saw, cut the floor to shape. If you want a longer floor, cut a longer piece of stock, but keep the front profile the same. Glue and clamp the floor stops (H) into place; then set the assembly aside.

3. COUPLING ARM

Lay out the profile of the coupling arm (B) on a piece of stock. For additional strength in the arm, place the coupling arm on the stock so the grain runs diagonally across it. Cut out the arm and drill a 3/8"-diameter hole in the end of it for a coupling pin (C). Glue the pin into place; then glue and clamp the coupling arm to the trailer floor.

After the glue has thoroughly dried, drill a 2-1/2"-deep hole through the bottom of the floor up through the coupling arm. Glue a reinforcing pin (I) into the hole and sand flush.

4. AXLE HOLDER

After you've prepared the stock for the axle holder (D), clamp it securely to a drill press table and drill the 5/16"-diameter axle holes in it. Next, glue and clamp the holder (D) to the spacer (E). After the glue

has dried, glue and clamp the assembly to the floor.

5. WHEELS

Make the wheels (F) by first forming the 1/8"-deep wheel rims with a 3/4"-diameter hole saw. Next, use a 1-3/8"-diameter hole saw to cut out the 1-1/4"-diameter wheels. After the wheels have been cut out, sand them smooth. Finally, cut the axles (G) to length and assemble them with glue to the wheels and the axle holder.

The low-boy trailer is ready to go to work for your construction crew and provide much-needed assistance in transporting all that equipment to the next site.

MATERIALS

Part	Description	Pieces	Dimensions
			(finished dimensions in inches)
A	Floor	1	3/4 × 5-3/4 × 12
B	Coupling arm	1	3/4 × 2 × 4-3/4
C	Coupling pin	1	3/8 dia. × 1-5/8
D	Axle holder	1	3/4 × 2-1/4 × 4
E	Axle spacer	1	3/8 × 1-1/2 × 3-1/2
F	Wheels	4	1-1/4 dia. × 3/4
G	Axles	2	1/4 dia. × 5-5/8
H	Floor stops	2	3/8 × 3/8 × 5-3/4
I	Reinforcement pin	1	3/8 dia. × 2-1/2

CONSTRUCTION NOTES

1. The floor (A) can be made any length to accommodate various sizes of equipment.

2. Lay out the coupling arm (B) diagonally across the grain for strength.

FLATBED TRAILER

This style of trailer leaves most of the designing up to you. It serves as a starting point for many trailers— flatbed, stake, container, tandem, and others. For example, drill holes around the perimeter of the bed, and you've created a stake bed trailer. Or, add a box with a hinged door to get a container trailer. Just let your imagination go with designing.

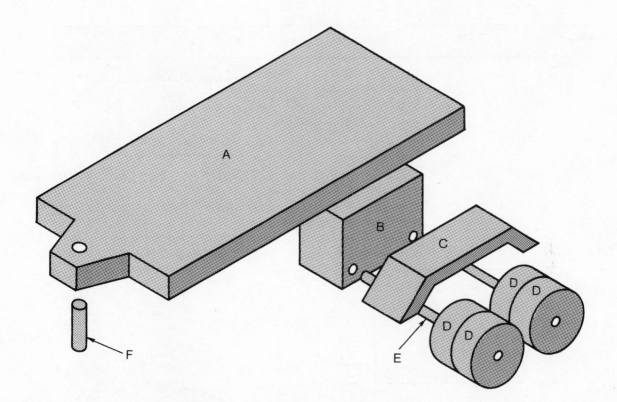

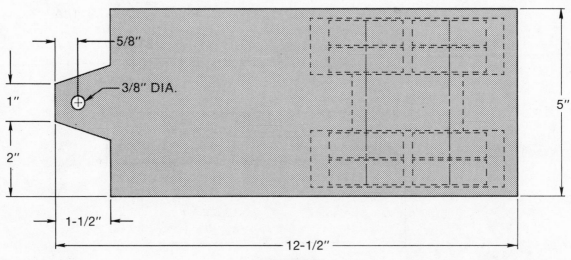

TOP VIEW

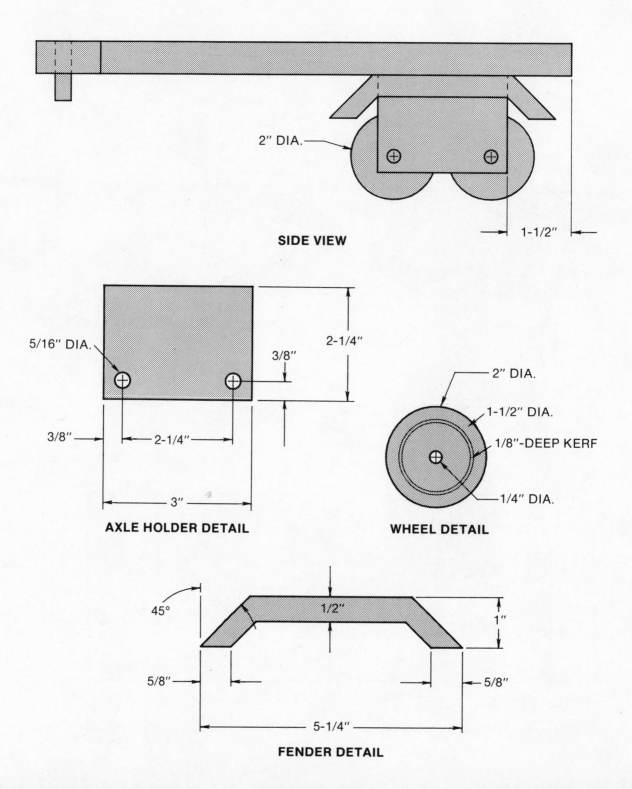

SIDE VIEW

AXLE HOLDER DETAIL

WHEEL DETAIL

FENDER DETAIL

PROCEDURE

1. FLOOR

Cut all the stock to size according to the materials list. On the front of the stock for the floor (A) draw the contours according to the plans. If you're going to build several trailers, make a template for this contour using stiff cardboard or a piece of hardboard. Cut out the floor contour with a bandsaw or scroll saw. Then drill a 3/8"-diameter hole for the coupling pin (F). If you want to make a stake bed, drill 1/4"-deep holes for the stakes around the perimeter of the floor. Use ten stakes—five on each side. Glue the coupling pin (F) and stakes into place.

2. AXLE HOLDER

To make the axle holder (B), glue up three pieces of 3/4" stock to form the 1-1/2" × 2-1/4" × 3" block. Sand the block square, and drill the two 5/16"-diameter axle holes as shown. Glue and clamp the axle holder to the floor.

3. FENDERS

The fenders for the flatbed trailer and tanker trailer are identical in construction. For each fender (C), glue together two pieces of 3/4" stock to form a 1-1/2" × 1" × 5-1/4" block. On the 1" × 5-1/4" side of the block, draw the fender profile that's shown. Next, using a bandsaw or scroll saw,

cut the fenders to shape. Finally, sand the fenders; then glue and clamp them to the floor snug to the axle holder.

4. WHEELS

The wheels (D) are made by a two-step process similar to the other projects. Begin by using a 1-1/2"-diameter hole saw to create a 1/8"-deep kerf for the tire rims. Next, use a 2-1/8"-diameter hole saw to cut out the 2"-diameter wheels. Sand the wheels after you've cut them out; then glue them onto the axles and mount in the axle holder.

The basic flatbed trailer is now complete and ready for loading.

MATERIALS

Part	Description	Pieces	Dimensions
			(finished dimensions in inches)
A	Floor	1	3/4 × 5 × 12-1/2
B	Axle holder	1	1-1/2 × 2-1/4 × 3
C	Fenders	2	1-1/2 × 1 × 5-1/4
D	Wheels	8	2 dia. × 3/4
E	Axles	2	1/4 dia. × 4-5/8
F	Coupling pin	1	3/8 dia. × 1-3/8

CONSTRUCTION NOTES

1. The floor (A) can be used as a base for most any trailer configuration.

2. Fenders could be cut by ripping a 2 × 4 into 1" strips, then crosscutting to length.

TANK TRAILER

Hauling fuel to your construction toys is important. And what better way to do the job than with a well-designed tank trailer?

The biggest design problem with this toy was making it light enough to be practical; a solid wooden tank would weigh several pounds. The solution: Build up the tank, then bevel the sides. You can also round the sides, leaving flat areas on the top and bottom.

This trailer features a nozzle system. Nylon hoses equipped with couplers and nozzles plug into a control panel on the back or into filler pipes on the top of the trailer. Drilling matching filler holes in the sides of your construction equipment and trucks makes "filling 'er up" easy.

Remember, no design is static. These plans can be a starting point for designing your own toys. For example, if you extend the base of the tractor cab or cab-over-engine truck, you can put a shortened version of the tank trailer on the truck bed. (Measure 7-1/2" from the back of the tank, keep the control panel, and eliminate the hose platform.)

No matter how you treat this project, it's sure to add a lot of fun to any child's toy collection.

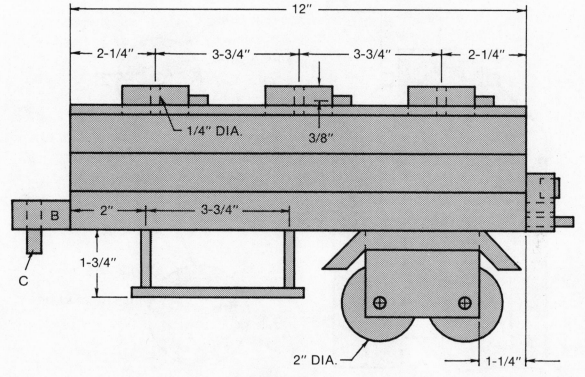

SIDE VIEW

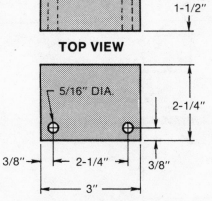

TOP VIEW

SIDE VIEW
AXLE HOLDER DETAIL

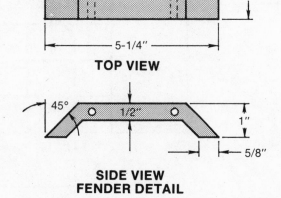

TOP VIEW

SIDE VIEW
FENDER DETAIL

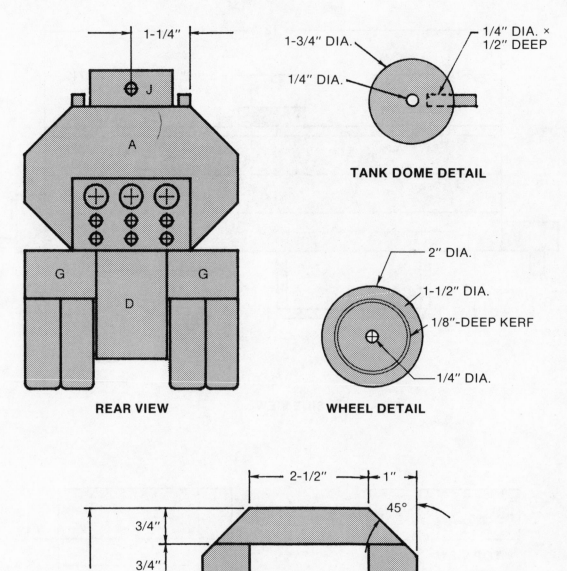

REAR VIEW

TANK DOME DETAIL

WHEEL DETAIL

TANK CONSTRUCTION DETAIL

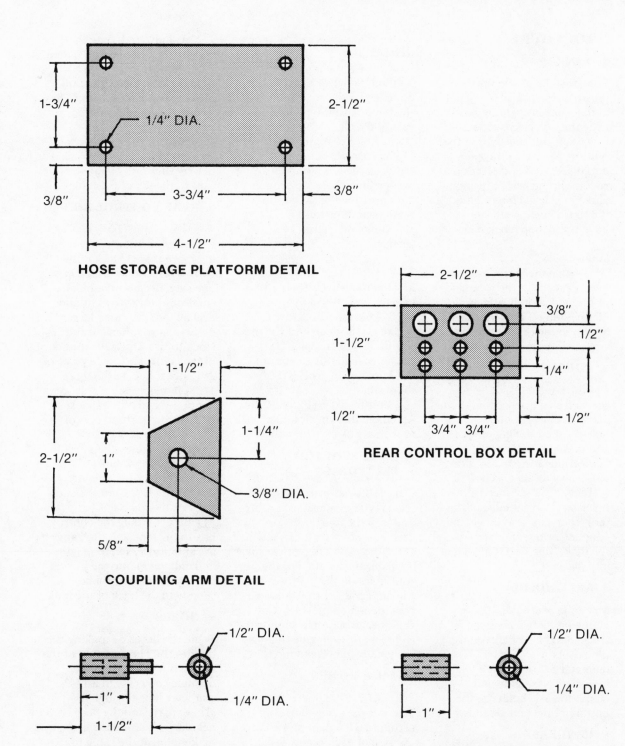

HOSE STORAGE PLATFORM DETAIL

REAR CONTROL BOX DETAIL

COUPLING ARM DETAIL

HOSE NOZZLE DETAIL

HOSE CONNECTOR DETAIL

PROCEDURE

1. TANK

Cut the stock to size for the tank (A), and follow the detail in the planks for gluing it up. Glue the side pieces together first; then glue the sides to the bottom. Next, glue the ends into place. (The end pieces may require fitting before being glued in place.) Finally, glue the top in place. You should have a glued-up block measuring 3" high × 4-1/2" wide × 12" long.

With a table saw, cut a 45° bevel on each of the four sides of the tank as indicated in the plans. Sand off the saw marks, and sand the ends flush and smooth. Set the tank aside.

2. COUPLING ARM

Cut the coupling arm (B) to size and shape according to the plans. Drill a 3/8"-diameter hole for the coupling pin (C) and two 1/4" holes in the back edge of the arm for 1/4" dowel pins. Next, locate and drill matching 1/4"-diameter dowel holes on the front edge of the tank; then glue and dowel the coupling arm to the front of the tank. Glue the coupling pin into place.

3. AXLE HOLDER

Make the axle holder (D) by gluing up three pieces of 3/4" stock. Sand the block square; then drill the two 5/16"-diameter axle holes in it where indicated. Next, glue and clamp the axle holder to the bottom of the tank as shown.

4. FENDERS

For each fender (G), glue to-gether two pieces of 3/4" stock to form a 1-1/2" × 1" × 5-1/4" block. Draw the fender profile on the 1" × 5-1/4" side; then cut each fender to shape. Sand the fenders smooth; then lo-cate and drill 3/16"-diameter dowel holes to match the axle holders. Dowel pins are needed between the fender and axle holder since there isn't much gluing surface between the fenders and the tank.

Glue and clamp the fenders into position.

5. WHEELS

Making the wheels (F) is a two-step process. Begin by using a 1-1/2"-diameter hole saw to create a 1/8"-deep kerf for the tire rims. Next, use a 2-1/8"-diameter hole saw to cut out the 2"-diameter wheels. Sand them smooth.

Cut the axles (E) to length. Assemble the wheels and axles to the axle block with glue.

6. HOSE STORAGE PLATFORM

Cut the stock for the platform (H) to final dimensions. Locate and drill the four 1/4"-diameter holes on it as shown. Place the platform on the tank. Transfer the location of the four holes on the platform to the underside of the tank, and drill the matching holes. Cut the storage platform supports (I) to length; then glue the plat-form and supports to the tank.

7. TANK DOMES

With a 1-7/8"-diameter hole saw, cut the three tank domes (J) out of 3/4"-thick stock. Into the side of each dome, drill a 1/4-diameter hole to a depth of 1/2" as indicated. Glue the nozzles (K) into the holes; then glue and clamp the three domes to the top of the tank. Make extra domes and nozzles to have on hand for other tanks.

Finish off the tanker top by cutting the tank top rails (L) to size. Glue and clamp the rails to the top of the tank.

8. REAR CONTROL BOX

The rear control box (M) looks complicated but is really noth-ing more than a block of wood with several holes drilled in one side. Because the block is small, it's best to lay out and drill all the holes on a larger piece of stock; then cut the stock to size. Draw the outline of the control box on a piece of 3/4" stock. Locate the three 1/2"-diameter gauge holes at the upper end of the block; then locate the two rows of 1/4"-diameter holes. Drill 3/8"-deep gauge holes; then drill the two rows of 1/4" holes all the way through the stock. After drilling the holes, cut the con-trol box to size.

Before gluing the control box to the tank, cut the gauges (N) and nozzles (O) to length, and glue them into the box. Fi-nally, glue the control box as-sembly to the back of the tank.

9. HOSES

Begin the hoses by making the nozzles (P). The first part of the nozzle is a piece of 1/2"-diameter dowel with a 1/4"-diameter hole through it. (These parts and the hose con-nectors [Q] are identical, so make them at the same time.) Clamp the 1/2"-diameter dowel to a drill press table and drill a 1/4″-diameter hole through it. Use long (2″ to 4″) lengths of 1/2″-diameter dowel; then cut the stock to length after drilling. For the second part of the nozzle, cut two 1″-long pieces of 1/4″-diameter dowel. Glue the 1/4″-diameter dowels into the two 1/2″-diameter dowels, and the nozzles are complete.

Cut the nylon line to two 18″ lengths, and use a candle to melt the end of one of the pieces. When it's melted, stick it into the open end of a nozzle. The hot nylon will "glue" itself into the dowel as it cools. Melt the other end of the line, and stick it halfway into one of the connectors (Q). Repeat the process for the other line.

CAUTION: Be very careful when working with molten nylon. It is extremely **HOT** and can cause severe burns.

MATERIALS

Part	Description	Pieces	Dimensions
			(finished dimensions in inches)
A	Tank	2	3/4 × 4-1/2 × 12
		4	3/4 × 1 × 12
		2	3/4 × 1-1/2 × 2-1/2
B	Coupling arm	1	3/4 × 1-1/2 × 2-1/2
C	Coupling pin	1	3/8 dia. × 1-3/8
D	Axle holder	1	1-1/2 × 2-1/4 × 3
E	Axles	2	1/4 dia. × 4-5/8
F	Wheels	8	2 dia. × 3/4
G	Fenders	2	1-1/2 × 1 × 5-1/4
H	Hose storage platform	1	1/4 × 2-1/2 × 4-1/2
I	Storage platform supports	4	1/4 dia. × 2-1/2
J	Tank domes	3	1-3/4 dia. × 3/4
K	Tank dome nozzles	3	1/4 dia. × 1
L	Tank top rails	2	1/4 × 1/4 × 12
M	Rear control box	1	3/4 × 1-1/2 × 2-1/2
N	Rear control box gauges	3	1/2 dia. × 1/2
O	Rear control box nozzles	3	1/4 dia. × 1-1/4
P	Hose nozzles	2	1/2 dia. × 1
		2	1/4 dia. × 1
Q	Hose connectors	2	1/2 dia. × 1
R	Hose (nylon line)	2	1/4 dia. × 18

BIPLANE

The Stearman Trainer Biplane was the standard training plane for the Air Force and Navy prior to and during World War II. Because the original color of the plane was yellow and so many students scared so many instructors during training flights, the aircraft picked up the nickname *Yellow Peril.*

This biplane design is generic and uses only the general features of the Stearman Trainer. Since special construction techniques are required for this toy, read all the instructions before making any cuts. Also, it's quite easy to make more than one of these planes at a time.

Here is the flight plan for the biplane.

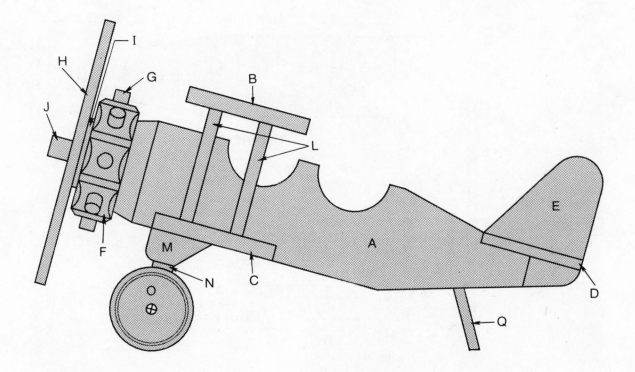

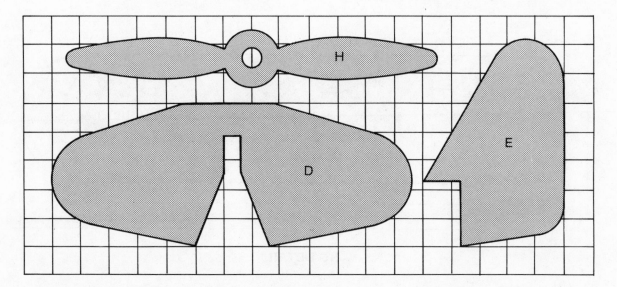

ONE SQUARE = 1/2"

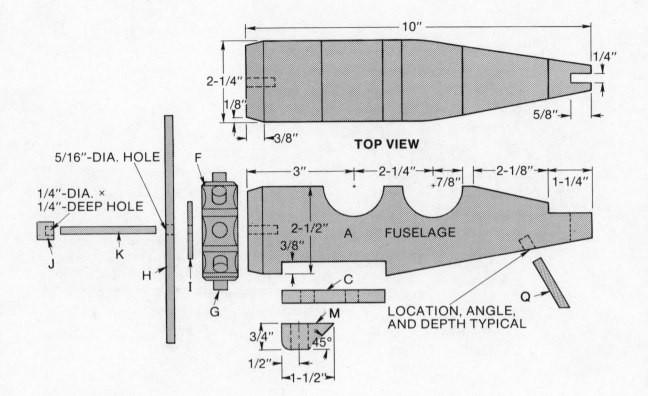

10"

2-1/4"

1/8"

1/4"

5/8"

3/8"

TOP VIEW

5/16"-DIA. HOLE

F

1/4"-DIA. ×
1/4"-DEEP HOLE

3"   2-1/4"   +7/8"   2-1/8"   1-1/4"

2-1/2"   A   FUSELAGE

3/8"

J   K   H   I   G   C

M

3/4"

1/2"

1-1/2"   45°

LOCATION, ANGLE,
AND DEPTH TYPICAL

Q

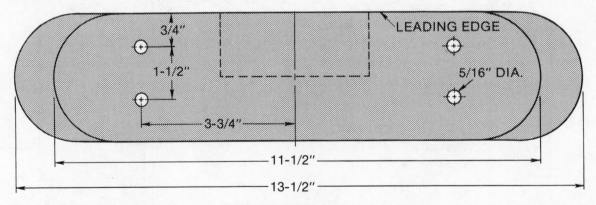

3/4"

LEADING EDGE

1-1/2"

5/16" DIA.

3-3/4"

11-1/2"

13-1/2"

WING DETAIL

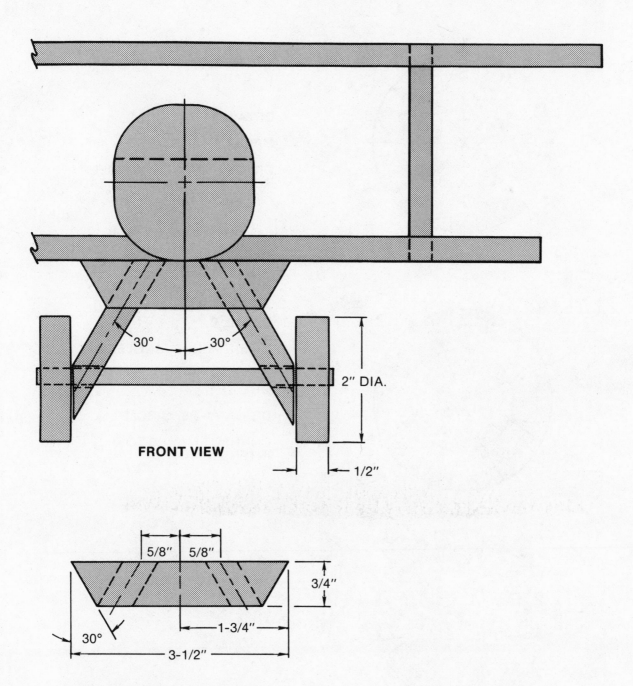

FRONT VIEW

2" DIA.

1/2"

WHEEL STRUT BLOCK DETAIL

5/8" 5/8"

3/4"

1-3/4"

30°

3-1/2"

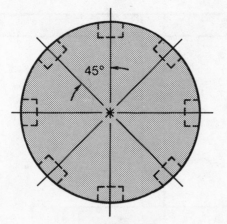

DETAIL A

MARK OFF LINES EVERY 45°

DRILL 7/16"-DIA. × 1/4"-DEEP
HOLES FOR CYLINDER HEADS

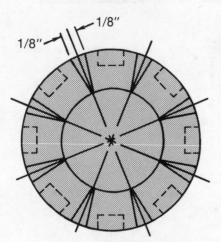

DETAIL B

DIVIDE THE 45° ANGLES

MARK 1/8" ON EACH SIDE
OF LINE

DRAW A 1-5/8" CIRCLE

CONNECT MARKS TO
INTERSECTION

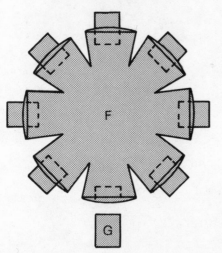

PROCEDURE

1. FUSELAGE

Glue and clamp three pieces of 3/4" × 2-1/2" × 11" stock to form the fuselage block. If making more than one plane, allow about 11" length for each fuselage. Cut the block to finished dimensions; then draw the top and side profiles on it.

Cut out the wing notch on the bottom and the rear tail notches. Taper the sides of the fuselage with a scroll saw or bandsaw. Tape back the scrap pieces. Place the fuselage on its side and cut the side profile.

Finally, with a rasp or power sander, round off the edges of the fuselage; then bevel the nose.

Set the fuselage aside.

2. WINGS

Make the upper and lower wings (B, C) at the same time. Begin with a piece of stock at least 3/4" thick and 13-1/2" long. The proper width of the wings is determined by the notch already cut on the fuselage. Remove the excess width of the wing stock until it fits the notch.

Lay out the location of the wing strut holes and drill them with a 5/16"-diameter drill bit. Resaw the stock into two 3/8"-thick wing blanks. Form the round contour on the wing tips as shown; then sand the tips smooth.

Glue and clamp the lower wing (C) to the fuselage. Assemble the upper wing (B) to the fuselage with the wing struts (L). Sand the wing struts flush with the wings; set the assembly aside.

3. HORIZONTAL AND VERTICAL TAILS

Make a cardboard template as in the previous step and transfer the design to 3/4" stock. Cut out the contours with a bandsaw or scroll saw; sand the edges smooth. Resaw the stock to yield 1/4"-thick parts.

Glue and clamp the horizontal tail (D) to the fuselage; then glue and clamp the vertical tail (E) in place. Set the assembly aside.

4. ENGINE

Glue and clamp two pieces of stock to form a 1-1/2"-thick piece. Next, resaw the stock to a 1-1/4" thickness. With a compass and straightedge, draw the outside circumference of the block and locate the piston and cylinder positions. To do this, draw a 2-3/4"-diameter circle; then draw lines from the center of the circle to the circumference every 45°. These lines locate the centers of the cylinders.

Next, draw a 1-5/8"-diameter circle and bisect each of the 45° angles with another line to the outside circumference. Mark 1/8" on each side of these bisection marks and connect them to the 1-5/8"-diameter circle (see detail in the plans).

Now it's time to start machining. Use a scroll saw or bandsaw to cut the block round. Sand the edge smooth; then drill the 5/16"-diameter cylinder holes 1/4" deep. After drilling the holes, form the pistons with a scroll saw or bandsaw (see Fig. 1).

Finish the engine block by chamfering the edges with a power sander or rasp. Glue the cylinder heads (G) into place; then set the engine block aside.

5. PROPELLER

Lay out the profile of the propeller (H) on a piece of 1/4" plywood or clear stock. Drill the 5/16"-diameter shaft hole in the center of the piece; then cut out the propeller with a

Fig. 1. Cut out the wedges in the engine block to create the cylinders. Make the cuts with a bandsaw or scroll saw.

scroll saw. Sand the edges smooth.

Drill a 1/4"-diameter hole into the end of a length of 1/2" dowel stock to make the propeller hub (J). Cut the hub to length; cut and glue the propeller shaft (K) into the hub.

With a 1-3/4" diameter hole saw, cut a 1-5/8"-diameter blank from 1/8"-thick stock to make the propeller spacer (I). Glue and clamp the spacer to the engine block.

To assemble the engine and the propeller parts to the fuselage, glue the engine block to the fuselage assembly. The spacer has a 1/4"-diameter hole that can be used as a guide for drilling the propeller shaft hole through the engine and into the fuselage. Use a 1/4"-diameter drill bit and make the hole according to the plans. Glue the propeller shaft and propeller into place, being careful not to get glue on the propeller.

6. WHEEL STRUT ASSEMBLY

This plane has a wheel strut block that goes under the fuselage. To fabricate the piece, cut stock to the proper length and width. Set up a drill press to drill holes in the block at a 30° angle as shown. After drilling the holes, form the con-

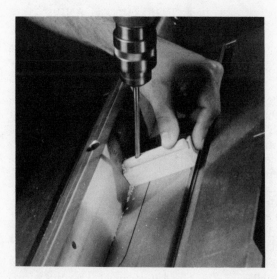

Fig. 2. With the table tilted 30°, secure the wheel strut in a V-block to drill the axle hole.

tours by tapering the sides 30° and the trailing edge 45°. Round the bottom front edge with a power sander or a rasp to contour.

Make a V-block to hold round stock, and drill the 5/16"-diameter axle holes in the wheel struts (N) at 30° (see Fig. 2). After drilling the holes, glue the struts into the wheel strut block, using the axle to keep the struts aligned. When the glue dries, sand any excess strut sticking through the block. Glue and clamp the block to the fuselage.

7. WHEELS

With a 1-1/2"-diameter hole saw, make 1/8"-deep kerfs on 1/2"-thick stock. Use a 2-1/8"-diameter hole saw to cut out the wheels; sand them smooth; glue the wheels and the axle to the struts.

8. FINAL TOUCHES

To finish, put the tail skag (Q) on the plane; its location and angle are not critical. Drill the 5/16"-diameter holes and glue the skag in place.

If painting is your finishing choice, paint the entire aircraft yellow, engine and tires flat black, and the propeller silver. Make insignias out of contact paper and vinyl lettering.

MATERIALS

Part	Description	Pieces	Dimensions
			(finished dimensions in inches)
A	Fuselage	1	2-1/4 × 2-1/2 × 10
B	Upper wing	1	3/8 × 3 × 13-1/2
C	Lower wing	1	3/8 × 3 × 11-1/2
D	Horizontal tail	1	1/4 × 2-1/2 × 6-1/4
E	Vertical tail	1	1/4 × 2-1/2 × 3-5/8
F	Engine block	1	2-3/4 dia. × 1-1/4
G	Engine cylinder heads	8	7/16 dia. × 1/2
H	Propeller	1	1/4 × 1 × 6-1/2
I	Propeller spacer	1	1-5/8 dia. × 1/8
J	Propeller hub	1	1/2 dia. × 1/2
K	Propeller shaft	1	1/4 dia. × 2-3/4
L	Wing struts	4	5/16 dia. × 3-1/2
M	Wheel strut block	1	3/4 × 1-1/2 × 3-1/2
N	Wheel struts	2	1/2 dia. × 3
O	Wheels	2	2 dia. × 1/2
P	Wheel axle (not shown)	1	1/4 dia. × 5
Q	Tail skag	1	5/16 dia. × 1-1/2

SPIRIT OF ST. LOUIS

The "Spirit of St. Louis," designed and built by the Ryan Aircraft Company of San Diego, California, was flown nonstop by Charles Lindbergh from New York to Paris in 1927.

The toy aircraft on these pages captures the magic of that heroic flight. It features the exposed cylinders of the engine, the streamlined fuselage (without a cockpit windscreen break), the wing struts, and the large enclosed wheel strut shock absorbers.

Attaching the wing struts to the fuselage and the wheel shock absorbers to the wing struts appears complex but involves only drilling holes at a shallow angle. The wing struts are cantilevered from the holes in the fuselage and butt-glued to the wings to avoid extreme drilling angles in the wings as well as alignment problems. When the aircraft is complete, it has a good dimension for play and provides a great opportunity to pass on aviation lore.

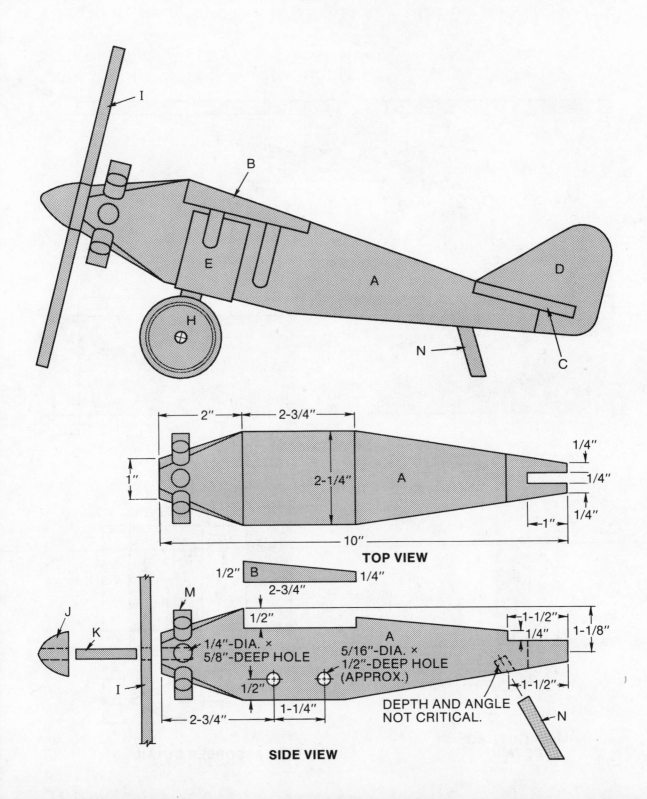

TOP VIEW

SIDE VIEW

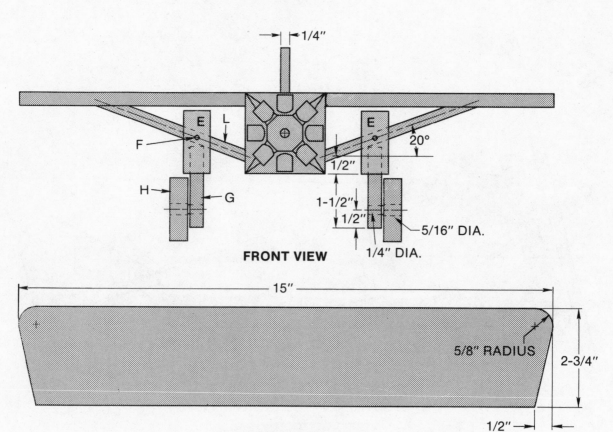

1/4"

E   L   E   20°

F

1/2"

H   G

1-1/2"

1/2"

5/16" DIA.

1/4" DIA.

FRONT VIEW

15"

5/8" RADIUS

2-3/4"

1/2"

WING DETAIL

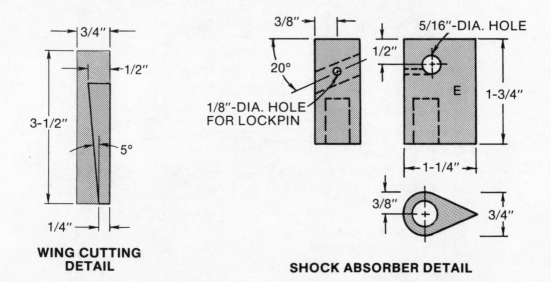

3/4"

1/2"

3-1/2"

5°

1/4"

**WING CUTTING
DETAIL**

3/8"

5/16"-DIA. HOLE

1/2"

20°

1/8"-DIA. HOLE
FOR LOCKPIN

E

1-3/4"

1-1/4"

3/8"

3/4"

SHOCK ABSORBER DETAIL

PROPELLER DETAIL   **ONE SQUARE = 1/2"**

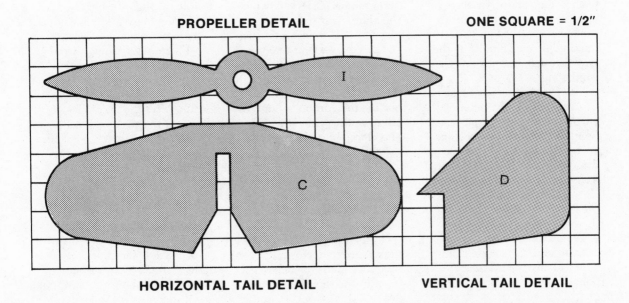

HORIZONTAL TAIL DETAIL   **VERTICAL TAIL DETAIL**

PROCEDURE

1. FUSELAGE

Glue up three pieces of 3/4" × 2-1/4" × 10" stock to form a 2-1/4" square block for the fuselage (A). Draw the top and side profiles on the block along with all hole locations— engine cylinder holes, tail skag, propeller, and wing strut holes—then drill the holes. (Because the fuselage block is square here, drilling the holes now is easier than waiting until a future step.)

The drilling sequence is as follows: drill the propeller hole first, then the wing strut holes. (Tilt the drill press table 20°.) Finally, drill the 7/16"- diameter cylinder holes 1/4"

deep and 45° apart. To do this, tilt the table 45° and drill the holes in the corners of the fuselage. Then line up the fuselage to drill the holes on the four flat sides.

After drilling all the holes, cut out the top and side profiles using a scroll saw or bandsaw. When cutting, stop sawing just before the saw blade completes the cut. This

Fig. 1. Cut out the profile, but stop just before cutting off the waste stock. Leaving the waste stock intact provides support to the block when cutting the profile on the next side.

leaves stock on the fuselage to provide support when cutting the next side (see Fig. 1). After making the cuts almost all the way through, go back and finish the cuts.

Begin shaping the fuselage by drawing a 1"-diameter circle on the nose of the piece. Sand or rasp the nose section corners to meet the 1" circle drawn on the nose. Then, using a rasp or power sander, round all the corners and edges of the fuselage. Be sure to keep the edges sharp around the wing and tail notches. Finally, cut and glue the engine cylinders (M) into the cylinder holes.

2. WING

The wing (B) for the "Spirit" is made by tapering a piece of 3/4" × 3-1/2" × 15" stock. Taper the wing when resawing the stock. To resaw, tilt the bandsaw table 5° and cut the stock, resulting in one 1/4"-thick edge (see plans). Once the wing is tapered, measure over 2-3/4" from the 1/4" edge and rip the stock to the proper width.

NOTE: Check the measurement of the wing notch on the fuselage before making this cut.

Once the wing is cut to the proper width, transfer the wing tip contours to it from the plans. Using a scroll saw or bandsaw, cut out the contours and sand the edges smooth. Set the wing aside.

3. HORIZONTAL AND VERTICAL TAILS

Make cardboard or paper patterns for the horizontal and vertical tails (C, D) following the plans. Transfer the patterns to 1/4"-thick stock; then cut out the parts. If making more than one plane, transfer the pattern to thicker stock; then resaw the pieces after cutting the contours. Sand the edges of the parts, then glue and clamp into place.

4. WHEEL SHOCK ABSORBERS

There is a left and a right shock absorber. Each is different because of the way the wing strut angles through it, so make sure to perform the correct operations to each one.

Cut the strut blocks to 3/4" × 1-1/4" × 1-3/4". In the bottom of each absorber, drill a 7/16"-diameter × 3/4"-deep hole for the wheel strut.

Next, drill the wing strut holes in the shock absorber. Tilt the drill press table 20° and drill the block. Be careful when doing this because the right and left struts have the angled hole going in opposite directions. Drill 1/8"-diameter holes for the lockpins in the front of each absorber.

With a rasp or power sander, contour the shock absorbers according to the plans. Set the absorbers aside.

5. PROPELLER ASSEMBLY

Transfer the propeller pattern from the plans to the stock. Make a template for the propeller (I) out of cardboard if you want more than one. Cut with a scroll saw or bandsaw and resaw the stock, if necessary, to obtain a 1/4" thickness. Sand the edges of the propeller and round off the sharp points. Finally, drill a 5/16"-diameter

hole through the center.

Next, use a 1-1/8"-diameter hole saw and cut out a 1"-diameter blank for the propeller hub (J). Glue the 1/4"-diameter × 1-1/2"-long propeller shaft (K) into the hub. After the glue dries, mount the shaft in a drill chuck; then use a rasp or file to contour the hub. Set the propeller and shaft hub assembly aside.

6. WHEELS

Make the wheels (H) with a 1-1/2"-diameter hole saw to form a 1/8"-deep kerf in 1/2"-thick stock. Next, with a 1-7/8"-diameter hole saw, cut out the wheels. (Make extras now.) Sand them and set aside.

Cut the wheel struts (G) to length and drill an 11/64" pilot hole in each one for the wheel mounting screw. Mount the wheels to the struts with #12 × 1-1/4" roundhead wood screws. File off the protruding screw points. Glue the struts into the shock absorbers and set the assemblies aside.

7. ASSEMBLY

Dry-fit the wing struts (L) into the fuselage. Cut the struts a little long so they can be trimmed. With the struts in place, hold a straightedge across the wing notch and mark a line across each strut. Remove the struts and cut or sand them to the line just marked; then dry-fit them again. Make a final check of the lengths by dry-fitting the wing in place. If the struts fit, glue them in place, but don't glue the wing yet.

After the glue dries, slide the shock absorber/wheel assemblies onto the front struts. When their proper position is located, slide them out of the way and spread glue on the strut. Put the absorbers in position, aligning them up and down. After the glue dries, drill a 1/8" locking pin hole into the strut using the hole in the shock absorber as a guide. Glue the lockpins (F) into place and sand flush.

Finally, spread glue in the wing notch and on the tops of the struts. Clamp the wing into place. After the glue dries, drill a 5/16" hole in the tail for the tail skag (N); then glue the tail skag into place; its position and angle are not critical. Glue the propeller into place.

The aircraft is ready for flight. For further finishing de-

tails you can paint the aircraft silver or light gray and the cylinder heads and wheels flat black. Vinyl stick-on letters complete the detailing. NX-211 is the registration number, RYAN the manufacturer, NYP stands for *New York to Paris* and, of course, the name is *Spirit of St. Louis.*

MATERIALS

Part	Description	Pieces	Dimensions
			(finished dimensions in inches)
A	Fuselage	1	2-1/4 × 2-1/4 × 10
B	Wing	1	1/2 × 2-3/4 × 15
C	Horizontal tail	1	1/4 × 2-1/4 × 6-1/4
D	Vertical tail	1	1/4 × 2-3/4 × 2-3/4
E	Wheel shock absorbers	2	3/4 × 1-1/4 × 1-3/4
F	Shock absorber lockpins	2	1/8 dia. × 3/4
G	Wheel struts	2	7/16 dia. × 2
H	Wheels	2	1-3/4 dia. × 1/2
I	Propeller	1	1/4 × 1 × 7
J	Propeller hub	1	1 dia. × 3/4
K	Propeller shaft	1	1/4 dia. × 1-1/2
L	Wing struts	4	5/16 dia. × 5
M	Engine cylinders	8	7/16 dia. × 3/4
N	Tail skag	1	5/16 dia. × 1-1/2

MISCELLANEOUS
#12 × 1-1/4 roundhead wood screws (2)

CONSTRUCTION NOTES
1. The two shock absorbers (E) are different—one is for the left side of the plane, one is for the right side.

2. The wing (B) is cut from a 3/4" × 3-1/2" piece of stock (see procedure).

P-40 FIGHTER

During the early stages of World War II, there was a volunteer group of American aviators named the "Flying Tigers." This group defended the skies over China against the Japanese and became world-famous by scoring many combat victories against tremendous odds. The distinctive shark mouth insignia became a symbol associated with complex aerial maneuvers, aggressiveness, and superior skill in airwar tactics.

You can recreate images of that past by building this P–40 Fighter. The design for the P–40 features some fine detailing in the armament and exhaust pipes—but nothing beyond the grasp of the average woodworker. The only special construction note is that the propeller must be made out of plywood for strength.

As with the other toys in this book, the P–40 is easy to mass-produce—and think of the effect of two or more of these suspended from a ceiling in a child's room. Once again complex air maneuvers can take place as the sound of heavy machine guns is heard in aerial dogfights.

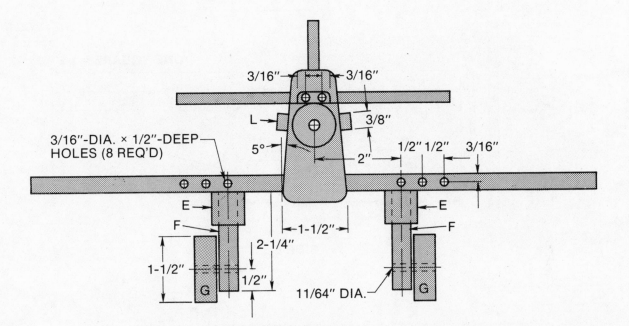

FRONT VIEW

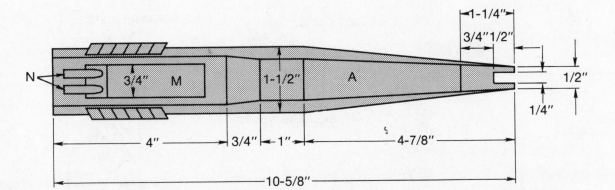

TOP VIEW

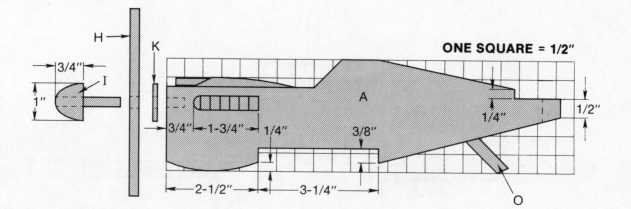

ONE SQUARE = 1/2"

SIDE VIEW

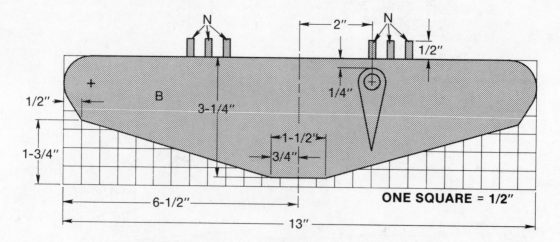

ONE SQUARE = 1/2"

WING

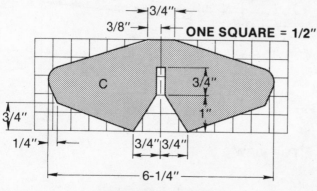

ONE SQUARE = 1/2"

HORIZONTAL TAIL

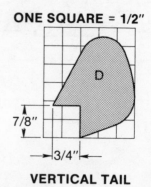

ONE SQUARE = 1/2"

VERTICAL TAIL

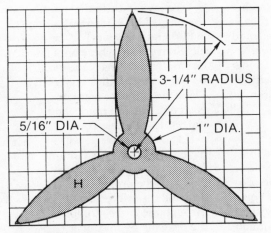

ONE SQUARE = 1/2"

PROPELLER

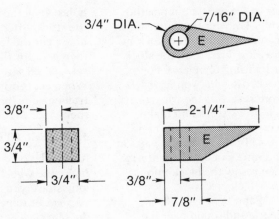

WHEEL FAIRING DETAIL

PROCEDURE

1. FUSELAGE

Glue up and clamp 1 × 4 stock, allowing about 11" of length for each plane you want to make. If you wish, skip gluing up the stock and use 2 × 4 stock. If you do this, use only the clear parts of the stock; and avoid knots and cracks.

Rip and crosscut the stock to the final 1-1/2" × 3" × 10-5/8" block. Transfer the top and side profiles onto the stock as indicated in the plans. If you're making more than one of the planes, make cardboard or hardboard templates and trace around them.

Once you lay out the pattern, cut the notches for the main wing and horizontal tail with a bandsaw or scroll saw. After cutting the notches, form the curved cowling under the engine area in the front of the fuselage. Make one final cut by forming the notch on the rear

for the vertical tail. Stop cutting at this point, because you'll need the rest of the stock to provide support while beveling the sides.

To bevel the sides, tilt the table of either a bandsaw or scroll saw 5°. Bevel both sides of the fuselage, saving the scrap. After you've beveled the sides, tape the scrap to the fuselage with masking tape. The scrap now holds the fuselage parallel to the saw table as you cut out the rest of the side profile.

After completing all the bevels and profiles, round the edges of the fuselage. Sand the fuselage, being careful to keep the edges of the wing notches sharp.

2. WING

Rip a 3/4" × 3-1/2" × 13" (1" × 4" × 13") piece of stock to the proper width for the wing (B). The width of the wing should equal the width of the wing notch on the fuselage.

Continue to cut and test-fit the wing until the fit is snug. Next, draw all the contours on the top of the wing. (If you're building several planes, make a template out of cardboard or hardboard; then use the template to transfer the pattern.)

Locate and drill the 3/16" × 1/2"-deep holes for the wing guns (N); then resaw the wing so it's 3/8" thick. (Save the scrap to make the tail wings.) After drilling the holes, cut the wing to shape using a scroll saw or bandsaw. Round off all the edges of the wing (except where the wing fits in the notch).

Cut six of the guns (N) to size, and glue them into the holes on the wing. With the wing now complete, glue and clamp it to the fuselage; then set the assembly aside.

3. HORIZONTAL AND VERTICAL TAILS

Making the horizontal tail (C) and vertical tail (D) is very similar to the way you made the wing. Transfer the patterns from the plans to the stock by drawing directly on the stock or by using templates. For stock, use what you have left from resawing the wing; or use 3/4"-thick stock and make several of these parts at one time. (To make several parts at one time, cut out the pattern; then resaw the block into 1/4"-thick pieces.)

Sand the edges of the pieces, and round over the edges if you want. When rounding the edges, be careful not to round any portion of the wing that fits in the notch.

Glue and clamp the horizontal tail into place; then glue and clamp the vertical tail into place. Set the assembly aside.

4. WHEEL FAIRINGS

To make the wheel fairings (E), mark off a 3/4" × 3/4" × 15" piece of stock into 2-1/2" sections. The extra length of the stock is necessary for safe handling while machining; but it also yields enough fairings for three planes.

Next, make a template for the fairings out of cardboard; and on the template, mark the center of the 7/16"-diameter strut hole. When you use the template to transfer the pattern to the 3/4"-square stock, secure the template with a tack stuck through the wheel strut hole mark. The tack transfers the hole location and also secures the template while you transfer the design.

Before cutting the fairings to length, drill the 7/16"-diameter holes you just located with the tack. Use a backup board, since these

holes go all the way through the stock. After drilling the holes, cut the fairings to length; then contour them using a rasp, scroll saw, or disc sander. When contouring, bevel the trailing edge (bottom) first; then taper the sides.

5. WHEEL STRUTS

Although you don't have to make the wheel struts from long stock, you'll find the process easier to perform if you do. Mark a length of dowel into 2-5/16" lengths (that's enough stock for the strut plus a 1/16" kerf). Locate and drill the 11/64" pilot holes for the wood screw axles that you'll add later. Cut the struts to length; but don't glue them into place yet.

6. WHEELS

Prepare 1/2"-thick stock. Then, using a 1"-diameter hole saw, create a 1/8"-deep wheel rim kerf for each wheel you make. Next, using a 1-5/8"-diameter hole saw, cut out the wheels and sand them smooth.

Attach the wheels to the struts with #12 × 1-1/4"-long roundhead wood screws. For a decorative look, use brass screws. The screws will protrude a little on the other side of the strut, so grind them off with a power sander or a grindstone.

Glue and clamp the struts into the wheel fairings, and check for alignment.

7. PROPELLER

Make the propeller (H) of 1/4"-thick plywood. Plywood, with its different laminations, has grain running in both directions and, therefore, has the strength required for this part.

To lay out the pattern for the propeller, set a compass at 3-1/4" and draw a 6-1/2" circle. Starting anywhere on the circumference, mark the circle on either side of the compass. Place the compass point on each one of these marks and repeat the process. Your 6-1/2"-diameter circle will have six marks on its circumference. Next, delineate the blades of the propeller by drawing three intersecting arcs through the circle. Complete the drawing by making a 1"-diameter circle in the middle of the prop.

Drill a 5/16"-diameter hole through the center of the propeller; then cut out the piece using a scroll saw or coping saw. Sand the sawn edges and set the prop aside.

8. PROPELLER HUB/SHAFT

To make the propeller hub (I), cut two 1"-diameter blanks out of 3/4"-thick stock with a 1-1/8"-diameter hole saw. Set one plug aside, and glue a 1/4"-diameter dowel into the other one. After the glue dries, place the shaft in an electric drill or drill press and shape the hub as indicated in the plans with a rasp or file. Set the hub and shaft aside.

9. PROPELLER BEARING SPACER

Resaw the other 1" plug you made in step 8 into 1/8"-thick pieces. Glue the spacer to the front of the fuselage where indicated in the plans.

Now, using the hole in the spacer as a guide, drill a 1/4"-diameter hole about 3/4" deep into the nose of the fuselage.

Dry-fit the propeller shaft in the hole to assure that the propeller moves satisfactorily. If everything works properly, glue the shaft into place.

10. ENGINE EXHAUST STACKS

Make a 1/4"-thick × 3/8"-wide piece of stock 12" long (for safe handling). Using a scroll saw or coping saw, cut kerfs in the stock every 1/4" at 45 °. Round the two top edges of the exhaust stack stock; then cut the stacks to length. Glue and clamp the exhaust stacks into place on the fuselage.

11. FUSELAGE GUN COWLING

Lay out the gun cowling (M) on a 3/4" × 3/4" × 2-3/4" piece of stock according to the plans. Drill two 3/16"-diameter holes for the guns. Taper the back of the block; then form the bevel on the front with a rasp, file, or power sander. After completing all the drilling and contouring, cut the cowling from the block; then glue and clamp the part to the fuselage. Glue the guns into place.

12. FINAL TOUCHES

You can make all the decorations for this model from vinyl contact paper obtainable at an office supply store. The star insignias on the wings are blue and white, the shark's mouth is red and white, and the letters are black.

MATERIALS

Part	Description	Pieces	Dimensions
			(finished dimensions in inches)
A	Fuselage	1	1-1/2 × 3 × 10-5/8
B	Wing	1	3/8 × 3-1/4 × 13
C	Horizontal tail	1	1/4 × 2-1/2 × 6-1/4
D	Vertical tail	1	1/4 × 2-1/4 × 2-3/4
E	Wheel fairings	2	3/4 × 3/4 × 2-1/4
F	Wheel struts	2	7/16 dia. × 2-1/4
G	Wheels	2	1-1/2 dia. × 1/2
H	Propeller	1	6-1/2 dia. × 1/4
I	Propeller hub	1	1 dia. × 3/4
J	Propeller shaft (not shown)	1	1/4 dia. × 1-3/4
K	Propeller spacer	1	1 dia. × 1/8
L	Engine exhaust stacks	2	1/4 × 3/8 × 1-3/4
M	Fuselage gun cowling (not shown)	1	1/4 × 3/4 × 2-3/4
N	Guns	8	3/16 dia. × 7/8
O	Tail skag	1	5/16 dia. × 1-1/2

MISCELLANEOUS
#12 × 1-1/4 roundhead wood screws (2)

F-16 FIGHTER

This F-16 fighter is actually a composite: Its stream-lined fuselage, large box-like engine intakes, and double vertical tails reflect the jets in the sky today.

Powerful and functional-looking, this plane will fire the young imagination and provide a lot of enjoyable playtime. Because these jets fly in formation, consider making more than one. If the jets are for a child's room, eliminate the landing gear and drill 1/32"-diameter holes to suspend the craft from the ceiling with nylon line.

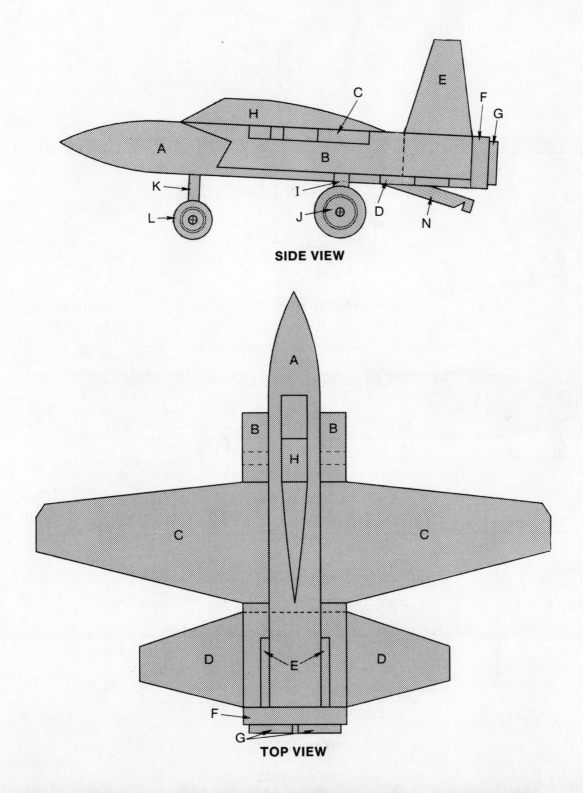

SIDE VIEW

TOP VIEW

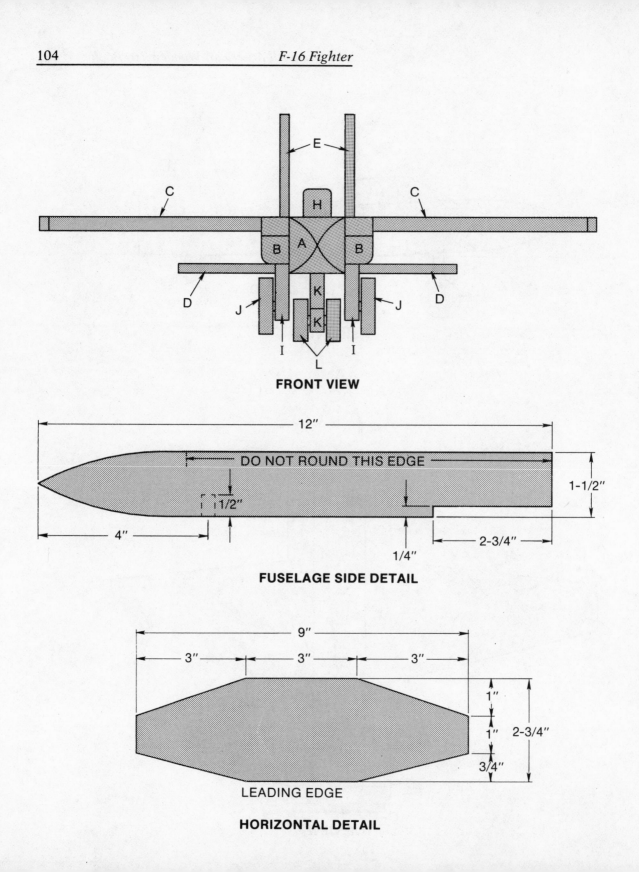

FRONT VIEW

12"

DO NOT ROUND THIS EDGE

1-1/2"

1/2"

4"

1/4"

2-3/4"

FUSELAGE SIDE DETAIL

9"

3"   3"   3"

1"

1"   2-3/4"

3/4"

LEADING EDGE

HORIZONTAL DETAIL

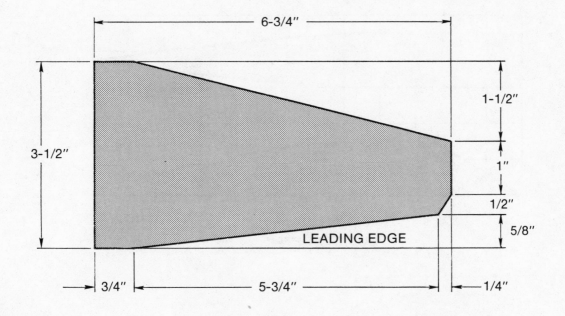

WING DETAIL

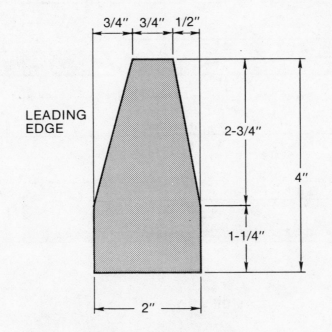

VERTICAL TAIL DETAIL

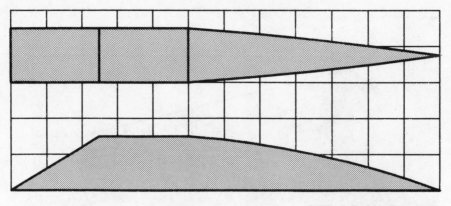

ONE SQUARE = 1/2"

COCKPIT DETAIL

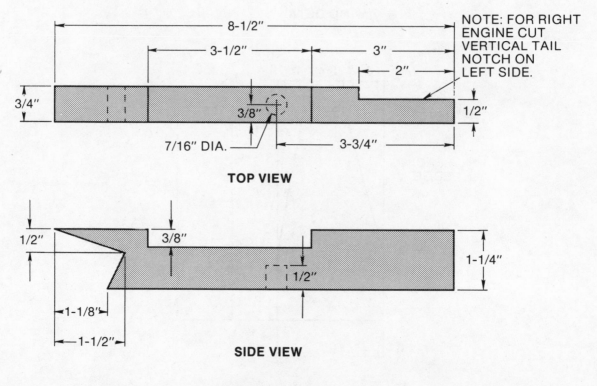

NOTE: FOR RIGHT ENGINE CUT VERTICAL TAIL NOTCH ON LEFT SIDE.

8-1/2"

3-1/2"

3"

2"

3/4"

3/8"

1/2"

7/16" DIA.

3-3/4"

TOP VIEW

1/2"

3/8"

1-1/4"

1/2"

1-1/8"

1-1/2"

SIDE VIEW

ENGINE DETAIL

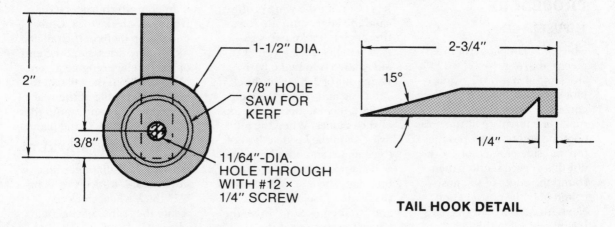

1-1/2" DIA.

7/8" HOLE
SAW FOR
KERF

2"

3/8"

11/64"-DIA.
HOLE THROUGH
WITH #12 ×
1/4" SCREW

MAIN WHEEL

2-3/4"

15°

1/4"

TAIL HOOK DETAIL

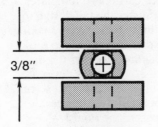

3/8"

TOP VIEW

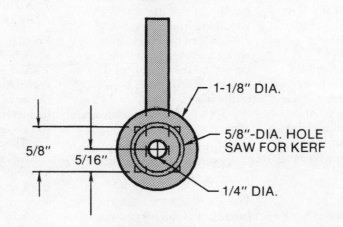

1-1/8" DIA.

5/8"-DIA. HOLE
SAW FOR KERF

1/4" DIA.

5/8"

5/16"

SIDE VIEW

NOSE WHEEL ASSEMBLY

PROCEDURE

1. FUSELAGE

Glue and clamp together two pieces of 3/4″ × 1-1/2″ × 12″ stock to form a 1-1/2″ square block for the fuselage (A). Because the block is square, make one template of the nose contour and trace it onto the top and side of the block. Cut out this curved section; then round the edges of the nose—round only the nose section. Next, round the bottom edges from the nose to the tail. Cut the horizontal tail notch in the rear bottom of the fuselage. Turn the fuselage over and drill the 5/16″-diameter × 1/2″-deep nose wheel strut hole.

2. ENGINES

Prepare the engine stock and transfer the engine profile to it using a cardboard pattern made from the plans. The vertical tail notches go on the inside, creating a left and right engine.

Cut the wing notches in the engine's top. Cut the vertical tail notches on the inside edges, being sure to keep the edges sharp.

Cut out the side profiles. Drill the landing gear holes as shown. Round the top outside edge of each engine from the rear of the wing notch to the tail. Round the bottom outside edge of each engine with a rasp or Surform tool.

3. WINGS

Transfer the wing pattern from the plans to a 3/4″ × 3-1/2″ × 6-3/4″ block of wood. (A cardboard template saves time, especially if making more

jets.) Cut out the wing profile; sand the edges smooth. Resaw the stock to make two separate, equally thick pieces. (An alternative is to make both wings out of 3/8″-thick stock.)

Glue and clamp the wings (C) into the notches on the top of the engines. When the glue dries, sand the inside edges of the engines smooth; then glue and clamp the engines to the fuselage. The assembly consists of the fuselage, engine, and front wing. Sand flush the entire top surface of the assembly; then set aside.

4. HORIZONTAL AND VERTICAL TAILS

Cut out cardboard templates and transfer the tail design to 1/4″-thick stock. When making more than one part (like the vertical tail), transfer the design to 3/4″ stock, if desired. Cut out the parts with a scroll saw or bandsaw; then resaw the parts to the final 1/4″ thickness.

Glue and clamp the vertical tail (E) into the notches between the fuselage and engines. Clean off excess glue with a wet rag. Then glue and clamp the horizontal tail (D) into the notch on the bottom of the fuselage.

Set the assembly aside and allow the glue to dry.

5. FUSELAGE TAIL CAP/ AFTERBURNER ASSEMBLY

Transfer the pattern for the fuselage tail cap (F) to a piece of 1/2″ stock. Cut out the part and sand the edges smooth.

With a 1-3/8″-diameter hole saw, cut out the 1-1/4″-

diameter afterburners (G) from 1/4″-thick stock. Glue and clamp them to the tail cap. As the glue dries, sand the end of the fuselage/engine assembly flush. Trim the tail cap to match the profile of the rear of the plane. Glue and clamp the tail cap assembly to the plane.

6. MAIN WHEELS/STRUTS

With a 1-1/2″-diameter hole saw, make 1/8″-deep kerfs on 1/2″-thick wheel stock to create the "rims" of the main wheels (J). Use a 1-7/8″-diameter hole saw to cut out the wheels. Sand them flush and set aside.

Cut the 7/16″-diameter main wheel struts (I) to length and drill 11/64″-diameter holes as shown. Attach the wheels to the struts with #12 × 1-1/4″ roundhead wood screws. The screws will protrude through the other side of the strut; file or sand off the excess.

Glue the completed wheels into the holes in the engines.

7. NOSE WHEEL ASSEMBLY

Form the 1/8″-deep "rim" kerfs in 3/8″-thick stock with a 1″-diameter hole saw. After completing the kerf, cut out the nose wheels with a 1-1/4″-diameter hole saw. Sand the wheels and set aside.

The nose wheel strut (K) consists of two parts. Cut a 2″ length of 5/16″-diameter dowel stock and drill a 5/16″-diameter hole into its end. Glue the 5/16″-diameter dowel rod into this hole to a 5/8″ depth. Cut the 5/8″ dowel to length; then place the strut assembly into a V-block and drill a

5/16″-diameter axle hole through it as shown. Sand or file flats on each side of the 5/8″ dowel. Glue the nose wheels (L), nose wheel axle (M), and nose wheel strut (K) into place.

8. COCKPIT

Transfer the top and side pro-files of the cockpit (H) to a length of 3/4″ square stock. With a scroll saw or bandsaw, cut out the part and sand all surfaces. Glue and clamp the cockpit to the top of the plane.

9. TAIL HOOK

An optional part on this air-craft is the tail hook (N). This part is vital if your fighter is to see duty on a carrier. Cut out the part according to the plans and taper one end. Glue and clamp to the rear of the craft.

10. FINAL TOUCHES

If preferred, cut out identifying letters and numbers for the finished craft.

MATERIALS

Part	Description	Pieces	Dimensions
			(finished dimensions in inches)
A	Fuselage	1	1-1/2 × 1-1/2 × 12
B	Engines	2	3/4 × 1-1/4 × 8-1/2
C	Wings	2	3/8 × 3-1/2 × 6-3/4
D	Horizontal tail	1	1/4 × 2-3/4 × 9
E	Vertical tails	2	1/4 × 2 × 3-1/2
F	Fuselage tail cap	1	1/2 × 1-1/2 × 3
G	Engine afterburners	2	1-1/4 dia. × 1/4
H	Cockpit	1	3/4 × 3/4 × 6
I	Main wheel struts	2	7/16 dia. × 1-3/4
J	Main wheels	2	1-1/2 dia. × 1/2
K	Nose wheel strut	1	5/16 dia. × 2
		1	5/8 dia. × 5/8
L	Nose wheels	1	1-1/8 dia. × 3/8
M	Nose wheel axle	1	1/4 dia. × 1-3/8
N	Tail hook	1	3/8 dia. × 2

MISCELLANEOUS
#12 × 1-1/4″ roundhead wood screws (2)

STERNWHEELER

Interesting to build and to receive, this sternwheeler peaks interest in America's exciting pioneer river history. You can hear the chug of the engines, the splash of the paddle wheel, and that whistle blowin' as a riverboat comes 'round the bend. Pittsburgh, Cincinnati, St. Louis, New Orleans, Vicksburg, Hannibal—all stopping points for pioneers on their way to settle a new land.

This sternwheeler project is designed with a paddle wheel that revolves as you push or pull the boat across carpet or sand. Its balance and weight make it unsuitable for water. And if it's taken out for a "spin," the paddle wheel will most likely lock up as the wood swells. Luckily, it'll move again once the wood dries.

Construction of this boat involves using a simple jig with the table saw when cutting slots in the paddle wheel ends (see step 9). And the delicate-looking upper deck railings can withstand moderate abuse and are easy to make and install.

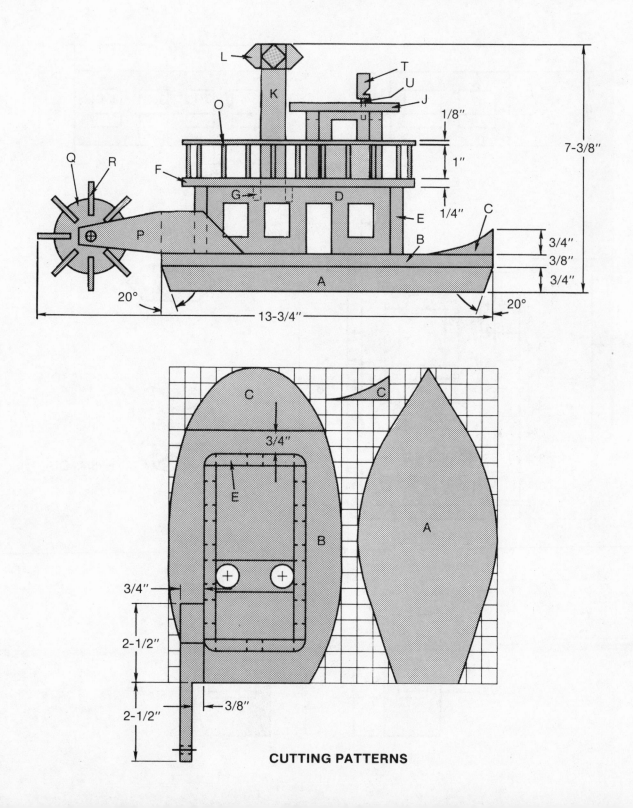

CUTTING PATTERNS

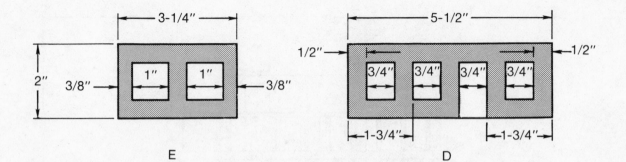

E

D

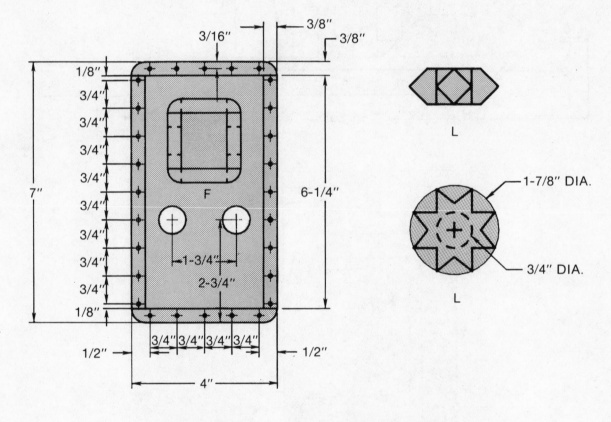

F

L

L

1-7/8" DIA.

3/4" DIA.

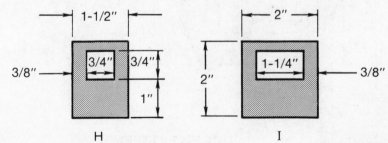

H

I

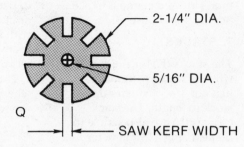

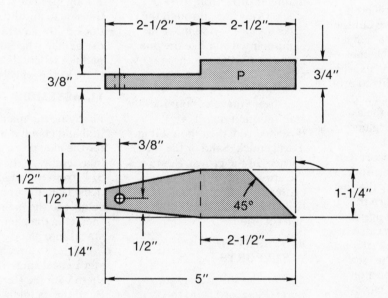

PROCEDURE

1. HULL

Start construction with the hull (A), using the drawings provided to make a template and transferring the hull pattern to the stock. With a bandsaw or scroll saw, cut out the hull at a 20° angle. Sand the edge of the hull smooth and set aside.

2. MAIN DECK

Make a template for the main deck (B) from the pattern in the plans. Fold a piece of paper in half and draw out half the pattern; then cut out the pattern and transfer it to the stock. After cutting out the deck and sanding the edges, set it aside.

3. FOREDECK

Start the foredeck (C) with a 3/4″ × 2″ × 5″ piece of stock. Cut a slight curve diagonally from one corner to the other on the 3/4″ × 2″ side. Transfer the pattern from the main deck to the top of the pattern. Cut out the foredeck, but leave the pattern line. Glue and clamp the foredeck to the main deck; sand the entire deck flush after the glue dries.

4. MAIN DECK CABIN

Cut 3/4″ stock to length and width (but not thickness) for the cabin sides (D) and ends (E). Cut out the windows and doors with a scroll or coping saw; then resaw the stock into two 3/8″-thick pieces. Glue and clamp together the cabin parts. After the glue dries, sand the sides flush and round the corners. Keep the top and bottom edges of the cabin sharp.

5. UPPER DECK

Transfer the pattern for the upper deck (F) to 1/4" stock. Cut out the upper deck and set aside.

Cut out the railing parts (M, N), and glue and clamp them together. Once the glue thoroughly dries, locate holes for the rail uprights (O). Place the railing on top of the upper deck and carefully drill both parts at the same time. Cut the rail uprights about 1/8" longer than required; assemble the deck, railing, and uprights with glue. Allow the uprights to protrude through the deck and the railing; then sand the assembly flush after the glue dries.

Cut the stack support (G) to final dimension. Test-fit it in the main cabin assembly—the fit should be snug. Turn the upper deck assembly upside down, place the main cabin assembly (with the stack support in place), and mark the location of the stack support on the underside of the upper deck. Glue and clamp the stack support to the upper deck. After the glue dries, locate and drill 3/4"-diameter stack holes.

6. PILOT HOUSE

Make the pilot house (H, I) the same way that you made the main deck cabin in step 4. As with the main deck cabin, sand all parts flush after gluing and round the corners.

Use either 1/8" or 1/4" plywood or solid stock for the roof (J). Cut out and sand the roof according to the plans;

then glue and clamp it in place. Set the pilot house aside.

7. STACKS

The stacks (K) for the sternwheeler are easy to make—just cut 3/4"-diameter dowel stock to length. The stack crowns (L) are also simple to make. Using a 2"-diameter hole saw, make two 1-7/8"-diameter disks from 3/4" stock. Draw lines through the disks every 45°, and make an eight-pointed star like the one in the plans. Cut out the star shape using a scroll saw or bandsaw.

After you've cut out the star, mount it on a 1/4" threaded rod; then mount it in a drill chuck. Sand or file the corners of the crown. Remove the crown and drill out the center hole to a 3/4" diameter. Glue the crowns to the stack and set aside.

8. STERNWHEEL SUPPORTS

Cut out the sternwheel supports (P) according to the plans, using a bandsaw or jigsaw. Remember that there is a left support and a right support. Sand the parts and set them aside.

9. PADDLE WHEEL

Using a 2-3/8" hole saw, cut out a 2-1/4"-diameter blank. The two paddle wheels (Q) are made from this one blank.

Make the slots on the paddle wheel with a table saw and a jig to hold the disk. (You can also cut them on a bandsaw or a scroll saw, but they will vary

in size.) A simple board bolted or clamped to the miter gauge with a 1/4" bolt mounted directly in line with the blade is all you need for a jig. Cut the 1/2"-deep slots; then resaw the wheel into equal halves. Set the wheels aside.

10. PADDLES

Cut the paddles (R) from a 2'-long piece of 3/4" stock. Set the saw to cut the stock as thick as the saw kerf slots in the paddle wheel ends. Cut the paddles to length; then glue them to the wheels.

11. ASSEMBLY

First glue the main deck to the hull and clamp it in place. After the glue dries, glue the cabin assembly to the main deck 3/4" from the edge of the fore deck. Glue the upper deck assembly to the main deck cabin; then glue the pilot house and stacks into place.

Prior to attaching the sternwheel supports (P), test-fit them with the sternwheel. Sand the paddle wheel if necessary; then glue and clamp the assembly in place.

12. WHISTLE

No riverboat would be without a whistle to sound its arrival. Holding a short piece of 3/8" dowel with pliers, drill a 1/8"-diameter hole in one end about 3/8" deep. Carve or saw a notch in the dowel. Finally, drill a 1/8"-diameter hole in the pilot roof; glue the whistle in place.

MATERIALS

Part	Description	Pieces	Dimensions
			(finished dimensions in inches)
A	Hull	1	3/4 × 4-1/2 × 10
B	Main deck	1	3/8 × 5-1/2 × 10
C	Foredeck	1	3/4 × 2 × 4-1/2
D	Main deck cabin sides	2	3/8 × 2 × 5-1/2
E	Main deck cabin ends	2	3/8 × 2 × 3-1/4
F	Upper deck	1	1/4 × 4 × 7
G	Stack support	1	1/2 × 1 × 2-1/2
H	Pilot house sides	2	3/8 × 2 × 1-1/2
I	Pilot house ends	2	3/8 × 2 × 2
J	Pilot house roof	1	1/8 × 2-1/2 × 3-1/4
K	Stacks	2	3/4 dia. × 4-3/4
L	Stack crowns	2	1-7/8 dia. × 3/4
M	Side railings	2	1/8 × 3/8 × 6-1/4
N	End railings	2	1/8 × 3/8 × 4
O	Rail uprights	28	1/8 dia. × 1-3/8
P	Sternwheel supports	2	3/4 × 1-1/4 × 5
Q	Paddle wheels	2	2-1/4 dia. × 3/8
R	Paddles	8	kerf × 1 × 4
S	Sternwheel axle	1	1/4 dia. × 4-3/4
T	Whistle	1	3/8 dia. × 3/4
U	Whistle stem	1	1/8 dia. × 1-1/4

CONSTRUCTION NOTES

1. May use solid stock or plywood for parts B, F, and J.
2. Cut contours for parts D, E, H, I, and Q out of 3/4″ stock; then resaw.
3. Use hardwood dowel for parts K, O, S, T, and U.
4. Form with hole saw for parts L and Q.
5. Cut long strip for part R; then crosscut to length.

"THE GENERAL"

T his locomotive was the mainstay of America's early railway system. During the Civil War, the "General" was a familiar sight carrying both Yankees and Rebels and their equipment to battle. Even though the Space Age competes with the excitement once kindled by trains, the General will always have active and enthusiastic fans—whether they're five or ninety-five.

The old-time train can be followed by a tender, plus the baggage, passenger, and observation cars.

This is an ideal project for the beginning woodworker. Be prepared, however, to spend some time in the workshop—it's not a one-evening project. Procedures are designed for all of the parts to be made first, then assembled, car by car. Many of these parts can be mass-produced, making overall construction easier.

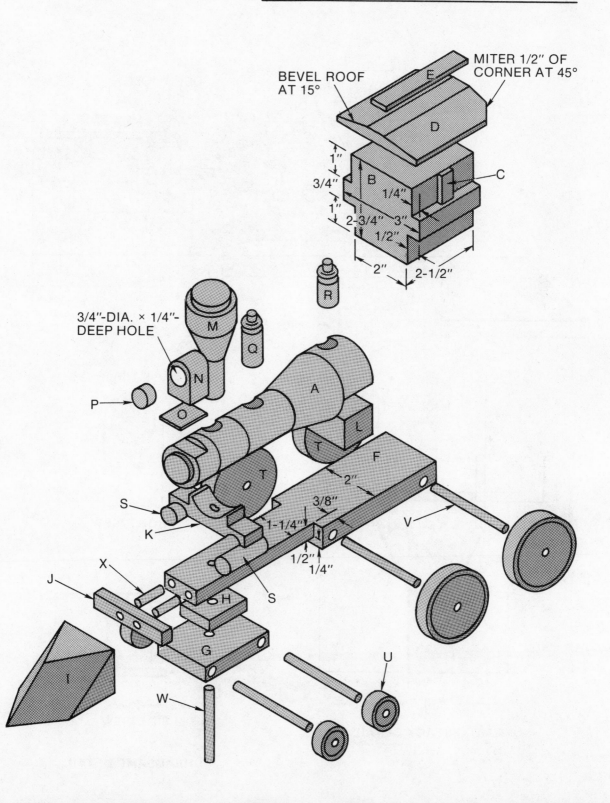

BEVEL ROOF AT 15°

MITER 1/2" OF CORNER AT 45°

E

D

1"

3/4"

1"

B

C

1/4"

2-3/4"

3"

1/2"

2"

2-1/2"

R

3/4"-DIA. × 1/4"-DEEP HOLE

M

N

P

A

L

T

T

F

2"

S

3/8"

K

1-1/4"

V

X

1/2"

J

1/4"

H

S

G

I

W

U

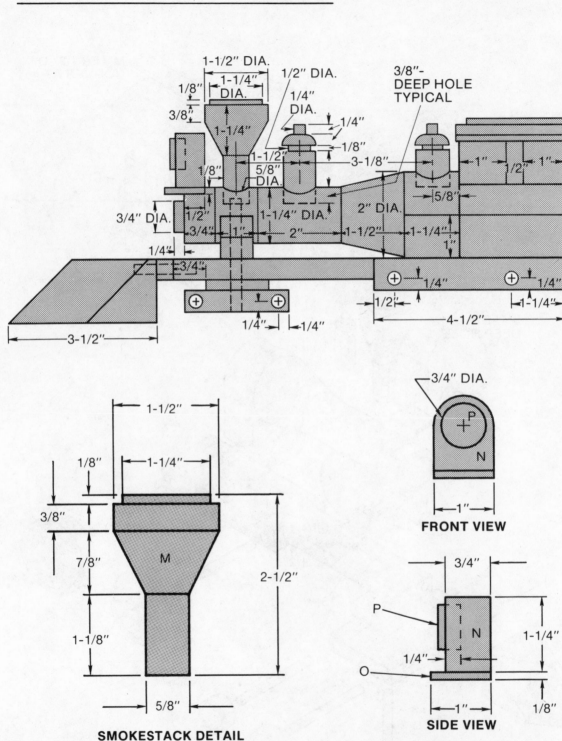

1-1/2" DIA.

1-1/4" DIA.

1/8"

3/8"

1-1/4"

1/2" DIA.

1/4" DIA.

1/4"

1/8"

3/8"- DEEP HOLE TYPICAL

1-1/2"

5/8" DIA.

3-1/8"

1"

1/2"

1"

1/8"

1/8"

3/4" DIA.

1/2"

1-1/4" DIA.

2" DIA.

5/8"

3/4"

1"

2"

1-1/2"

1-1/4"

1"

1/4"

3/4"

1/4"

1/4"

1/4"

1/4"

1/2"

1-1/4"

4-1/2"

3-1/2"

SMOKESTACK DETAIL

1-1/2"

1/8"

1-1/4"

3/8"

7/8"

M

2-1/2"

1-1/8"

5/8"

FRONT VIEW

3/4" DIA.

P

N

1"

SIDE VIEW

3/4"

P

N

1/4"

O

1"

1-1/4"

1/8"

HEADLAMP DETAIL

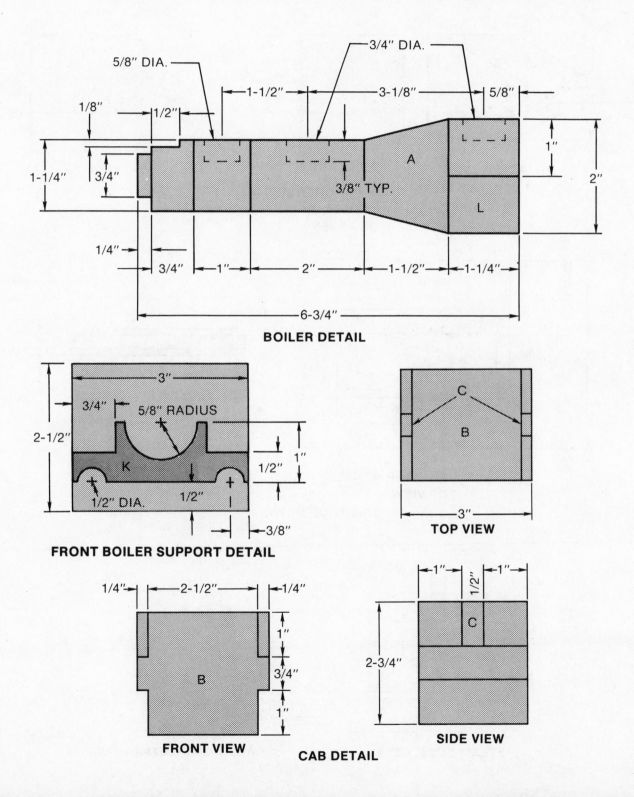

BOILER DETAIL

FRONT BOILER SUPPORT DETAIL

TOP VIEW

FRONT VIEW

CAB DETAIL

SIDE VIEW

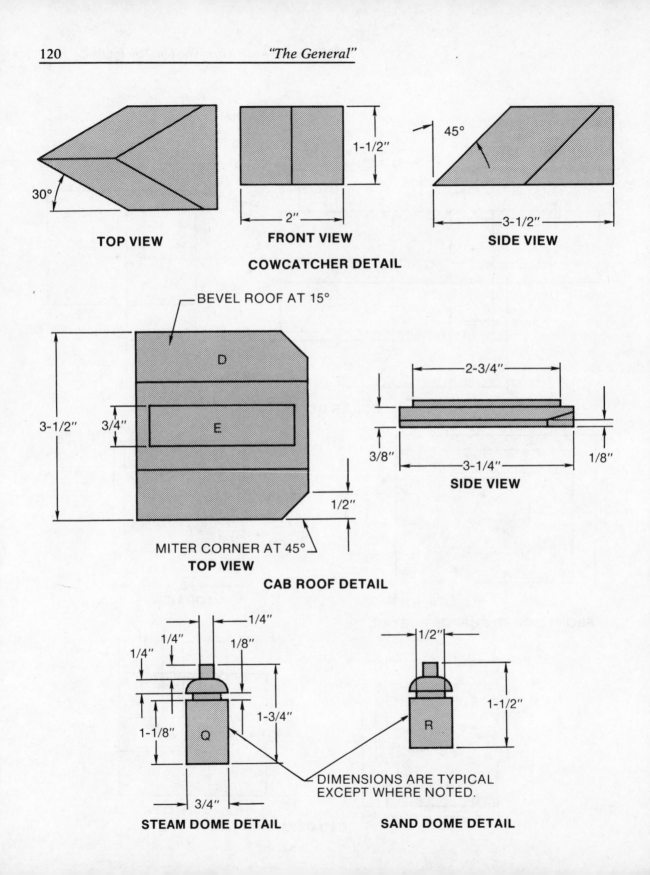

TOP VIEW   **FRONT VIEW**   **SIDE VIEW**

1-1/2"

2"

45°

3-1/2"

30°

COWCATCHER DETAIL

BEVEL ROOF AT 15°

D

E

3-1/2"

3/4"

1/2"

2-3/4"

3/8"

3-1/4"

1/8"

SIDE VIEW

MITER CORNER AT 45°

TOP VIEW

CAB ROOF DETAIL

1/4"

1/4"   1/8"

1/4"

1-3/4"

1/2"

1-1/8"

Q

R

1-1/2"

3/4"

DIMENSIONS ARE TYPICAL
EXCEPT WHERE NOTED.

STEAM DOME DETAIL   **SAND DOME DETAIL**

PROCEDURE

1. BOILER/SMOKESTACK

Turn the boiler (A) and smoke-stack (M), a simple process when both are turned at the same time from one piece of stock (see Fig. 1). To form the turning blank, glue up three pieces of 3/4" stock and clamp securely overnight. When the glue is dry, turn the two parts according to the plans, then sand them. With a parting tool, cut the parts and set aside.

2. CAB

Glue up four pieces of stock to form a 2-1/2" × 2-3/4" × 3" block. After the glue dries, sand the block flush. On the 2-3/4" × 3" sides, locate the 1" × 1-1/2" notches for the drive wheels. Then, locate the 1/4" × 1" notches for the windows just above the wheel notches, and cut with a band-saw or scroll saw.

From scraps or new stock, cut two pieces of 1/4" × 3/8" × 1" strips to form the window strips (C). Glue them into the notches as shown.

3. CAB ROOF

Prepare a length of 3/8" × 3-1/2" stock. All car roofs are made from this size of stock, so prepare several 3' lengths. Tilt the bandsaw table 10° and form bevels according to the plans.

NOTE: If the stock isn't the exact width or the table isn't tilted 10°, the roof size will be off. Just remember there must be a 3/4" flat area on center of the roof and a 1/8" edge on the sides.

Cut the roof (D) to length; glue and clamp it to the cab. Cut the roof vent (E) to size and glue and clamp to the roof.

4. BASE

With a bandsaw or scroll saw, resaw the 1/2" × 4-3/4" step in the base (F) as shown. Place the base upside down on the saw table and cut 3/8" from each side of the step. Lay out and drill the 5/16" axle holes where indicated. Set the part aside.

5. AXLE HOLDER/SPACER

In the axle holder (G), drill 5/16" holes 1/4" from the bottom, front, and rear edges of the block. Cut out the axle spacer (H); glue and clamp to the holder. Glue and clamp this assembly to the base (F).

6. COWCATCHER

Glue up two pieces of 3/4" × 2" × 10" pieces of stock. (The extra length is for the safe handling of the stock while cutting

the profile on the end.) Tilt the bandsaw table 30° and adjust the miter gauge to 30°. Make the compound cut to form the cowcatcher (see Fig. 2).

NOTE: This is a difficult procedure to explain. Be sure to use a scrap piece of stock to make all trial cuts. Whether working with scrap stock or the real thing, **DO NOT ATTEMPT THIS CUT ON A TABLE SAW OR RADIAL ARM SAW.**

Cut the cowcatcher to the proper length. Assemble the cowcatcher, cowcatcher crossbar (J), and base (F) using 1/4"-diameter dowels and glue. Set the assembly aside.

7. FRONT SUPPORT

Cut a piece of stock twice the size you need (3/4" × 2-1/2" × 3"). With a 1-1/4"-diameter hole saw, cut a hole into the center of the stock. Drill the two 1/2"-diameter holes for the pistons (S). Cut the excess stock from the top. (Save the

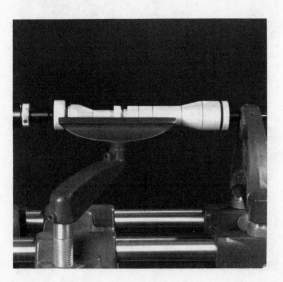

Fig. 1. The boiler and the smokestack can both be turned at the same time from one piece of stock.

top as a temporary support for assembly later.) Glue the front support (K) to the boiler; clamp securely.

8. HEADLAMP

Drill a 1/4"-deep × 3/4"-diameter hole in the stock for the headlamp case (N) as indicated. Round off the top of this case with a power sander or rasp.

Glue the headlamp (P) into the hole just drilled; then glue and clamp the assembly to the headlamp base (O).

9. STEAM/SAND DOMES

The domes (Q, R) are turned from an 8" long piece of 3/4"-diameter dowel. Turn the two domes as shown. While still on the lathe, sand them smooth. Cut the parts to length with a parting tool and set aside.

10. WHEELS

Delineate the rims for the main drive wheels (T) using a 2"-diameter hole saw. Form 1/8"-deep saw kerfs in 3/8"-thick stock. Next, use a 2-1/2"-diameter hole saw to cut out the wheels. Sand thoroughly and set aside.

The front truck wheels (U) and all the rest of the wheels on the old-time train are the same. You need four wheels for the engine and eight for each car, so determine the quantity you want (a typical train will require 36) and pre-pare the 3/8"-thick stock for them. Use a 1"-diameter hole saw for the rim kerf and a 1-3/8"-diameter hole saw to cut the wheels. Sand them and set aside.

11. ASSEMBLY

Cut out the notch in the back of the boiler (A) with a band-saw or scroll saw. Place the rear support (L) in the notch and make sure the boiler is level. Sand, if necessary, then glue the rear support in place.

Drill the 5/8"-diameter smokestack hole and the 3/4"-diameter steam and sand dome holes.

At the front of the boiler, make a 1/8"-deep saw kerf 1/2" back from the edge. With a chisel, cut back to the saw kerf to form a flat area for the headlamp assembly.

Glue the headlamp assembly (N, O, P), smokestack (M), and domes (Q, R) in place. Anchor the headlamp by drilling a 3/16" hole down from the top of the assembly into the boiler. Glue a 3/16" dowel into this hole; sand flush when dry.

Glue and clamp the cab assembly to the base. After the glue dries, glue and clamp the boiler assembly to the base.

Next, glue and clamp the front axle holder (G) to the front of the engine assembly. After the glue sets up, drill a 1/4"-diameter hole up through the base into the front boiler support, boiler, and smoke-stack. Glue a dowel pin (W) into this hole. An alternative to the dowel is to drill a pilot hole and use a #12 × 2" flathead wood screw to anchor the parts in place.

Fig. 2. To form the cowcatcher, tilt a bandsaw table 30° and set the miter gauge at 30°. Experiment with scrap stock to double-check your settings.

The cowcatcher assembly is attached to the front of the engine with 1/4"-diameter dowel pins. Drill matching dowel holes in both parts; then glue and clamp these together.

Finally, glue the wheels and axles into place; then glue and clamp the pistons (S) to the front support.

The engine is complete. Before giving this toy to a child, make sure you have sanded all of the sharp edges thoroughly—especially the point and edges of the cowcatcher.

MATERIALS

Part	Description	Pieces	Dimensions
			(finished dimensions in inches)
A	Boiler	1	2-1/4 dia. × 6-3/4
B	Cab	1	2-1/2 × 2-3/4 × 3
C	Cab window strips	2	1/8 × 1/2 × 1
D	Cab roof	1	3/8 × 3-1/2 × 3-1/4
E	Cab roof vent	1	1/8 × 3/4 × 2-3/4
F	Base	1	3/4 × 2 × 9-1/4
G	Axle holder	1	1/2 × 2 × 2-1/2
H	Axle spacer	1	1/4 × 1-1/4 × 1-1/2
I	Cowcatcher	1	1-1/2 × 2 × 3-1/2
J	Cowcatcher crossbar	1	1/2 × 1/2 × 2-3/4
K	Front support	1	3/4 × 1 × 3
L	Rear support	1	1-1/4 × 1 × 2
M	Smokestack	1	1-1/2 dia. × 2-1/2
N	Headlamp case	1	3/4 × 1 × 1-1/4
O	Headlamp base	1	1/8 × 1 × 1
P	Headlamp	1	3/4 dia. × 3/8
Q	Steam dome	1	3/4 dia. × 1-3/4
R	Sand dome	1	3/4 dia. × 1-1/2
S	Pistons	2	1/2 dia. × 1-1/2
T	Drive wheels	4	2-3/8 dia. × 3/8
U	Front wheels	4	1-1/4 × 3/8
V	Axles	4	1/4 dia. × 2-7/8
W	Dowel pin	1	1/4 dia. × 2-5/8
X	Dowel pins	2	1/4 dia. × 1-1/2

TENDER

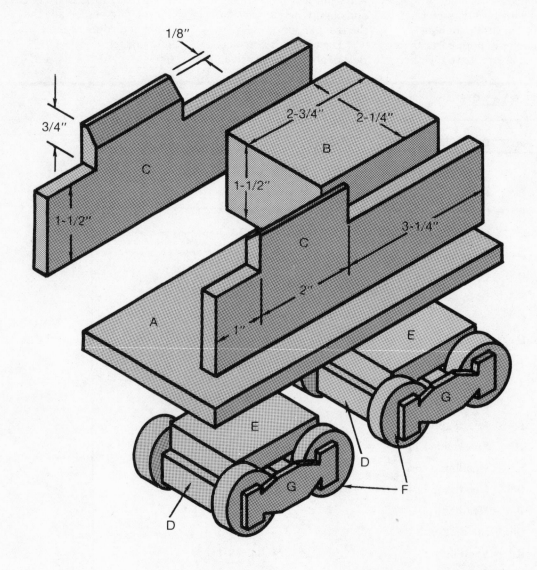

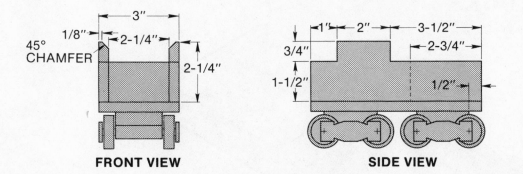

FRONT VIEW   **SIDE VIEW**

TENDER DETAIL

PROCEDURE

1. TANK

Glue together three pieces of 3/4" × 1-1/2" × 2-3/4" stock. When the glue dries, sand the block smooth and set aside.

2. SIDES

From a 3/4"-thick piece of stock, cut out the profile as shown. Resaw the stock to form the two sides. Bevel the top inside edges of the sides; then sand the parts smooth.

3. ASSEMBLY

Glue and clamp the sides to the tank. When the glue dries, sand the bottom of the assembly flush; then glue and clamp the assembly to the base. Leave a 1/4" ledge on the front and rear of the base. Next, glue and clamp the wheel assemblies to the base. For couplers, drill a 3/32" hole in the front and rear of the base for a screw hook and screw eye.

MATERIALS

Part	Description	Pieces	Dimensions
			(finished dimensions in inches)
A	Base	1	3/8 × 3 × 6-1/2
B	Tender tank	1	1-1/2 × 2-1/4 × 2-3/4
C	Sides	2	3/8 × 2-1/4 × 6-1/4
D	Axle holders	2	1/2 × 2-1/2 × 2-3/4
E	Axle spacers	2	1/2 × 1-3/4 × 2
F	Wheels	4	1-1/4 dia. × 3/8
G	Wheel covers	4	1/8 × 3/4 × 2-1/4
H	Axles	4	1/4 dia. × 2-5/8

MISCELLANEOUS
1-5/8" screw hook
1-1/8" screw eye

TRUCKS

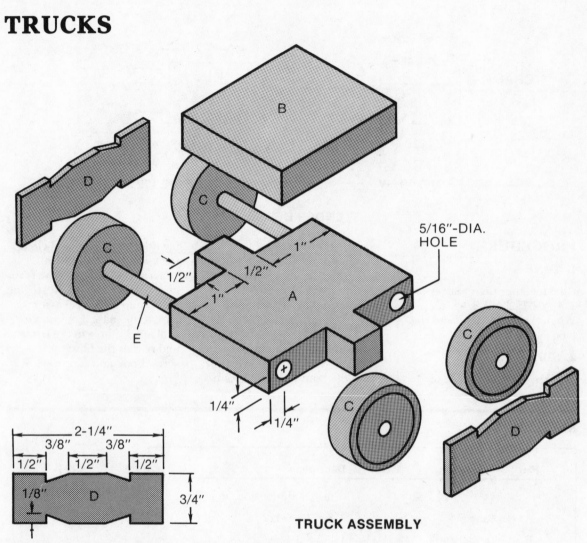

5/16"-DIA. HOLE

TRUCK ASSEMBLY

WHEEL COVER DETAIL

Wheel assemblies on a train are called *trucks*. The trucks for the train cars are easy to make; you'll need two per car. Requirements for one truck are listed under the materials.

PROCEDURE

1. AXLE HOLDERS

Prepare as much 1/2" stock as needed. Cut the axle holder (A)

and spacer (B) to size. Drill 5/16"-diameter axle holes and cut notches on the axle holders as shown.

2. WHEELS

Use a 1"-diameter hole saw to score kerfs in 3/8"-thick stock. Cut out the wheels with a 1-3/8"-diameter hole saw. Sand the wheels and set aside.

3. WHEEL COVERS

Make either one or several at a time. To make one, prepare 1/8"-thick stock; then cut each to shape with a scroll saw or bandsaw. To make several at once, cut the cover profile on a 3-1/2"-wide block of stock with a bandsaw or scroll saw. When done, slice 1/8"-thick pieces from the block. Sand smooth.

4. ASSEMBLY

Glue and clamp the axle holders together; install the axles and wheels. Glue and clamp the wheel covers in place. When the glue dries, tack the cover to the axle holder with a brad to reinforce the construction.

5. AN ALTERNATIVE

For an easier way to make the trucks, use 3/4″ × 1-3/4″ × 2-1/2″ blocks for the axle holders and drill the 5/16″-diameter axle holes 1/4″ from the bottom edge. Use 1/4″-thick plywood for the spacers and skip the kerf on the wheels.

MATERIALS

Part	Description	Pieces	Dimensions
			(finished dimensions in inches)
A	Axle holder	1	1/2 × 2-1/2 × 2-3/4
B	Axle spacer	1	1/2 × 1-3/4 × 2
C	Wheels	4	1-1/4 dia. × 3/8
D	Wheel covers	2	1/8 × 3/4 × 2-1/4
E	Axles	2	1/4 dia. × 2-5/8

MISCELLANEOUS PARTS

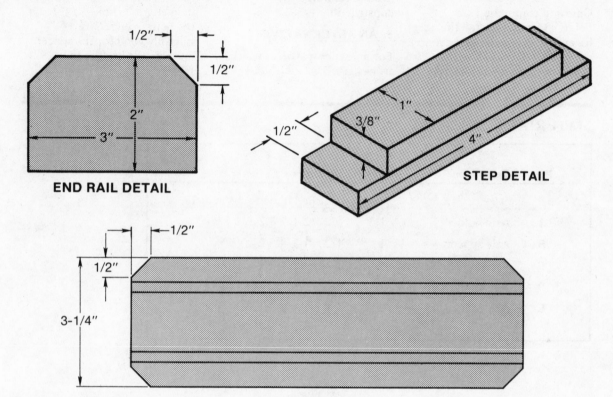

1/2"

1/2"

2"

3"

END RAIL DETAIL

1"

3/8"

1/2"

4"

STEP DETAIL

1/2"

1/2"

3-1/4"

TOP VIEW

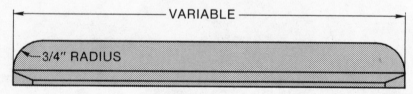

VARIABLE

3/4" RADIUS

SIDE VIEW

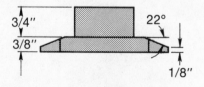

3/4"

22°

3/8"

1/8"

FRONT VIEW

ROOF DETAIL

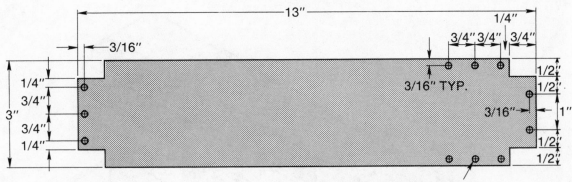

3/16"-DIA. DOWEL HOLES

BASE DETAIL

END RAILINGS

Cut a piece of 3/4" × 3" × 2" stock and chamfer the corners as shown.

NOTE: For strength, the grain of the railings must be vertical.

Resaw the block to yield 1/8"-thick pieces. One block yields the four railings needed for the cars shown here, but make extra railings for more cars.

STEPS

Prepare 3/8" × 1" stock and cut a 3" and 4" piece for each unit. Glue and clamp the pieces together. If using pine, 3/8" × 3/4" stock is available at most home centers and lumberyards. Whether stock is bought or made, you'll need

about 30" of it just for the three cars on this train.

ROOF ASSEMBLIES

It's best to mass-produce the roofs. For three, prepare two pieces of stock—3/8" × 3-1/4" × 36" and 3/4" × 1-1/2" × 36". Then, bevel the edges of the 3/8" stock 22° to get stock with 1/8"-thick edges and a flat on top at least 1-1/2" wide. Crosscut the roofs into required lengths. (Refer to the materials lists for individual cars.) When the roof lengths are correct, miter the corners as shown; then sand the edges smooth.

Cut the roof vents to length and round over each end of these to a 3/4" radius. Glue and clamp the vents to

the roofs. Set the assemblies aside.

BASES

Crosscut a 3/8" × 3" × 40" length of stock to appropriate lengths for the tender and cars. Cut notches for the steps where indicated. Note that the base for the baggage car is 1/4" narrower than the others. Set the bases aside. (The "Santa Fe" requires the same size stock for its cars, so consider preparing a lot of extra stock.)

These are parts that can be made in advance. Don't be frustrated because you've done a lot of work and have no train cars to show for it. The results of this advance work will come fast.

PASSENGER CAR

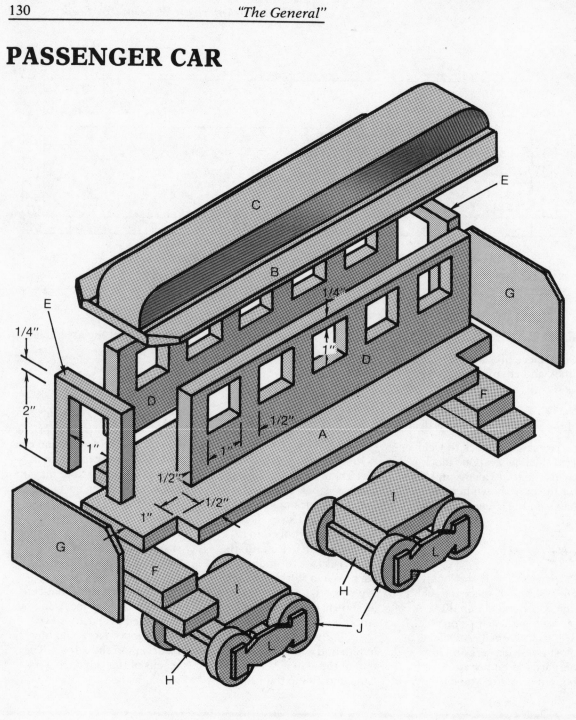

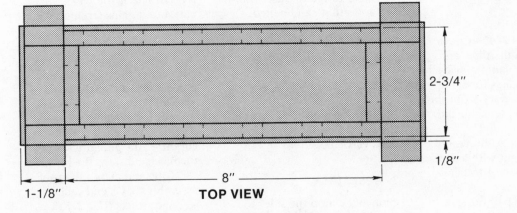

2-3/4"

1/8"

8"

1-1/8"

TOP VIEW

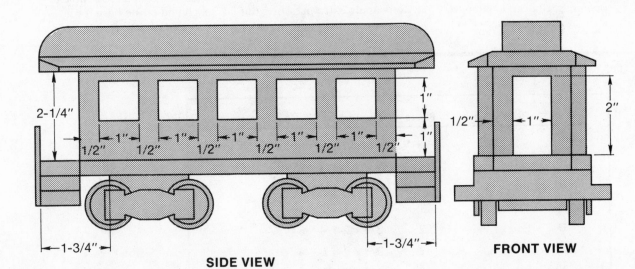

2-1/4"

1"

1"

1"   1"   1"   1"   1"

1/2" 1/2" 1/2" 1/2" 1/2" 1/2"

1-3/4"

1-3/4"

SIDE VIEW

1/2"   1"   2"

FRONT VIEW

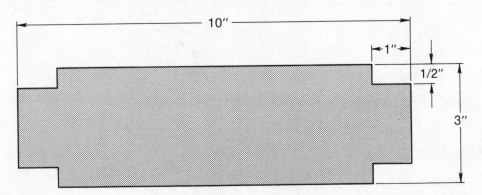

10"

1"

1/2"

3"

PASSENGER CAR BASE

PROCEDURE

1. SIDES

Rip a length of 3/4" stock to the proper width. Allow approximately 9" length for each car. (Extra stock is for squaring up and saw kerfs). Cut the stock to length; set aside the remainder.

Lay out the windows on the stock and cut with a coping saw or scroll saw. Another method is to saw a 1/4" strip of stock off the top of the side stock and cut out the window openings. Glue and clamp the strip in place. Or, use a 1"-diameter drill and make round windows that can be filed square with a rasp.

Resaw the side stock to make two 3/8"-thick pieces.

2. CAB ENDS

Make these ends (E) as you did the sides. Be sure the grain runs vertically.

3. ASSEMBLY

Glue and clamp the sides to the cab ends. When clamping, don't apply extra pressure; this could crack the ends.

NOTE: This is the weakest part, but it gains strength when assembled to the others.

Center the assembly and glue and clamp to the base with a 1" overhang at each end.

Glue and clamp the steps (F) flush with each end of the car. After the glue dries, sand the base and steps flush.

Glue and clamp the roof assembly (B, C), end railings (G), and trucks (H, I, J, K, L) together. Drill a 3/32" hole in each end of the base for a screw hook and screw eye.

MATERIALS

Part	Description	Pieces	Dimensions
			(finished dimensions in inches)
A	Base	1	3/8 × 3-1/4 × 10
B	Roof	1	3/8 × 3-1/4 × 10
C	Roof vent	1	3/4 × 1-1/2 × 10
D	Sides	2	3/8 × 2-1/4 × 8
E	Ends	2	3/8 × 2 × 2-1/4
F	Steps	2	3/8 × 1 × 3
		2	3/8 × 1 × 4
G	End railings	2	1/8 × 3 × 2
H	Axle holders	2	1/2 × 2-1/2 × 2-3/4
I	Axle spacers	2	1/2 × 1-3/4 × 2
J	Wheels	8	1-1/4 dia. × 3/8
K	Axles (not shown)	4	1/4 dia. × 2-5/8
L	Wheel covers	4	1/8 × 3/4 × 2-1/4

MISCELLANEOUS
1-5/8" screw hook
1-1/8" screw eye

BAGGAGE CAR

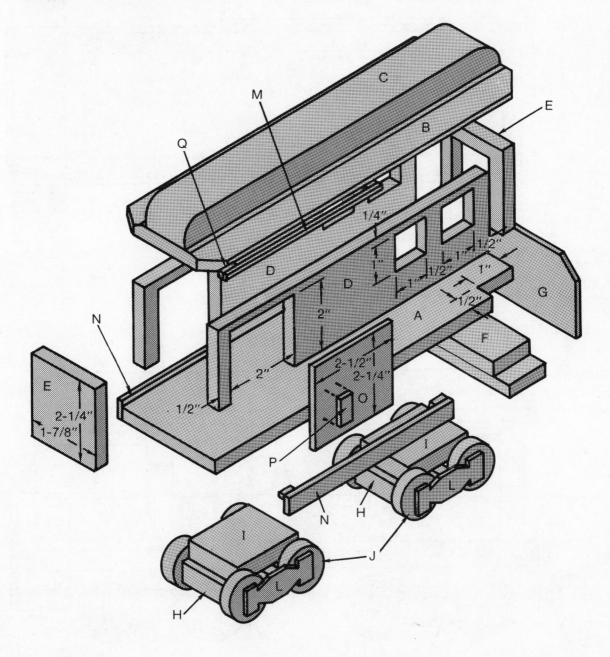

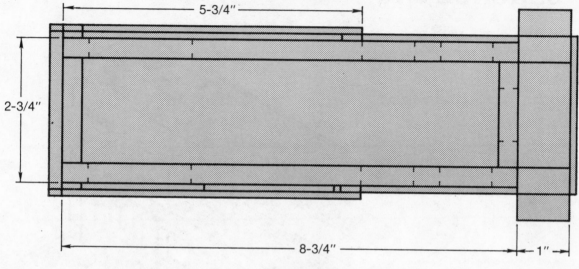

TOP VIEW

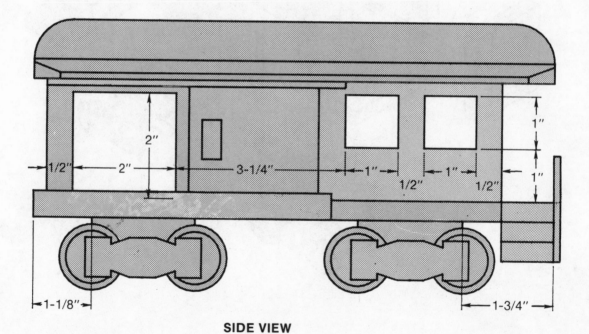

SIDE VIEW

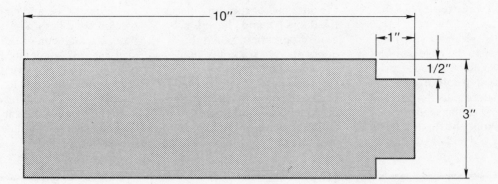

BAGGAGE CAR BASE

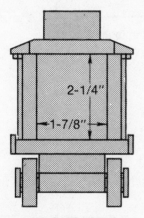

FRONT VIEW

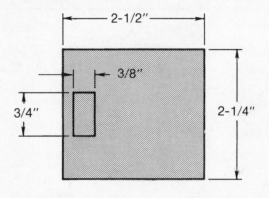

BAGGAGE DOOR

PROCEDURE

1. BASE

Cut the base (A) to the proper width and length. Locate and cut out the notches for the steps on the back end of the car as shown.

2. SIDES

Prepare a 3/4″ × 2-1/4″ × 8-3/4″ piece of stock for the sides (D). Lay out the window and door openings. Cut out the openings with a scroll saw or coping saw. Resaw the stock into two 3/8″-thick pieces.

Sand the sides and openings smooth and set aside.

3. CAB ENDS

Resaw the stock; then cut out the door on one of the ends.

NOTE: To allow room for the sliding doors, the cabin ends for this car are 1/8″ narrower than those of the passenger car or observation car.

Glue and clamp the parts together. When applying clamping pressure, don't over-tighten the clamp. Excessive pressure will crack the parts.

4. SLIDING DOORS

Prepare a 3/4″ × 2-1/4″ × 2-1/2″ piece of stock. With a bandsaw or scroll saw, resaw the stock into 1/8″-thick pieces. Glue and clamp the door handles (P) in place. Set the doors aside.

5. ASSEMBLY

Glue the roof subassembly to the cabin subassembly, being careful to center the roof. Glue and clamp the top door rails (M) under the roof overhang at least 1/8″ from the cabin sides.

Sand off any excess glue, if necessary.

Glue the entire cab/roof assembly to the base with the window end of the cab flush with the step cutout. Glue the bottom door rails (N) into place and clamp securely. (Rails should be flush with the bottom and end of the base at the door end of the cab.) Insert the doors (O) and check for ease of operation. When the doors operate smoothly, glue the stops (Q) in place.

Glue the steps (F) to the end of the base. When the glue dries, sand the end flush. Glue and clamp the end railings (G) into place.

Finally, glue and clamp the truck assemblies under the base. On each end of the base, drill the 3/32"-diameter pilot holes for the screw eye and screw hook couplers. Remember that the sliding door is on the front of the car and that end should couple with the tender.

MATERIALS

Part	Description	Pieces	Dimensions
			(finished dimensions in inches)
A	Base	1	3/8 × 3 × 10
B	Roof	1	3/8 × 3-1/4 × 10
C	Roof vent	1	3/4 × 1-1/2 × 10
D	Sides	2	3/8 × 2-1/4 × 8-3/4
E	Ends	2	3/8 × 1-7/8 × 2-1/4
F	Steps	1	3/8 × 1 × 3
		1	3/8 × 1 × 4
G	End railings	2	1/8 × 3 × 2
H	Axle holders	2	1/2 × 2-1/2 × 2-3/4
I	Axle spacers	2	1/2 × 1-3/4 × 2
J	Wheels	8	1-1/4 dia. × 3/8
K	Axles (not shown)	4	1/4 dia. × 2-5/8
L	Wheel covers	4	1/8 × 3/4 × 2-1/4
M	Top door rails	2	1/8 × 1/8 × 5-3/4
N	Bottom door rails	2	1/8 × 1/2 × 5-3/4
O	Doors	2	1/8 × 2-1/4 × 2-1/2
P	Door handles	2	1/8 × 3/8 × 3/4
Q	Door stops (not shown)	4	1/8 × 1/8 × 3/8

MISCELLANEOUS
1-5/8" screw hook
1-1/8" screw eye

OBSERVATION CAR

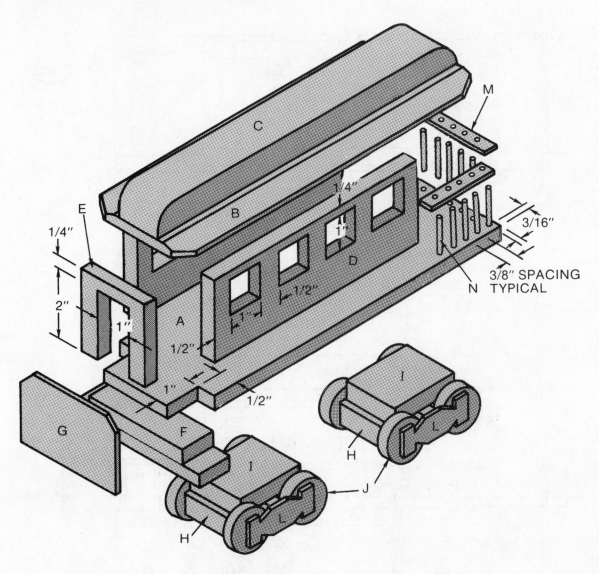

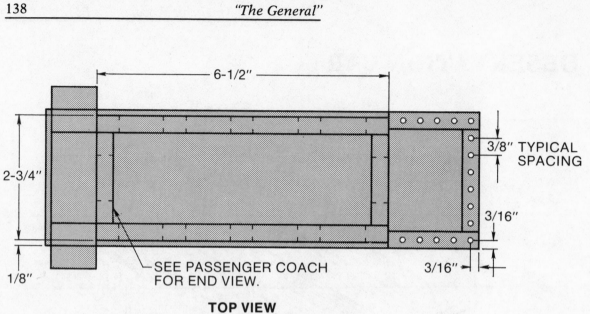

6-1/2"

2-3/4"

3/8" TYPICAL
SPACING

3/16"

3/16"

SEE PASSENGER COACH
FOR END VIEW.

1/8"

TOP VIEW

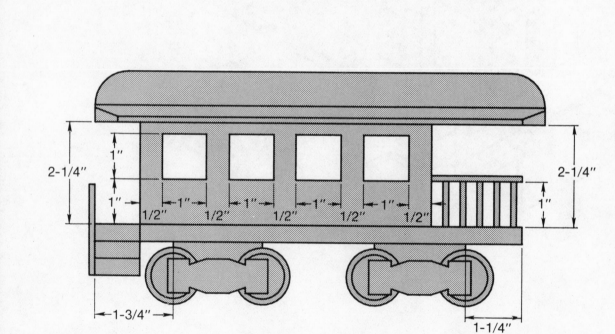

1"

2-1/4"

1"

1"

1/2"   1/2"   1/2"   1/2"   1/2"

1"   1"   1"   1"

2-1/4"

1"

1-3/4"

1-1/4"

SIDE VIEW

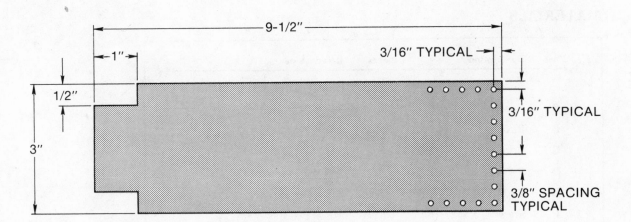

OBSERVATION CAR BASE

PROCEDURE

1. RAILING

Lay out the hole locations and step cutouts for the base (A). With a scroll saw, cut the notches for the steps on the front of the base. Drill the 1/8"-diameter holes on the opposite end as indicated.

Drill 1/8"-diameter holes in the railings (M) to match the holes in the base. Take the 1/8"-diameter dowel and push it through the bottom of the base into the rail. With the rail at the correct height, clip the dowel just above the top of the rail; then clip the rail below the base. Repeat this process until all the railings are in place.

Power-sand all protruding dowels smooth with the top of the railing and the bottom of the base.

2. SIDES

Rip a length of 3/4" stock to the proper width. Cut the stock to length.

Lay out the windows on the stock and cut with a coping saw or scroll saw. Or, saw a 1/4" strip of stock off the top of the side stock; then cut out the window openings. Glue and clamp the strip in place. (Or form round windows with a 1"-diameter drill and file square with a rasp.) Resaw the side stock to make two 3/8"-thick pieces.

3. CAB ENDS

Cab ends (E) are formed in much the same way as the sides. Be sure the grain runs vertically.

4. ASSEMBLY

Assemble the sides and ends with glue and clamps. Remember, excessive clamping pressure will crack the ends. Glue the roof, steps, end railing, and trucks into place.

MATERIALS

Part	Description	Pieces	Dimensions
			(finished dimensions in inches)
A	Base	1	3/8 × 3-1/4 × 10
B	Roof	1	3/8 × 3-1/4 × 9-1/2
C	Roof vent	1	3/4 × 1-1/2 × 9-1/2
D	Sides	2	3/8 × 2-1/4 × 6-1/2
E	Ends	2	3/8 × 2 × 2-1/4
F	Steps	1	3/8 × 1 × 3
		1	3/8 × 1 × 4
G	End railing	1	1/8 × 3 × 2
H	Axle holders	2	1/2 × 2-1/2 × 2-3/4
I	Axle spacers	2	1/2 × 1-3/4 × 2
J	Wheels	8	1-1/4 dia. × 3/8
K	Axles (not shown)	4	1/4 dia. × 2-5/8
L	Wheel covers	4	1/8 × 3/4 × 2-1/4
M	Rear deck railings	3	1/8 × 3/8 × 2
N	Railing uprights	15	1/8 dia. × 1-1/4

MISCELLANEOUS
1-5/8" screw hook
1-1/8" screw eye

TRAIN WHISTLE

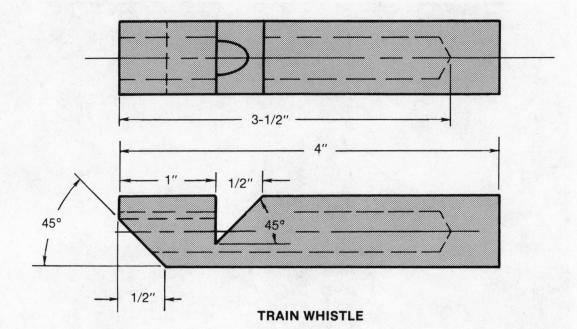

TRAIN WHISTLE

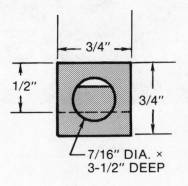

7/16" DIA. ×
3-1/2" DEEP

To make railroading more interesting for your little engineer, construct this train whistle to blow while moving the trains around. Drill a 7/16"-diameter hole in one end of a 3/4" × 3/4" × 4" piece of stock. Make a vertical cut 1" from the end and a 45° cut 1/2" from the vertical cut.

Sand a 1" piece of 7/16"-diameter dowel flat on one side. Glue the dowel into the hole flush with the end. After the glue dries, chamfer the end 45° as shown in the plans.

READING WORK TRAIN

T he design of the Reading Work Train and tender is based on an 0-8-0 switch engine. It features plenty of wheels, which are certain to make this toy entertaining for any child.

Before beginning, read through the instructions and check the parts that have the same dimensions. Ripping all pieces that are the same width at once lends accuracy to any project.

NOTE: Turning the boiler and the steam dome simultaneously from the same piece of stock saves time.

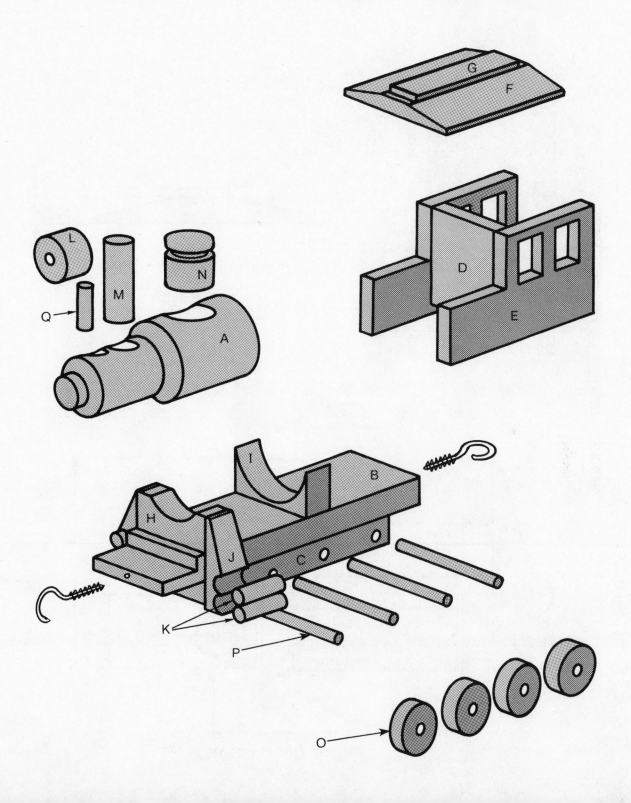

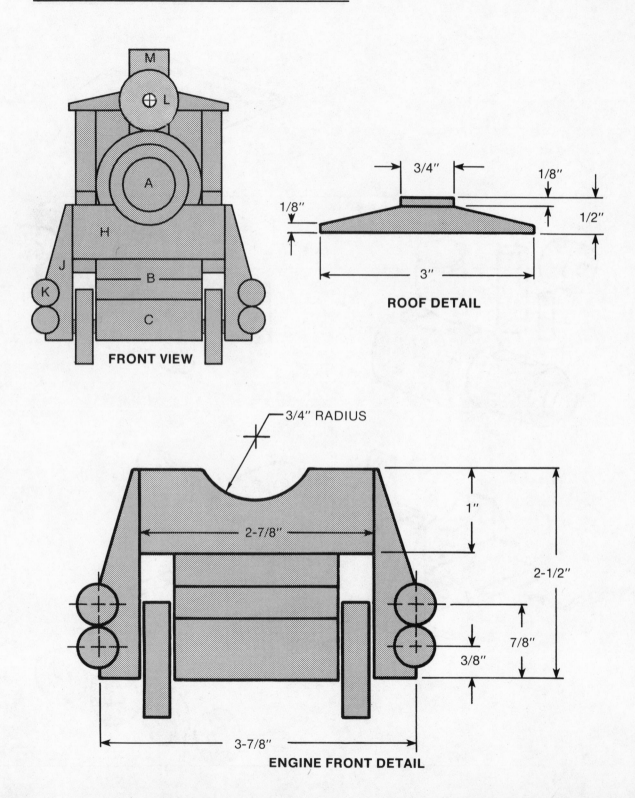

FRONT VIEW

ROOF DETAIL

3/4"

1/8"

1/8"

1/2"

3"

3/4" RADIUS

2-7/8"

1"

2-1/2"

7/8"

3/8"

3-7/8"

ENGINE FRONT DETAIL

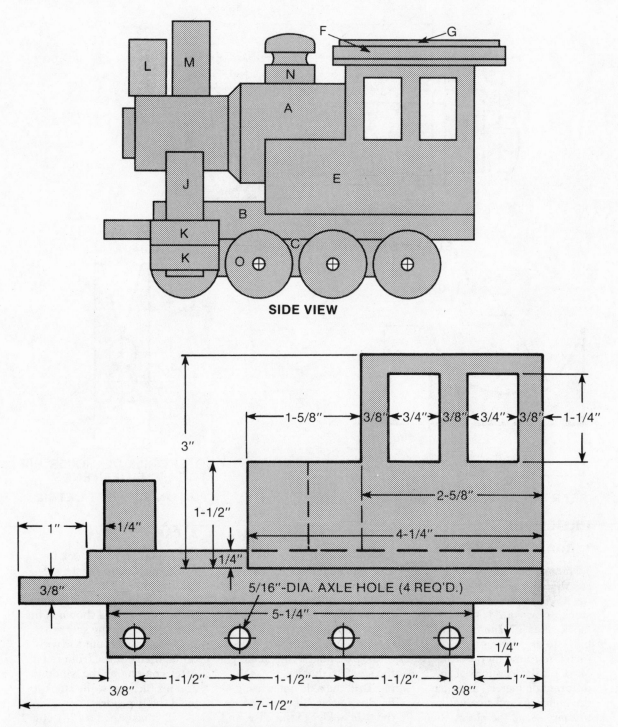

SIDE VIEW

ENGINE SIDE DETAIL

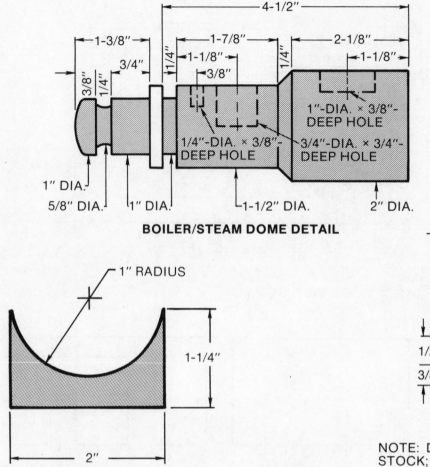

BOILER/STEAM DOME DETAIL

REAR BOILER SUPPORT DETAIL

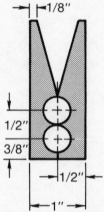

NOTE: DRILL 1/2" HOLES; RIP STOCK; CHAMFER ENDS.

PISTON SUPPORT DETAIL

PROCEDURE

1. BOILER/STEAM DOME

To make the engine's boiler/ steam dome, glue and clamp together three pieces of 3/4" stock to form a 2-1/4" square block at least 7" long. Allow the block to dry overnight; then turn it to round on the lathe. Mark off the locations of the different diameters, and turn the boiler (A) and steam dome to shape. Sand the pieces; then cut apart and set aside.

2. BASE/AXLE HOLDER

Cut the stock for the base (B) and axle holder (C) to width; then cut each piece to length. Using a bandsaw or scroll saw, cut the notch in the top front of the base as shown. Locate the 5/16"-diameter axle holes in the axle holder; then clamp the stock to the drill press table. Drill the axle holes using a brad-point bit. Glue and clamp the axle holder to the base, and set this assembly aside.

3. CAB

Cut a 3/4" piece of stock to width and length for the sides (E). Lay out the locations of the windows and the front profile of the sides as shown in the plans. Use a coping saw or scroll saw to cut out the windows; then cut the front notch. After completing the windows and profile, resaw the stock to yield the two sides.

To make the roof (F), cut 10° bevels on two edges of

3/4″ stock 3″ wide and at least 10″ long (for safe handling) according to the plans. The critical measurement here is keeping the flat on the top of the roof at least 3/4″ wide. After beveling the top, resaw the stock to make two 3/8″-thick pieces. Cut the cab roof to length and store the remaining roof stock for other train cars.

Cut the remaining stock to size to form the cab front (D). Cut the roof vent (G) to size, and glue and clamp it to the roof. Since the roof and other cab parts can't be assembled yet, set them aside.

4. SUPPORTS

Cut the front and rear boiler and piston supports (H, I, J). Lay these parts on a piece of stock (see Fig. 1). Next, use 2″ and 1-1/2″ hole saws to make the circular cutouts for parts H and I. For the piston supports, use a 1/2″-diameter drill (see plan detail). After the holes are made, cut the supports to length and width using a bandsaw or scroll saw.

5. WHEELS

Prepare 3/8″-thick stock for making the wheels (O). Using a 1-1/2″ hole saw, make the eight wheels (O) out of 3/8″ stock. Sand and set aside.

Change to a 1-1/4″-diameter cutter and cut the eight wheels for the tender out of 3/8″-thick stock.

Next, use a 1-1/4″-diameter hole saw to cut the headlamp (L) and the matching searchlight for the tender. Make these lights out of 3/4″ stock. Now use a V-block to drill the 1/4″ mounting holes for both lights. Sand the lights and glue the support (Q) into the headlamp (L). Set the wheels and lights aside.

6. ASSEMBLY

Glue and clamp the front boiler support (H) to the boiler (A). Wait for the glue to set (about 15 minutes); then glue and clamp the rear support (I) flush with the rear of the boiler. Be sure the supports are in line. To check alignment, set the boiler on a flat surface. If it's not level, slide the rear support into position; then clamp it securely.

With the boiler setting on its supports, drill the 1″-, 3/4″- and 1/4″-diameter holes in the top for the steam dome (N), smokestack (M), and headlamp support (Q). Then glue the boiler assembly to the base assembly.

After the glue dries, glue and clamp the cab front (D) to the back of the boiler. Be sure the sides of the rear boiler support and cab front are flush with the sides of the base. If not, sand them.

Next, glue the cab sides to the engine assembly, making sure the cab front and the top of the cab sides are flush. After the glue dries, sand the rear of the engine flush. Complete the cab by gluing and clamping the roof assembly to the cab.

Next, assemble the wheels and axles to the axle holder. (The wheels have to be glued into place before the piston supports are glued to the engine support.) Glue and clamp into place the searchlight, steam dome, and smokestack.

Finally, glue and clamp the pistons (K) to the piston supports (J). After the glue dries, glue and clamp the piston supports to the front boiler support. Since these pieces are tapered, dry-clamp them first. After gluing the piston supports in place, drill 1/4″ dowel holes in the supports and glue in dowels for reinforcement.

To finish the engine, drill 3/32″ holes in the front and back and install the screw hook and screw eye.

With the switch engine finished, build the tender to complete the set.

MATERIALS

Part	Description	Pieces	Dimensions
			(finished dimensions in inches)
A	Boiler	1	2 dia. × 4-1/2
B	Base	1	3/4 × 2 × 7-1/2
C	Axle holder	1	3/4 × 2 × 5-1/4
D	Cab front	1	3/8 × 2 × 2-3/4
E	Cab sides	2	3/8 × 3 × 4-1/4
F	Cab roof	1	3/8 × 3 × 3-1/2
G	Cab roof vent	1	1/8 × 3/4 × 3-1/4
H	Boiler front support	1	3/4 × 1 × 2-7/8
I	Boiler rear support	1	3/4 × 1-1/4 × 2
J	Piston supports	2	3/4 × 1/2 × 2-1/2
K	Pistons	4	1/2 dia. × 1-3/8
L	Headlamp	1	1-1/8 dia. × 3/4
M	Smokestack	1	3/4 dia. × 2-1/4
N	Steam dome	1	1 dia. × 1-3/8
O	Wheels	8	1-3/8 dia. × 3/8
P	Axles	4	1/4 dia. × 2-7/8
Q	Headlamp support	1	1/4 dia. × 1

MISCELLANEOUS
1-5/8″ screw hook
1-1/8″ screw eye
Vinyl stick-on letters

TENDER

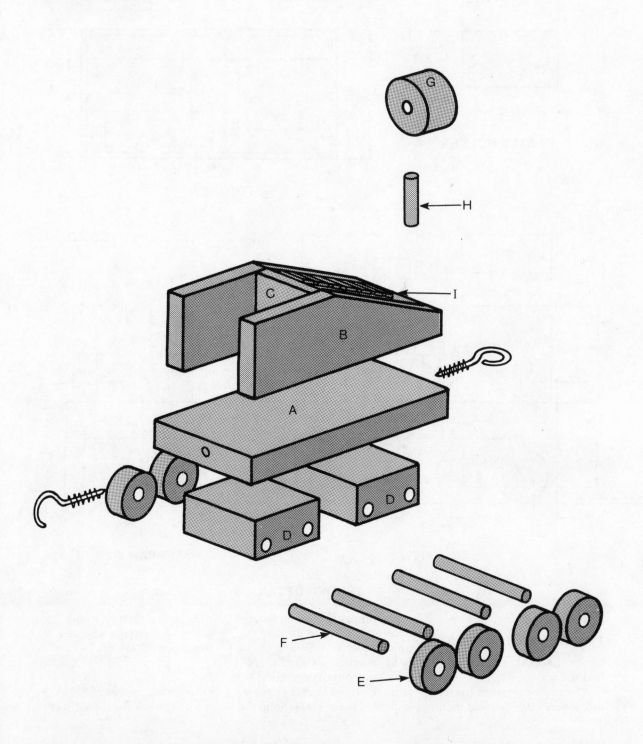

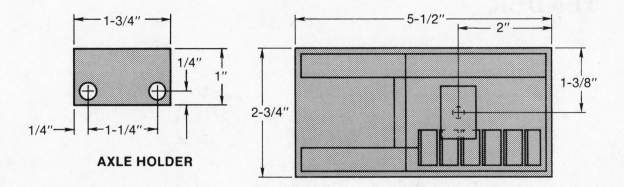

AXLE HOLDER

TOP VIEW

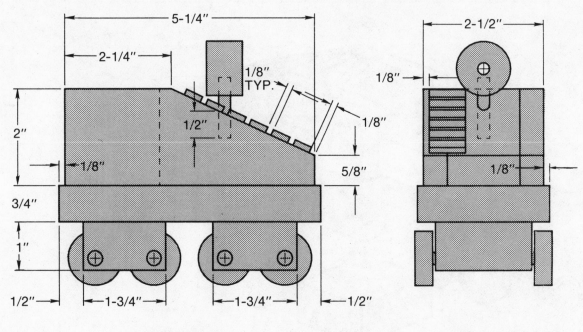

SIDE VIEW

REAR VIEW

TENDER DETAIL

PROCEDURE

1. BASE/AXLE HOLDERS

Cut the base (A) to the specified size.

Next, glue up stock for the axle holders (D); then cut them to the proper width and length before resawing to the required thickness. Drill the 5/16″-diameter axle holes 1/4″ from the bottom edge and 1/4″ from the front or rear edges as indicated in the plans. Sand the axle blocks; then glue and clamp them to the base. Set the assembly aside.

2. BODY

Glue up two pieces of 3/4″ × 2″ × 5-1/4″ stock for the sides (B).

Lay out and cut the side profile on this 1-1/2"-thick piece of stock; then resaw the contoured block to create the two side pieces.

Next, glue up and cut the tank (C) to size and shape. Glue and clamp the sides to the tank, and sand all the surfaces flush.

Drill the 1/4"-diameter × 1/2"-deep hole for the searchlight in the slope of the tank, about two-thirds of the way up from the bottom of the slope.

3. WHEELS

If you haven't already made the wheels, cut them out of 3/8"-thick stock using a 1-1/4"-diameter hole saw. Then, cut out the searchlight support (G). Next, cut the axles (F) and searchlight support (H) to length; then glue parts F, G, and H to the tender assembly.

4. ASSEMBLY

Cut the rungs (I) to the size indicated in the materials. Then glue them 1/8" from either the right or left edge (it makes no difference). Beginning 1/8" from the bottom of the slope, place the rungs 1/8" apart.

Glue the wheels (E) to the axles (F); then glue the searchlight support (H) to the searchlight (G), and glue the searchlight assembly in place.

Drill 3/32" holes in the front and rear of the tender base. Use the engine to gauge the proper height to locate the holes so they'll line up. Install the screw eye and screw hook.

Decorate the engine and tender with vinyl stick-on letters and cut a PRR logo for both sides of each car. If you choose to paint the engine and tender, use black for the base and wheels and perhaps a dark maroon for the upper parts.

The engine and tender are now ready to begin the arduous (or fun) task of moving other train cars around your switching yard.

MATERIALS

Part	Description	Pieces	Dimensions
			(finished dimensions in inches)
A	Base	1	3/4 × 2-3/4 × 5-1/2
B	Sides	2	1-1/2 × 2 × 5-1/4
C	Tank	1	1-1/2 × 2 × 3-1/4
D	Axle holders	2	1 × 2 × 1-3/4
E	Wheels	8	1-1/8 dia. × 3/8
F	Axles	4	1/4 dia. × 2-7/8
G	Searchlight	1	1-1/8 dia. × 3/4
H	Searchlight support	1	1/4 dia. × 1-1/4
I	Ladder rungs	7	1/8 × 3/8 × 3/4

MISCELLANEOUS
1-5/8" screw hook
1-1/8" screw eye
Vinyl stick-on letters

CRANE CAR

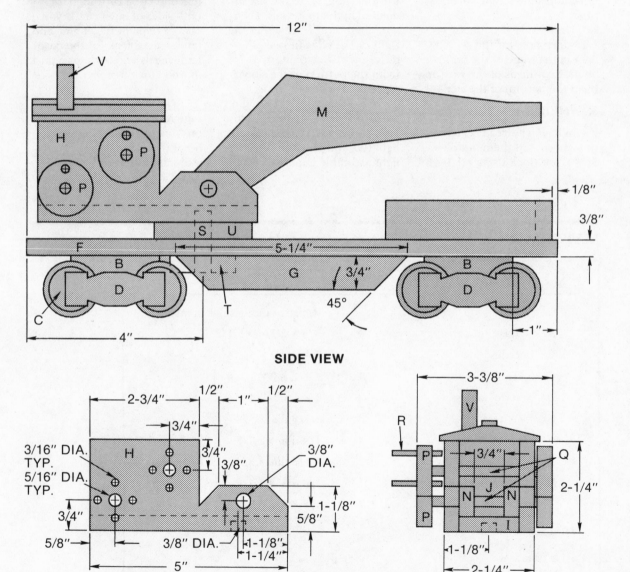

SIDE VIEW

3/16" DIA. TYP.
5/16" DIA. TYP.

3/8" DIA.

3/8" DIA.

SIDE VIEW   **CAB DETAIL**   **FRONT VIEW**

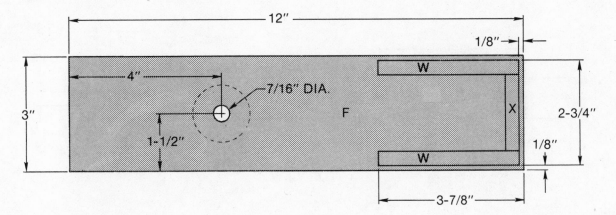

TOP VIEW

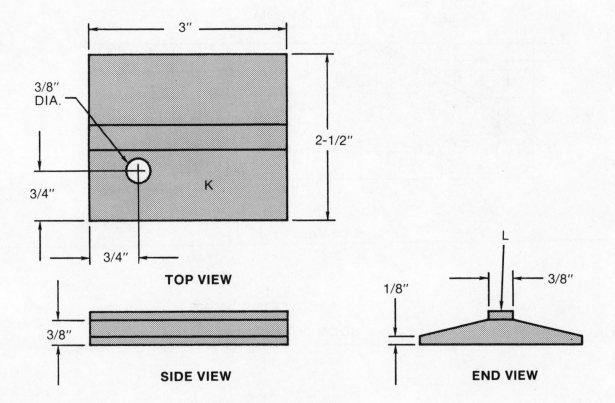

TOP VIEW

SIDE VIEW

END VIEW

ROOF DETAIL

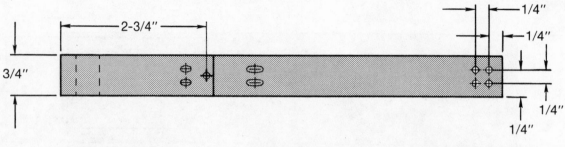

TOP VIEW

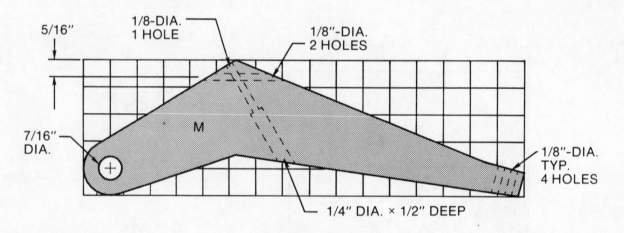

SIDE VIEW

BOOM DETAIL

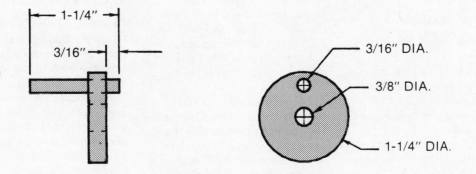

1-1/4"

3/16"

3/16" DIA.

3/8" DIA.

1-1/4" DIA.

CRANK WHEEL DETAIL

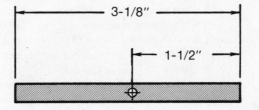

3-1/8"

1-1/2"

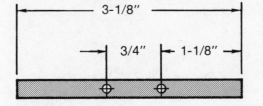

3-1/8"

3/4"

1-1/8"

CRANK WHEEL AXLES

PROCEDURE

1. BASE ASSEMBLY

Make the two truck assemblies (A–E). Next, resaw the stock for the base (F), and cut the part to final dimension according to the materials list. Drill the 7/16"-diameter hole for the cab pivot pin.

Make the base supports (G) by cutting the base support profile from a 3/4" × 3/4" × 5" piece of stock according to the plans and resawing the stock. Sand the parts. Next, make the three parts for the sides (W) and end (X).

Glue and clamp the trucks and base supports to the base. The base supports should be in line with the wheels. Finish assembly of the base by gluing and clamping the sides (W) and end (X) into place.

2. CAB

Transfer the pattern for the sides (H) to a piece of 3/4"-thick stock, carefully locating all the angles and holes except the crank lock holes.

Next, drill all the holes; then, using a bandsaw or scroll saw, cut out the side contours. Resaw the parts to 3/8" thick with a bandsaw or a scroll saw.

You can also make the sides from 3/8" stock. Just cut out the parts first; then stick them together with carpet tape and drill the holes—this keeps the holes in alignment.

Make the cab roof (K) from a 10" length of 3/8" stock (the extra length for safe handling) that's beveled on the top. The flat area on the top should be at least 1/2" wide. Once you've beveled the roof, cut the part to length and drill the 3/8"-diameter exhaust stack hole as indicated. Glue and clamp the roof vent (L) to the roof.

Next, make the cab floor (I) and rear panel (J). After cutting the parts to size, drill the cab pivot pin hole in the floor as indicated in the plans.

Set all the cab parts aside.

3. WHEELS

Make the blanks for the hook and boom crank wheels (P) 1-1/4" in diameter with a 1-3/8"-diameter hole saw. Drill a 3/16"-diameter crank hole in each of the two crank wheels.

Next, using a 2-1/2"-diameter hole saw, cut out the cab pivot platform (U). With a 1-5/8"-diameter hole saw, cut out the cab pivot pinlock (T). Both of these parts require a 3/8"-diameter hole in the center of them, so drill out the 1/4"-diameter pilot holes in each using a 3/8" twist drill bit.

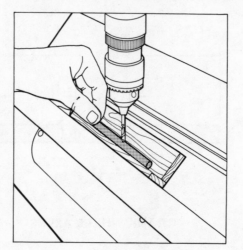

4. CAB ASSEMBLY

Glue and clamp the cab sides (H) to the floor (I) and rear panel (J). After the glue dries, sand the back of the assembly flush; then glue and clamp the boom anchor supports (N) in place. Again after the glue dries, drill the 3/8" boom anchor pin holes using the holes already drilled in the sides as guides. Set the partially assembled cab aside for now.

5. CRANK ASSEMBLIES

Sand the crank wheels you made in step 3, if you haven't already done so. In order for the locking crank system to work, the axles must slide back and forth to engage or disengage the axle locks. Since the axles slide back and forth, the holes for the boom and hook cables are not located in the centers of the axles. Locate the holes according to the plans; then drill them using a V-block, or tilt the table (see Fig. 1).

Fig. 1. When drilling the holes in the axles, use a V-block or some other piece of wood to back up the stock.

Dry-assemble the crank wheels to the axles, and locate the crank locking holes on the cab sides. If the crane is for a right-handed child, locate these holes on the right side of the cab. If the child is left-handed, locate the holes on the left side. Remove the crank assemblies and drill the 3/16"-diameter holes in the cab sides.

Assemble the crank assemblies with glue. The axle with the single-cable hole (boom axle) goes in the bottom rear position, and the axle with the two-cable hole (the hook axle) goes in the top front position. If you use a hook instead of a pulley, reverse the positions of the axles.

6. CRANE BOOM

After cutting the stock to size for the crane boom (M), make a template of the contour from the plans and transfer this contour to the stock. Use a scroll saw or bandsaw to cut out the part; then locate and drill the 7/16" anchor hole and all the 1/8" cable holes.

Sand the boom, and slide it into position between the boom anchor supports located on the cab. Check the fit and sand the boom if the fit is too tight. Once the boom fits between the supports, secure it in place by gluing the anchor pin (O) into position.

7. ASSEMBLY

First, glue and clamp the cab pivot platform (U) to the cab floor (I). Make sure the holes align with each other. Next, glue the cab pivot pin (S) into the bottom of the cab floor.

Place the cab assembly on the base (F) with the pivot pin through the hole drilled earlier. Glue the cab pivot pinlock (T) to the pivot pin.

8. HOOK AND BOOM ASSEMBLY

Cut a 30" length of nylon cord for the crane boom. Slightly singe both ends of the cord with a match to prevent it from unraveling. Next, thread one end of the line through one of the holes in the back crank axle. Bring the line up the boom and into the hole in the middle of the boom. This cable raises and lowers the boom. Adjust the cord and tie a knot in the end of it. Singe the cord with a match.

For the pulley assembly, cut a length of string about 3' long, and slightly singe both ends to prevent unraveling. Tie a knot in one end; then thread the other end through one of the holes on the front crank axle. Lead the line up through the boom, down through one of the back holes on the end of the boom, through one side of the pulley, and up through the front hole of the boom. Now cross over to the other front hole of the boom, down through the other side of the pulley, back up through the back hole on the front of the boom, back through the other hole in the middle of the boom, then back through the other holes on the axle. Tie a knot in the cord; then singe it with a match.

Once you thread the cables, glue the crank handles to the crank wheels; then glue the crank wheels to the axles. Finally, glue and clamp the roof to the cab assembly.

If you've used a hook arrangement for your crane, crimp one end of the hook around the washers. The S-hook will pick up a lot of items, so you may want to experiment. Try attaching a magnetic refrigerator message hook to the hook cable. Or try a little toy bucket. Whatever you and your little construction helper decide, you'll surely agree that this toy is a great deal of fun and a great addition to your train.

MATERIALS

Part	Description	Pieces	Dimensions
			(finished dimensions in inches)
A	Axle holders (not shown)	2	1/2 × 2-3/4 × 2-1/2
B	Axle spacers	2	1/2 × 1-3/4 × 2
C	Wheels	8	1-1/4 dia. × 3/8
D	Wheel covers	4	1/8 × 3/4 × 2-1/4
E	Axles (not shown)	4	1/4 dia. × 2-1/2
F	Base	1	3/8 × 3 × 12
G	Base supports	2	3/8 × 3/4 × 5
H	Cab sides	2	3/8 × 2-1/4 × 5
I	Cab floor (not shown)	1	3/8 × 1-1/2 × 5
J	Cab rear panel	1	3/8 × 1-1/2 × 1-7/8
K	Cab roof	1	3/8 × 2-1/2 × 3
L	Cab roof vent	1	1/8 × 1/2 × 3
M	Crane boom	1	3/4 × 2-1/2 × 8-1/4
N	Boom anchor supports	2	3/8 × 7/8 × 1-1/4
O	Boom anchor pin (not shown)	1	3/8 dia. × 2-1/4
P	Hook and boom crank wheels	4	1-1/4 dia. × 3/8
Q	Crank wheel axles	2	3/8 dia. × 3-1/8
R	Crank handles	2	3/16 dia. × 1-1/4
S	Cab pivot pin	1	3/8 dia. × 1-1/2
T	Cab pivot pinlock	1	1-1/2 dia. × 3/8
U	Cab pivot platform	1	2-3/8 dia. × 3/8
V	Exhaust stack	1	3/8 dia. × 1-1/4
W	Car sides	2	3/8 × 7/8 × 3-3/4
X	Car end	1	3/8 × 7/8 × 2-1/8

MISCELLANEOUS
1-5/8″ screw hook
1-1/8″ screw eye
#16 or #18 twisted nylon string (7′)
Medium S-hook or small pulley

CONSTRUCTION NOTES
1. For safe handling, cut part Q to size after drilling the 1/8″-diameter hole.
2. Refer to the crane project plan for more details on making this toy.

SIDE DUMP CAR

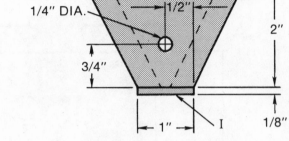

HOPPER END VIEW

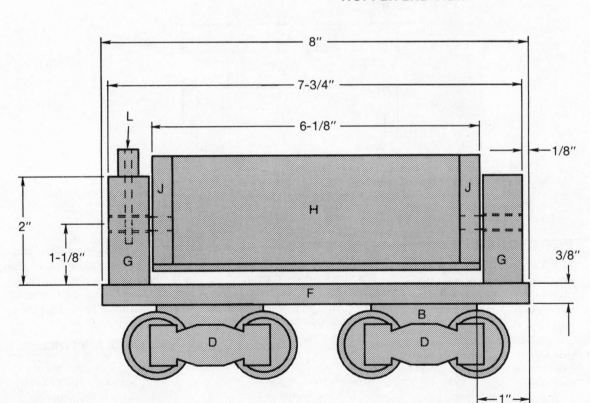

SIDE VIEW

SIDE DUMP CAR

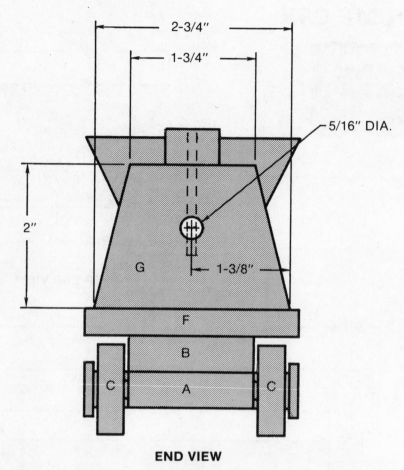

END VIEW

SIDE DUMP CAR

PROCEDURE

1. BASE ASSEMBLY

Make the two truck assemblies (A–E) and the base (F). Construction is the same as the flatcar with base supports omitted. Even though most side dump cars are short, you can always vary the length of them.

2. HOPPER

Begin with the sides (H) and ends (J). On 3/4"-thick stock, lay out the pattern for the ends as shown. Cut the angles; drill the pivot hole; then resaw the end stock into two equally thick pieces. Next, use 3/4" stock; cut the sides to length and width; then resaw the stock to form the two sides.

Glue and clamp the sides to the ends. Because the angles on the hopper are so slanted, use rubber bands as clamps.

After the glue dries, sand the top, bottom, and sides flush with a power belt or disc sander.

Cut the bottom (I) to proper thickness and size; then glue and clamp it to the hopper bottom. After the glue dries, sand the bottom flush and set the assembly aside.

3. HOPPER SUPPORTS

Transfer the pattern for the hopper supports (G) to 3/4" stock. Cut out the supports; then locate and drill the 3/8"-diameter pivot holes for the pivot pins. These holes must match so the hopper will operate smoothly. Finally, glue and clamp the supports to the base.

4. ASSEMBLY

For final assembly, hold the hopper in place; then slide in the pivot pins from each side through the supports. Check the length of the pins; if they fit, remove and reassemble

them with glue. Be sure not to get any glue in the support holes.

When the glue dries, drill a 1/8"-diameter hole in one support. The hole goes through the top of the support into the pivot pin (see plans).

Finally, make and assemble the pivot pinlock and lock the hopper in place.

5. FINISHING TOUCHES

Use a 3/32"-diameter bit and drill the ends of the base for the hook and eye. Paint the car, if desired, or add vinyl stick-on letters.

The side dump car is ready for a load of sand, gravel, or grain (birdseed will do).

MATERIALS

Part	Description	Pieces	Dimensions
			(finished dimensions in inches)
A	Axle holders	2	1/2 × 2-3/4 × 2-1/2
B	Axle spacers	2	1/2 × 1-3/4 × 2
C	Wheels	8	1-1/4 dia. × 3/8
D	Wheel covers	4	1/8 × 3/4 × 2-1/4
E	Axles (not shown)	4	1/4 dia. × 2-1/2
F	Base	1	3/8 × 3 × 8
G	Hopper supports	2	3/4 × 2-3/4 × 2
H	Hopper sides	2	3/8 × 2-1/4 × 5-3/8
I	Hopper bottom	1	1/8 × 1 × 6-1/8
J	Hopper ends	2	3/8 × 3 × 2
K	Pivot pins (not shown)	2	1/4 dia. × 1-1/4
L	Locking pin (not shown)	1	1/8 dia. × 1-3/4
		1	3/8 × 1/2 × 3/4

MISCELLANEOUS
1-5/8" screw hook
1-1/8" screw eye

"SANTA FE"

The "Santa Fe," or modern diesel locomotive, is easy to put together; it's really just three blocks on a platform. When completed, it can pull all of the train cars whose designs follow: flatcar, gondola, boxcar, hopper, tank car, and caboose.

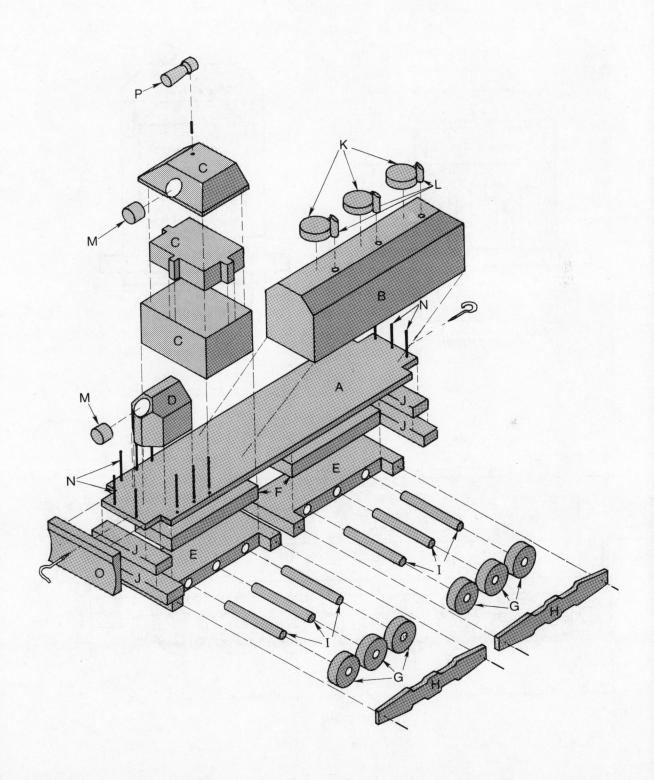

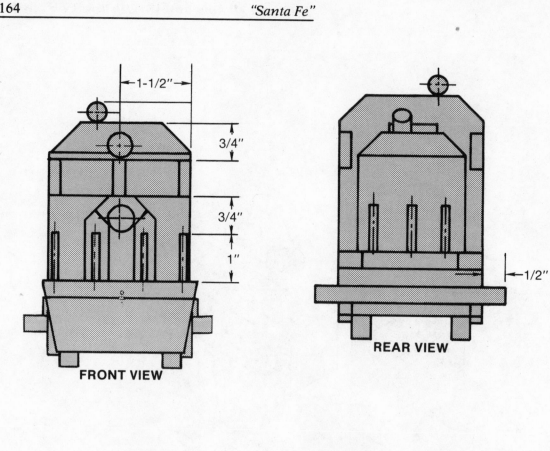

1-1/2"

3/4"

3/4"

1"

FRONT VIEW

1/2"

REAR VIEW

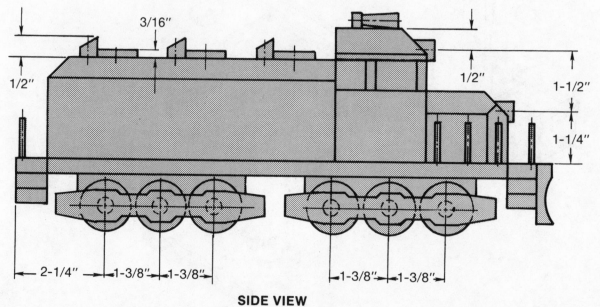

3/16"

1/2"

1/2"

1-1/2"

1-1/4"

2-1/4"   1-3/8" 1-3/8"   1-3/8"   1-3/8"

SIDE VIEW

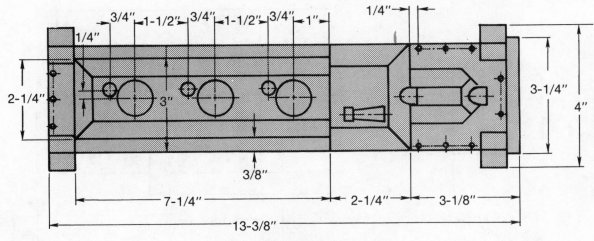

TOP VIEW

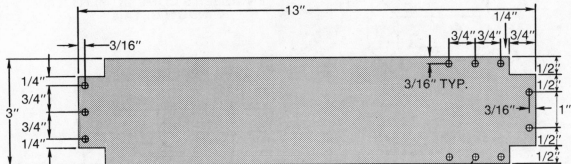
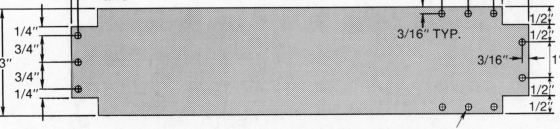

3/16"-DIA. DOWEL HOLES

BASE DETAIL

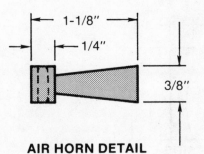

AIR HORN DETAIL

STEP DETAIL

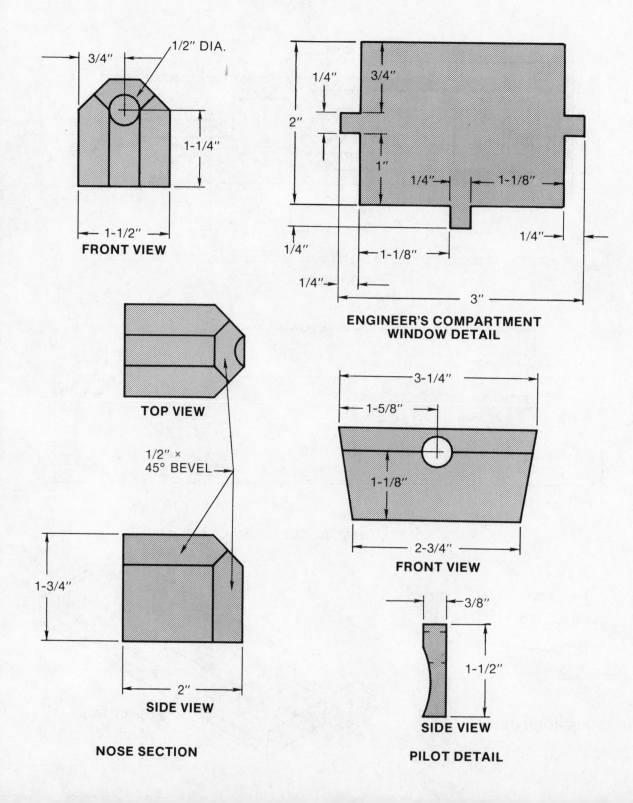

3/4"

1/2" DIA.

1-1/4"

1-1/2"

FRONT VIEW

1/4"

3/4"

2"

1"

1/4"

1-1/8"

1/4"

1-1/8"

1/4"

1/4"

3"

**ENGINEER'S COMPARTMENT
WINDOW DETAIL**

TOP VIEW

1/2" ×
45° BEVEL

1-3/4"

2"

SIDE VIEW

NOSE SECTION

3-1/4"

1-5/8"

1-1/8"

2-3/4"

FRONT VIEW

3/8"

1-1/2"

SIDE VIEW

PILOT DETAIL

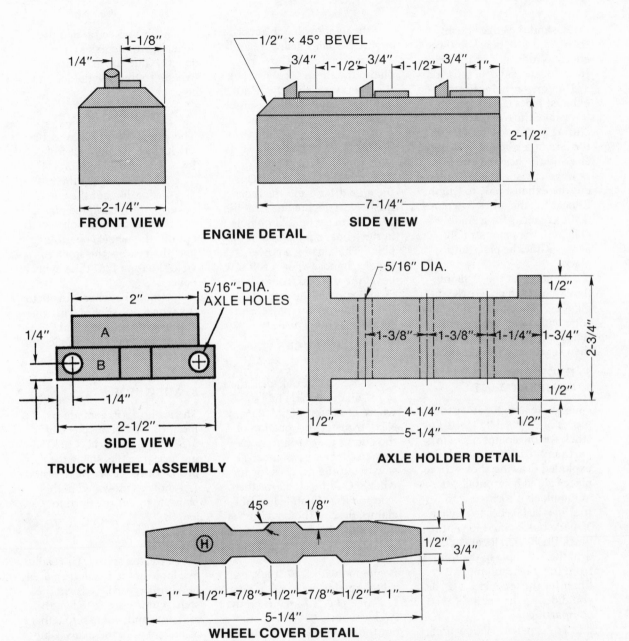

FRONT VIEW

1-1/8"
1/4"
2-1/4"

1/2" × 45° BEVEL

ENGINE DETAIL

3/4" 1-1/2" 3/4" 1-1/2" 3/4" 1"

SIDE VIEW

2-1/2"

7-1/4"

5/16"-DIA. AXLE HOLES

2"
1/4"
A
B
1/4"
2-1/2"

SIDE VIEW

TRUCK WHEEL ASSEMBLY

5/16" DIA.

1/2"
2-3/4"
1-3/8" 1-3/8" 1-1/4" 1-3/4"
1/2"
1/2" 4-1/4" 1/2"
5-1/4"

AXLE HOLDER DETAIL

45°   1/8"

H
1/2"
3/4"

1" 1/2" 7/8" 1/2" 7/8" 1/2" 1"
5-1/4"

WHEEL COVER DETAIL

PROCEDURE

1. BASE

Prepare the stock for the base (A); then lay out the notches. Using a bandsaw or scroll saw, cut out the notches in each corner. If you're making two engines, lay out and cut the notches on a piece of 3/4" stock; then resaw the stock into two bases.

After the base is cut to shape, locate and drill the elev-en handrail holes. Set the base aside for now.

2. ENGINE

Glue up three pieces of 3/4" × 2-1/2" × 7-1/4" stock to make the engine (B). After the glue dries, sand the edges flush; then cut a 1/2" bevel on three edges as indicated in the plans. Next, locate and drill the three 3/8"-diameter holes for the exhaust pipes (L).

Make the exhaust pipes by cutting about a 30° angle on the end of a piece of 3/8" dowel. Sand the beveled end to remove any sharp edges; then cut the exhaust pipe to length. Repeat for the other two pipes. If the engine is for a small child, cut the pipes straight across. Glue the pipes into place.

Finally, cut the 1"-diameter exhaust fan covers (K) using a 1-1/8"-diameter hole saw. Glue and clamp the fan covers to the engine compartment; then set the assembly aside.

3. ENGINEER'S COMPARTMENT

Glue and clamp together four pieces of 3/4" × 3-1/4" × 2-1/4" stock for the engineer's compartment (C). Even though the exploded drawing shows three pieces glued horizontally, the initial block is formed with four vertical pieces to make a 3"-wide block. Sand the entire block flush; then locate and drill the 1/2" hole in the top front for the headlamp (M). Chamfer the top edges 1/2" as you did with the engine compartment.

To form the window area, first, cut off the roof 3/4" from the top of the compartment. Next, form the block for the window area by taking another 3/4" from the block. Finally,

cut the window block according to the plans, using a bandsaw or scroll saw. Glue and clamp the three sections back together; then glue the headlamp in place. Set the assembly aside.

4. NOSE SECTION

Glue together two pieces of 3/4" × 1-3/4" × 2" stock. Once the glue dries, sand the faces flush. Next, locate and drill the 1/2"-diameter headlamp hole in the front as indicated in the plans. Then, using a power sander, bandsaw, or scroll saw, bevel the top and front edges as indicated in the plans. Glue the headlamp into place, and set the assembly aside.

5. AXLE HOLDERS

In two pieces of 1/2" × 2-3/4" × 5-1/4" stock, drill the 5/16"-diameter axle holes where indicated in the plans. Next, transfer the location of the cutout areas to the stock; then use a bandsaw or scroll saw to cut the notches for the wheels. Cut the stock for the axle spacers (F) and glue and clamp these to the holders. Set the holders aside.

6. WHEELS

Beginning with 3/8" stock, use a 1"-diameter hole saw to cut 1/8"-deep kerfs for rims on the twelve wheels (G). Then, cut out the 1-1/4"-diameter wheels using a 1-3/8"-diameter hole saw. Since these are the wheels used on most of the train cars, make several dozen extra and set them aside for later.

After you've sanded the wheels, cut the axles (I) to length. Glue the axles and wheels to the axle holder assemblies.

7. WHEEL COVERS

The wheel covers (H) may be made individually or as follows: Prepare a piece of 3/4" × 1" × 5-1/4" stock. On the 3/4" × 5-1/4" side, lay out the wheel cover pattern from the plans. Use a bandsaw or scroll saw to cut out the wheel cover outline, then resaw the stock to yield the four 1/8"-thick wheel covers.

Attach the wheel covers to the wheel assemblies with glue and brads; then glue and clamp the wheel assemblies to the base as indicated in the plans.

8. AIR HORN

The air horn (P) is made by mounting a 2"-long piece of 3/8" dowel in a drill chuck. Using a rasp or file, shape the profile of the horn. Next, drill a 1/8" hole as indicated in the plans; then cut the horn to length.

9. STEPS

Stock for the steps (J) is readily available in the finish trim area of a lumberyard. To form the steps, cut the stock to length and glue and clamp it together as indicated in the plans. Glue and clamp the assembled steps to the base flush with the ends.

10. PILOT

Prepare a 3/8" × 1-1/2" × 10"

piece of stock for the pilot (O) (more commonly known as a cowcatcher). The extra length is for safe machining and also for extra pilots. Lay out the pilot shapes on the stock; then locate and drill the 3/8"-diameter holes. Using the spindle end of a belt sander, remove stock to form the concave surface. Cut the pilots to length and shape; then set the extras aside. Glue and clamp the pilot to the base.

11. ASSEMBLY

Place the nose assembly, engineer's compartment, and engine assembly on the base. Mark the locations of the assemblies; then remove them. Glue and clamp the engineer's compartment to the base; then glue and clamp the other two sections. Glue the handrails (N) into place.

Drill a hole in the engineer's compartment to mount the horn.

Finally, drill a 3/32"-diameter hole in each end of the base for a screw hook and eye.

MATERIALS

Part	Description	Pieces	Dimensions
			(finished dimensions in inches)
A	Base	1	3/8 × 3 × 13
B	Engine	1	2-1/4 × 2-1/2 × 7-1/4
C	Engineer's compartment	1	3 × 3-1/4 × 2-1/4
D	Nose section	1	1-1/2 × 1-3/4 × 2
E	Axle holders	2	1/2 × 2-3/4 × 5-1/4
F	Axle spacers	2	1/2 × 1-3/4 × 4-1/4
G	Wheels	12	1-1/4 dia. × 3/8
H	Wheel covers	4	1/8 × 3/4 × 5-1/4
I	Axles	6	1/4 dia. × 2-1/2
J	Steps	2	3/8 × 3/4 × 3
		2	3/8 × 3/4 × 4
K	Exhaust fan covers	3	1 dia. × 3/16
L	Exhaust pipes	3	3/8 dia. × 1
M	Headlamps	2	1/2 dia. × 1
N	Handrails	11	3/16 × 1-3/8
O	Pilot (cowcatcher)	1	3/8 × 1-1/2 × 3-1/4
P	Air horn (not shown)	1	3/8 dia. × 1-1/8

MISCELLANEOUS
5/8" screw hook
1/4" screw eye

TRUCKS

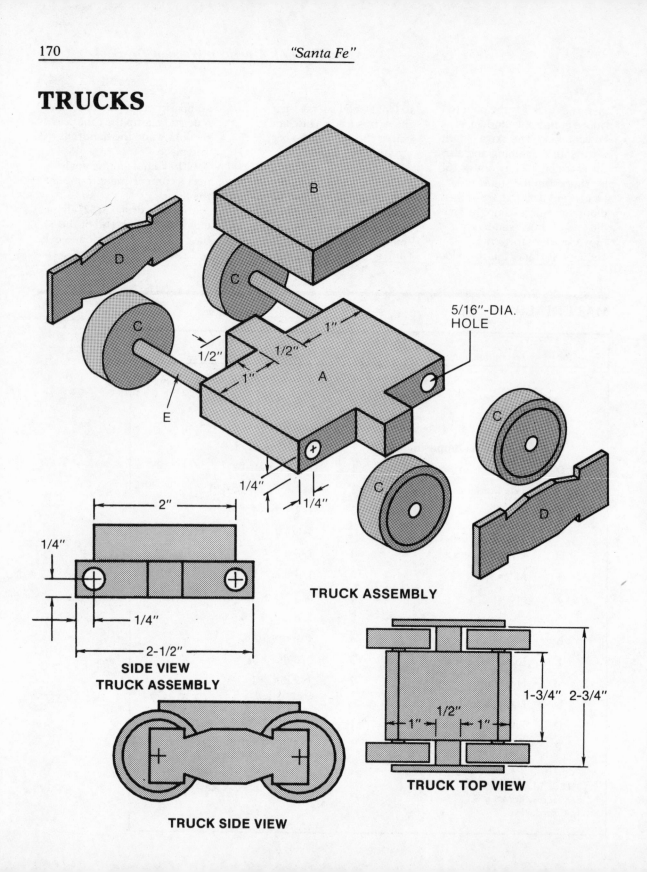

5/16"-DIA. HOLE

1/2"
1"
1/2"
1"
A
E
1/4"
1/4"

B
C
C
D
C
C
D

TRUCK ASSEMBLY

2"
1/4"
1/4"
2-1/2"

SIDE VIEW
TRUCK ASSEMBLY

1-3/4"   2-3/4"
1/2"
1"   1"

TRUCK TOP VIEW

TRUCK SIDE VIEW

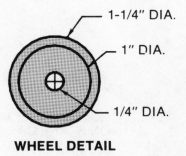

WHEEL DETAIL

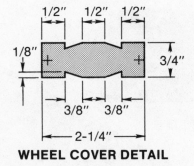

WHEEL COVER DETAIL

PROCEDURE

1. AXLE HOLDERS

Prepare as much 1/2" stock as needed for the spacers and holders. Cut the axle holders (A) and axle spacers (B) to size. Drill the 5/16"-diameter axle holes in the axle holders as indicated. Use a scroll saw or bandsaw to cut the notches on the axle holders.

2. WHEELS

Prepare enough 3/8"-thick stock for all the wheels needed (eight per car). With a 1"-diameter hole saw, make 1/8"-deep kerfs in the stock to delineate the rim of each wheel. Cut out the 1-1/4"-diameter wheels with a 1-3/8"-diameter hole saw. Sand the wheels and set aside.

3. WHEEL COVERS

To make the wheel covers (D) one at a time, transfer the pattern from the plan to 1/8"-thick stock and cut out the covers with a scroll saw. To make more than one wheel cover at a time, use a bandsaw or scroll saw to cut the cover profile on a 3-1/2"-wide block of stock. Slice 1/8"-thick pieces from the block.

4. ASSEMBLY

Glue and clamp the axle holders together. Install the axles and wheels. For smoother operation, rub parafin on the axle before gluing the wheels in place. Don't get any parafin on the axle—the glue won't stick to wax.

Glue and clamp the wheel covers into place. For reinforcement, secure the covers by tacking a brad into the wheel spacer.

MATERIALS

Part	Description	Pieces	Dimensions
			(finished dimensions in inches)
A	Axle holder	1	1/2 × 2-3/4 × 2-1/2
B	Axle spacer	1	1/2 × 1-3/4 × 2
C	Wheels	4	1-1/4 dia. × 3/8
D	Wheel covers	2	1/8 × 3/4 × 2-1/4
E	Axles	2	1/4 dia. × 2-5/8

FLATCAR

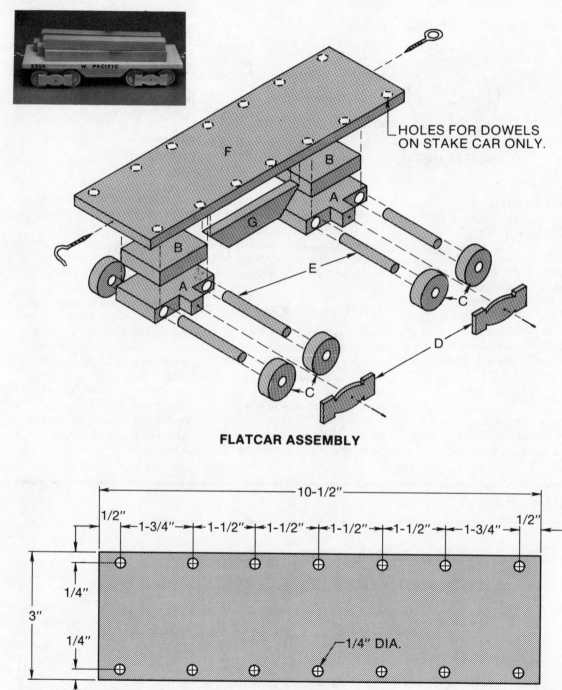

HOLES FOR DOWELS
ON STAKE CAR ONLY.

F

B

A

G

B

A

E

C

D

C

FLATCAR ASSEMBLY

10-1/2"

1/2" | 1-3/4" | 1-1/2" | 1-1/2" | 1-1/2" | 1-1/2" | 1-3/4" | 1/2"

1/4"

3"

1/4"

1/4" DIA.

TOP VIEW

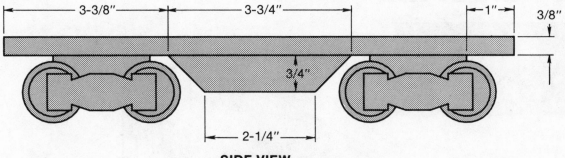

**SIDE VIEW
FLATCAR**

PROCEDURE

1. BASE ASSEMBLY

Make the two truck assemblies. Resaw the stock for the base (F), and cut the part to final dimension. A flatcar becomes a stake bed car by adding the stakes. To make a stake car, drill 1/4″-diameter holes as shown. For the base supports (G), take a 3/4″ × 3/4″ × 3-3/4″ piece of stock and cut the profile according to the plans. Resaw the stock for two supports and sand the parts.

2. ASSEMBLY

Glue and clamp the trucks to the base; glue and clamp base supports into place. The base supports should align with the wheels. (For the stake car, sand the stake's top edges and glue them into the holes.)

Drill a 3/32″-diameter hole in the front and rear of the base and install the screw hook and screw eye.

The flatcar is complete and ready for loading.

MATERIALS

Part	Description	Pieces	Dimensions
			(finished dimensions in inches)
A	Axle holders	2	1/2 × 2-3/4 × 2-1/2
B	Axle spacers	2	1/2 × 1-3/4 × 2
C	Wheels	8	1-1/4 dia. × 3/8
D	Wheel covers	4	1/8 × 3/4 × 2-1/4
E	Axles	4	1/4 dia. × 2-5/8
F	Base	1	3/8 × 3 × 10-1/2
G	Base supports	2	3/8 × 3/4 × 3-3/4
H	Stakes (not shown)	14	1/4 dia. × 1-3/4

MISCELLANEOUS
1-5/8″ screw hook
1-1/8″ screw eye

GONDOLA CAR

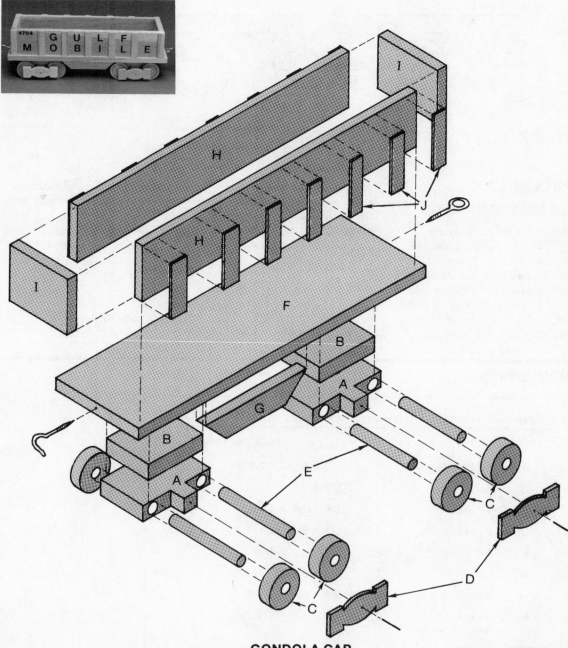

GONDOLA CAR

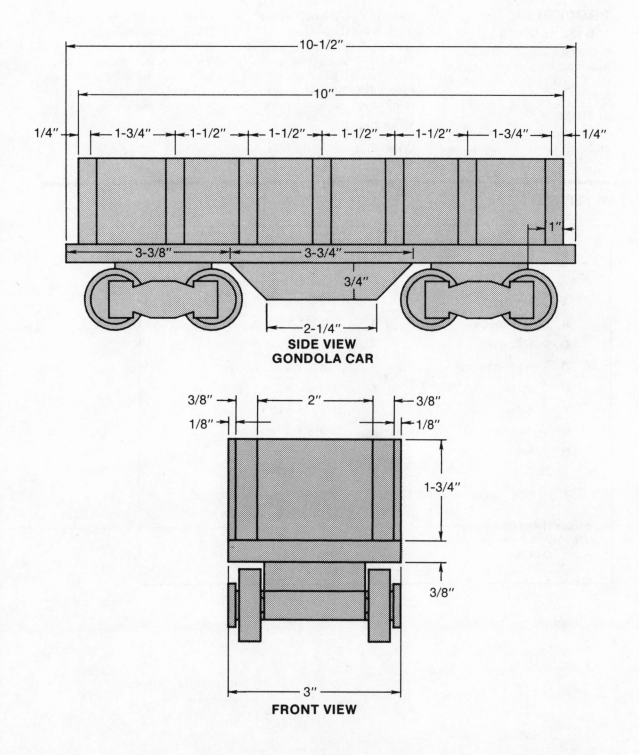

SIDE VIEW
GONDOLA CAR

FRONT VIEW

PROCEDURE

1. BASE ASSEMBLY

Follow the steps for the flatcar. Assemble the trucks (A–E) to the base (F) and add base supports (G).

2. SIDES

Cut 3/4"-thick stock to length and width for the sides (H) and ends (I); then resaw it to 3/8" thick. Sand the surfaces smooth. Prepare long strips of 1/8" × 3/8" stock for the reinforcements (J), and cut to length. Glue and clamp the reinforcements to the sides.

3. ASSEMBLY

When the glue for the reinforcements dries, glue and clamp the sides together. Power-sand the ends, top, and bottom square and flush. Finally, glue the body to the base and drill the pilot holes for the screw eye and screw hook.

MATERIALS

Part	Description	Pieces	Dimensions
			(finished dimensions in inches)
A	Axle holders	2	1/2 × 2-3/4 × 2-1/2
B	Axle spacers	2	1/2 × 1-3/4 × 2
C	Wheels	8	1-1/4 dia. × 3/8
D	Wheel covers	4	1/8 × 3/4 × 2-1/4
E	Axles	4	1/4 dia. × 2-5/8
F	Base	1	3/8 × 3 × 10-1/2
G	Base supports	2	3/8 × 3/4 × 3-3/4
H	Sides	2	3/8 × 1-3/4 × 10
I	Ends	2	3/8 × 1-3/4 × 2
J	Side reinforcements	14	1/8 × 3/8 × 1-3/4

MISCELLANEOUS
1-5/8" screw hook
1-1/8" screw eye

BOXCAR

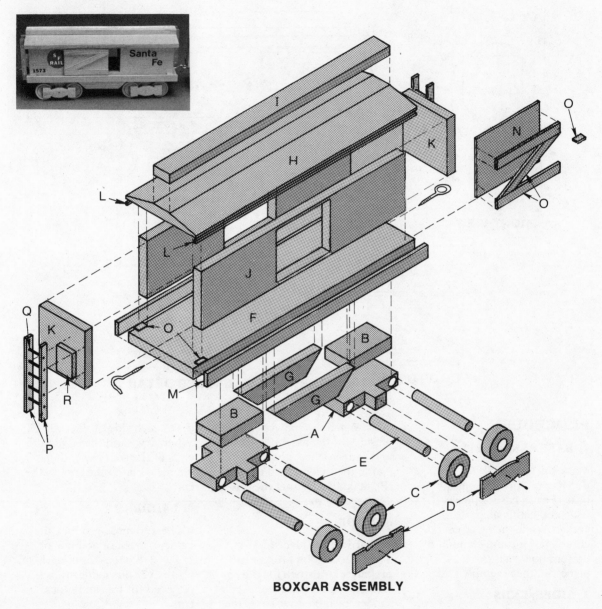

BOXCAR ASSEMBLY

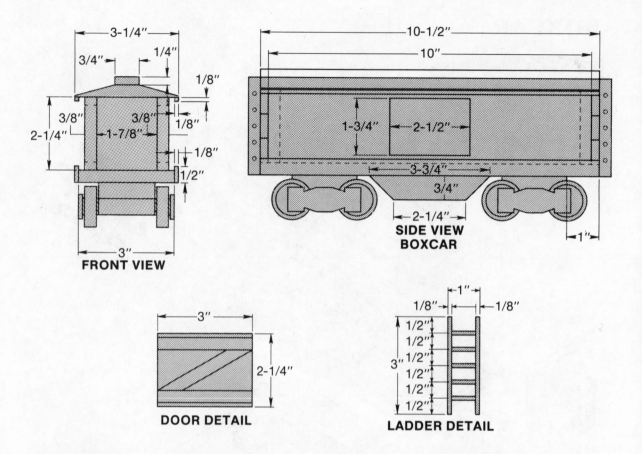

FRONT VIEW

SIDE VIEW BOXCAR

DOOR DETAIL

LADDER DETAIL

PROCEDURE

1. BASE ASSEMBLY

Make the flatcar—build the two trucks; then cut out the base (F) and base supports (G). Glue and clamp all parts together. When the basic car is complete, glue and clamp the bottom door rails (M) into place. Set the assembly aside.

2. SIDES/ENDS

Prepare a 3/4" × 2-1/4" × 16" piece of stock. Resaw it into two 3/8"-thick pieces; cut the sides (J) and ends (K) to length. Lay out the door openings in the sides and cut out with a scroll saw or coping saw. Glue and clamp the sides to the

ends. When dry, power-sand all sides of the assembly flush and square. Next, glue and clamp the assembly to the base (F), making sure that the box is centered on the base.

3. ROOF

Prepare an 11" piece of 3/4" × 3-1/4" stock (don't forget to prepare extra stock for the caboose). With a hand plane, belt sander, or table saw, bevel the edges of the roof about 15°, leaving a 3/4"-wide flat area on top. Resaw the stock to 3/8" thick; cut it to length. Finish the roof by gluing and clamping the roof vent (I) to the flat area on top of the roof. Glue and clamp the top door rails

(L) to each side of the roof. When dry, sand the edges and ends of the roof flush; then glue and clamp the roof to the car.

4. LADDERS

It's best to mass-produce the ladders. Prepare about 3' of 1/4" × 3/8" stock, and mark off the various ladder rails (P) required for this and other cars.

NOTE: Some of the ladders have six rungs, some have five.

Locate the ladder rung holes and ladder rail lengths on the 3/8" surface of the stock. Drill the 1/8"-diameter ladder rung holes. Resaw the stock into two equal halves, and cut the rails to length. Cut the rungs to 1-1/4" long (a bit oversized). Assemble the rails and rungs with glue, and adjust the rails so they measure 1" from one outside edge to the other.

Cut the stock for the ladder supports (R) to size. Glue and clamp them to the ends of the car. Glue one ladder onto each end of the boxcar as shown.

5. DOORS

Make the doors (N) from 1/8"-thick stock. Check the fit between the top and bottom rails. If the doors fit, remove them and glue optional 1/8" × 3/8" "bracing" into place on the outside of each door. Put the doors in place and glue the door stops (O) into place.

Using a 3/32"-diameter drill bit, drill the ends of the boxcar for the hook and eye. There are many ways to decorate the train cars—refer to catalogs or, better yet, use your imagination.

MATERIALS

Part	Description	Pieces	Dimensions
			(finished dimensions in inches)
A	Axle holders	2	1/2 × 2-3/4 × 2-1/2
B	Axle spacers	2	1/2 × 1-3/4 × 2
C	Wheels	8	1-1/4 dia. × 3/8
D	Wheel covers	4	1/8 × 3/4 × 2-1/4
E	Axles	4	1/4 dia. × 2-5/8
F	Base	1	3/8 × 3 × 10-1/2
G	Base supports	2	3/8 × 3/4 × 3-3/4
H	Roof	1	3/8 × 3-1/4 × 10-1/2
I	Roof vent	1	1/4 × 3/4 × 10-1/2
J	Sides	2	3/8 × 2-1/4 × 10
K	Ends	2	3/8 × 2-1/4 × 1-7/8
L	Top door rails	2	1/8 × 1/8 × 10-1/2
M	Bottom door rails	2	1/8 × 1/2 × 10-1/2
N	Doors (not shown)	2	1/8 × 2-1/4 × 3
O	Door stops	4	1/8 × 1/8 × 1/2
P	Ladder rails	4	1/8 × 3/8 × 3
Q	Ladder rungs	10	1/8 dia. × 1
R	Ladder supports	2	1/4 × 3/4 × 1-1/2

MISCELLANEOUS
1-5/8" screw hook
1-1/8" screw eye

HOPPER CAR

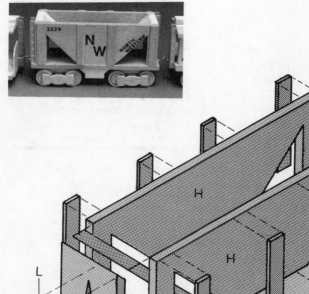

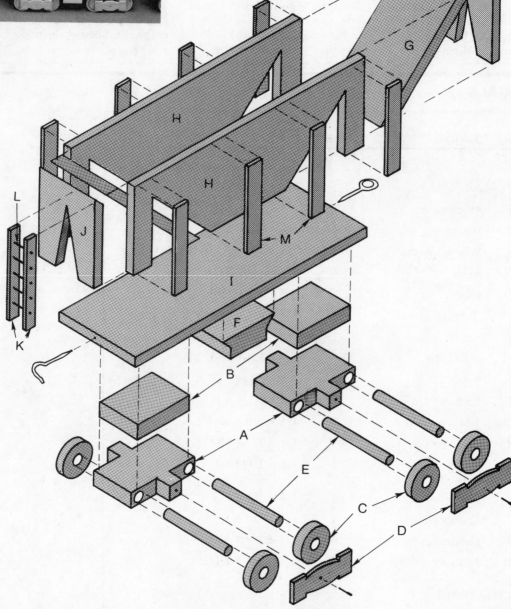

HOPPER CAR ASSEMBLY

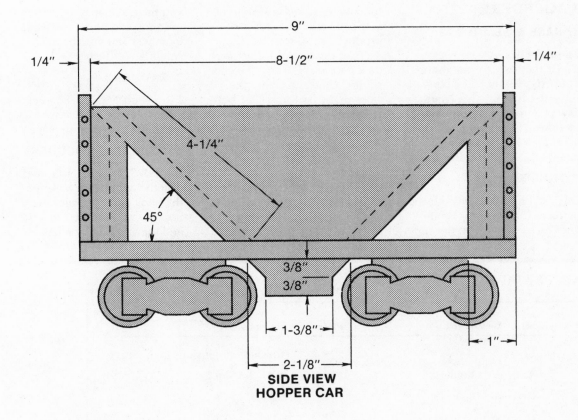

SIDE VIEW
HOPPER CAR

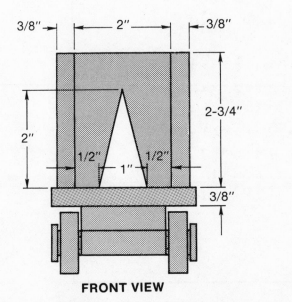

FRONT VIEW

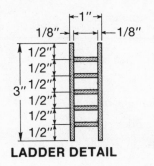

LADDER DETAIL

PROCEDURE

1. BASE ASSEMBLY

Make the truck assemblies (A–E), the base (F), and dump chute (G). Dump chute contours are made with a bandsaw or scroll saw. After completing all these parts, assemble with glue and clamps. Set the assembly aside.

2. HOPPER

On 3/4"-thick stock, lay out the patterns for the sides (H) and ends (J) as shown. Cut the contours with a bandsaw or scroll saw and resaw the stock to produce 3/8"-thick pieces.

Cut the stock for the diagonal bottoms (I); leave the ends square. Glue and clamp the sides to the bottoms. (The bottoms will overhang the top and bottom edges of the sides.) Bevel the top of the ends; glue and clamp them to the hopper assembly.

Cut 1/8" × 3/8" stock to length for the hopper reinforcements (M). Glue and clamp them to the sides. Now you have a hopper with an uneven top and bottom; solve this by power-sanding the top smooth and flush.

3. LADDERS

Begin with 1/4" × 3/8" stock; drill the holes; resaw the stock; then glue the rungs in place.

4. FINISHING TOUCHES

Use a 3/32"-diameter bit and drill the ends of the base for the hook and eye. Paint the hopper car, if desired, or just add the vinyl stick-on letters.

MATERIALS

Part	Description	Pieces	Dimensions
			(finished dimensions in inches)
A	Axle holders	2	1/2 × 2-3/4 × 2-1/2
B	Axle spacers	2	1/2 × 1-3/4 × 2
C	Wheels	8	1-1/4 dia. × 3/8
D	Wheel covers	4	1/8 × 3/4 × 2-1/4
E	Axles	4	1/4 dia. × 2-5/8
F	Base	1	3/8 × 3 × 9
G	Dump chute	1	3/4 × 2-3/4 × 2-1/8
H	Sides	2	3/8 × 2-3/4 × 8-1/2
I	Hopper bottom	2	3/8 × 2 × 4-1/4
J	Ends	2	3/8 × 2 × 2-3/4
K	Ladder rails	4	1/8 × 3/8 × 3
L	Ladder rungs	10	1/8 dia. × 1
M	Hopper reinforcements	8	1/8 × 3/8 × 2-3/4

MISCELLANEOUS
1-5/8" screw hook
1-1/8" screw eye

TANK CAR

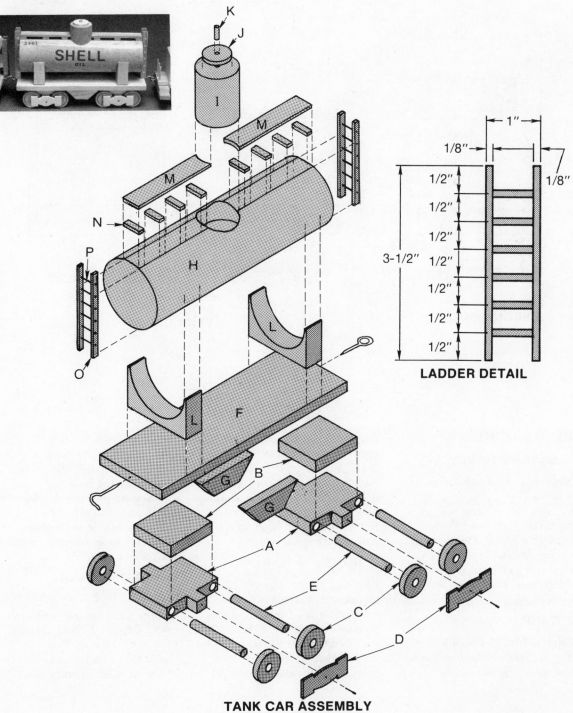

K

J

I

M

M

N

P

O

H

L

L

F

B

G

G

A

E

C

D

1"

1/8"

1/8"

1/2"

1/2"

1/2"

1/2"

3-1/2"

1/2"

1/2"

1/2"

LADDER DETAIL

TANK CAR ASSEMBLY

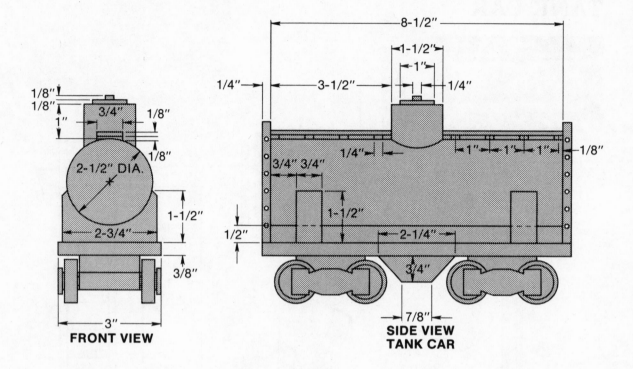

FRONT VIEW

SIDE VIEW TANK CAR

PROCEDURE

1. BASE ASSEMBLY

Make two truck (wheel) assemblies (A–E) and set aside. Cut the base (F) and base supports (G) to size and shape; then glue and clamp them together. When the glue dries, glue and clamp the trucks to the base assembly and set aside.

2. TANK

Glue up four pieces of 3/4" × 3" × 10" stock. Clamp securely and allow the block to set overnight. When the stock is ready, turn it on a lathe to 2-1/2" diameter. If you don't have a lathe, substitute an 8-1/2" length of an old rolling pin—the diameter doesn't have to be exact since you can adjust the other parts.

3. DOME

Glue and clamp together two pieces of 3/4" stock. Cut out the part with a 1-5/8"-diameter hole saw. Use a 1-1/8" hole saw, and cut out the tank dome cover (J) from 1/8" stock. Glue the dome cover to the dome, and drill a 1/4" hole into the top of the dome. Cut a 1/2" length of 1/4" dowel, and glue it into the hole.

Secure the tank in a V-block, and drill a 1-1/2"-diameter hole in the middle. Glue the dome assembly into the hole in the tank.

4. WALKWAY AND SUPPORTS

Cut the parts for the walkway (M,N). Glue and clamp them to the top of the tank. Some fitting with a small drum sander or the rounded surface of a rasp may be necessary to make the walkway fit up next to the dome.

Tank supports (L) are made from a single piece of 3/4″ × 2-3/4″ × 3″ stock. Use a 2-1/2″-diameter hole saw and cut a hole in the center of the block. Cut the block apart.

Glue the supports to the base assembly; glue the tank assembly into place.

5. ASSEMBLY

Drill six 1/8″-diameter holes in a 1/4″ × 3/8″ × 3-1/2″ piece of stock as shown. Resaw the stock and glue the rungs in place. Glue the ladders to the ends of the tanks.

Finally, drill a 3/32″-deep hole in the front and back of the base. Add the screw eye and screw hook. Apply vinyl letters as a final decoration, if desired.

MATERIALS

Part	Description	Pieces	Dimensions
			(finished dimensions in inches)
A	Axle holders	2	1/2 × 2-3/4 × 2-1/2
B	Axle spacers	2	1/2 × 1-3/4 × 2
C	Wheels	8	1-1/4 dia. × 3/8
D	Wheel covers	4	1/8 × 3/4 × 2-1/4
E	Axles	4	1/4 dia. × 2-5/8
F	Base	1	3/8 × 3 × 9
G	Base supports	2	3/8 × 3/4 × 2-1/4
H	Tank	1	2-1/2 dia. × 8-1/2
I	Tank dome	1	1-1/2 dia. × 1-1/2
J	Tank dome cover	1	1 dia. × 1/8
K	Tank dome cover wheel	1	1/4 dia. × 1/2
L	Tank supports	2	3/4 × 2-3/4 × 1-3/4
M	Tank walkway	2	1/8 × 3/4 × 3-1/2
N	Tank walkway supports	8	1/8 × 1/4 × 3/4
O	Ladder rails	4	1/8 × 3/8 × 3-1/2
P	Ladder rungs	12	1/8 dia. × 1

MISCELLANEOUS
1-5/8″ screw hook
1-1/8″ screw eye

CONSTRUCTION NOTES
1. Glue up four pieces of stock to turn the tank (H).

2. Tank supports (L) are cut from one piece of stock.

CABOOSE

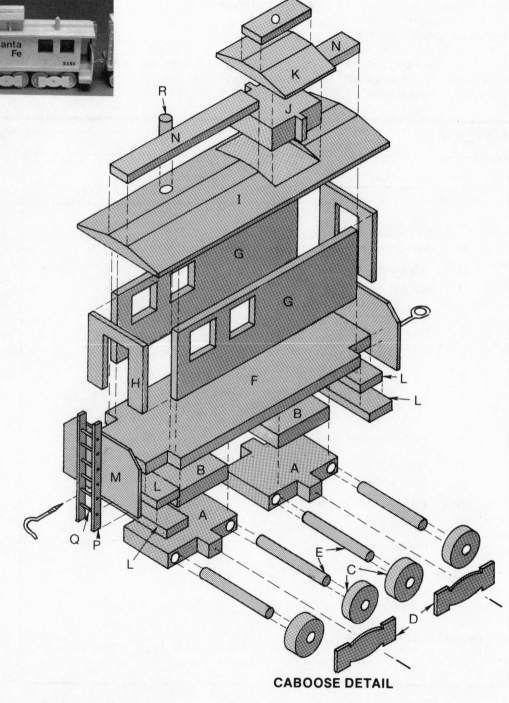

CABOOSE DETAIL

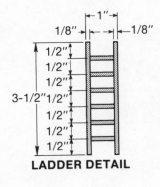

LADDER DETAIL

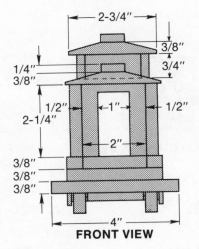

FRONT VIEW

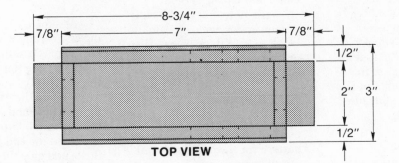

TOP VIEW

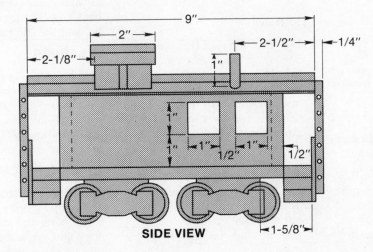

SIDE VIEW

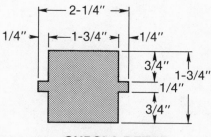

**CUPOLA DETAIL
TOP VIEW**

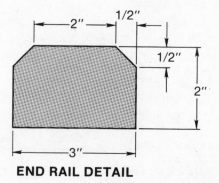

END RAIL DETAIL

PROCEDURE

1. BASE ASSEMBLY

Make the truck assemblies (A–E) and set them aside.

Prepare a 3/8"-thick piece of stock for the base (F) and lay out the positions of the notches on each end. Cut the steps (L) to length and glue and clamp together.

To assemble the base, glue and clamp the wheels in position. Finally, glue and clamp the steps into place and set the assembly aside.

2. SIDES AND ENDS

Lay out side (G) and end (H) contours on 3/4" × 2-1/4" × 10" stock. Use a coping saw or scroll saw to make the window openings.

NOTE: Use a 1"-diameter drill bit to cut out the windows and a rasp to file them square.

Resaw the stock into two 3/8"-thick pieces. Glue and clamp the sides to the ends. When dry, sand all sides smooth and flush; glue and clamp the body to the base.

3. END RAILS

Miter the corners of a 3/4" × 3"× 2" block of stock as indicated in the plans. For strength, note that the block is 2" long and 3" wide. Resaw the block to 1/8"-thick pieces; then glue and clamp the end rails to the caboose assembly.

4. CUPOLA

Take a 3/4" × 2-1/4" × 1-3/4" piece of stock and lay out the pattern for the cupola (J). Cut out the part using a bandsaw or scroll saw; then set the part aside.

5. ROOF

For the main roof (I), take a 3/8"-thick piece of stock and bevel the edges. When beveling, leave at least a 3/4" flat area on the top of the roof for the vent. Cut the roof to length and set aside. Drill a 3/8"-diameter hole as indicated in the plans for the smokestack (R).

Follow the same procedure for the cupola roof (K), but note that this roof is 2" wide instead of 3" like the main roof.

Since the cupola should be glued to a flat area, place it on the roof, mark its position, and use a chisel to create a flat area.

Assemble the roof by gluing and clamping the cupola roof vent (O) to the cupola roof (K). Glue this assembly to the cupola (J). Glue the cupola assembly to the caboose roof (I); then glue and clamp the roof vents (N) into place.

Sand the ends of the roof flush, and glue the smokestack into place. Glue the roof assembly to the caboose assembly and make sure that the back edge of the roof is lined up with the end rail.

6. LADDER

Drill holes in a 1/4" × 3/8" × 3-1/2" piece of stock as shown. Resaw the stock and glue the rungs (Q) into place. Glue and clamp the completed ladder to the end of the caboose.

7. FINAL TOUCHES

With a 3/32"-diameter drill bit, drill the pilot holes for the screw hook and eye. Install the hook and eye and apply decorations as desired.

MATERIALS

Part	Description	Pieces	Dimensions
			(finished dimensions in inches)
A	Axle holders	2	1/2 × 2-3/4 × 2-1/2
B	Axle spacers	2	1/2 × 1-3/4 × 2
C	Wheels	8	1-1/4 dia. × 3/8
D	Wheel covers	4	1/8 × 3/4 × 2-1/4
E	Axles	4	1/4 dia. × 2-5/8
F	Base	1	3/8 × 3 × 8-3/4
G	Sides	2	3/8 × 2-1/4 × 7
H	Ends	2	3/8 × 2-1/4 × 2
I	Main roof	1	3/8 × 3 × 9
J	Cupola	1	3/4 × 2-1/4 × 1-3/4
K	Cupola roof	1	3/8 × 2 × 2-3/4
L	Steps	2	3/8 × 3/4 × 3
		2	3/8 × 3/4 × 4
M	End rails	2	1/8 × 3 × 2
N	Roof vents	2	1/4 × 3/4 × 7-1/4
O	Cupola roof vent	1	1/4 × 3/4 × 2
P	Ladder rails	2	1/8 × 3/8 × 3-1/2
Q	Ladder rungs	6	1/8 dia. × 1
R	Smokestack	1	3/8 dia. × 1-1/4

MISCELLANEOUS
1-5/8″ screw hook
1-1/8″ screw eye

CONSTRUCTION NOTES
1. Grain direction on the end rails (M) must run vertically.

MODERN STEAM LOCOMOTIVE AND TENDER

This modern steam locomotive and tender are modeled after those used before World War II. The design, a 2-6-2 model, is a typical engine and tender of a general category of locomotive. Engines within this category have different numbers, wheel sizes, and cab and boiler configurations. Feel free to experiment with the design—that's what makes toy building such a personal hobby.

Before making the first cut, read all the instructions so you'll know how everything goes together as well as how simple it is to build this toy.

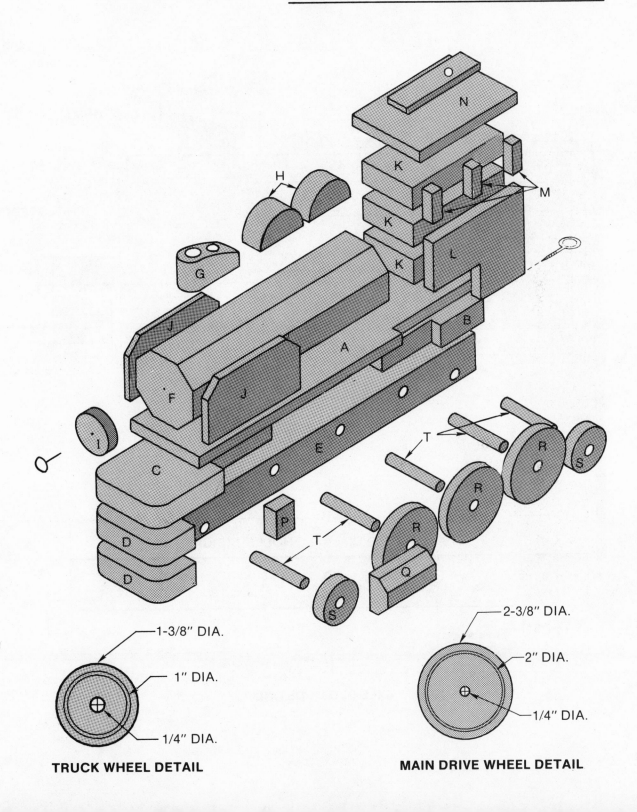

TRUCK WHEEL DETAIL

1-3/8" DIA.

1" DIA.

1/4" DIA.

MAIN DRIVE WHEEL DETAIL

2-3/8" DIA.

2" DIA.

1/4" DIA.

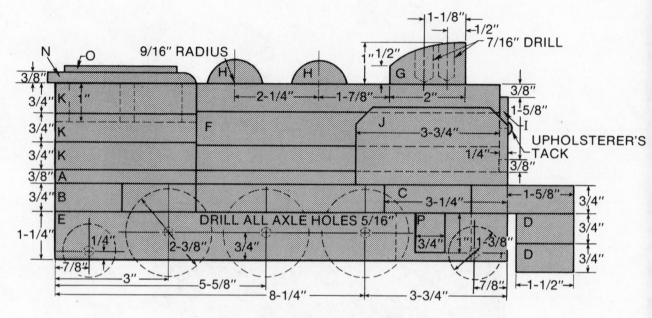

LOCOMOTIVE SIDE DETAIL

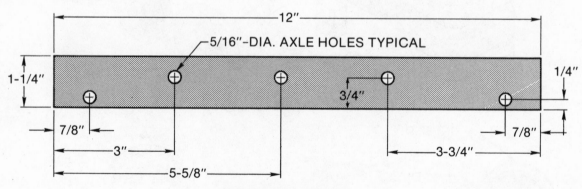

AXLE BLOCK DETAIL

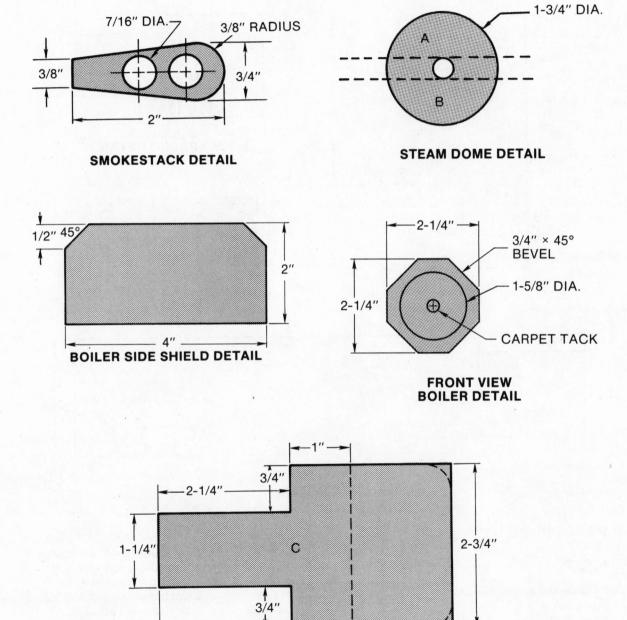

SMOKESTACK DETAIL

7/16" DIA.

3/8" RADIUS

3/8"

3/4"

2"

STEAM DOME DETAIL

1-3/4" DIA.

A

B

BOILER SIDE SHIELD DETAIL

1/2" 45°

2"

4"

FRONT VIEW BOILER DETAIL

2-1/4"

3/4" × 45° BEVEL

1-5/8" DIA.

2-1/4"

CARPET TACK

COWCATCHER DETAIL

1"

3/4"

2-1/4"

1-1/4"

C

2-3/4"

3/4"

5"

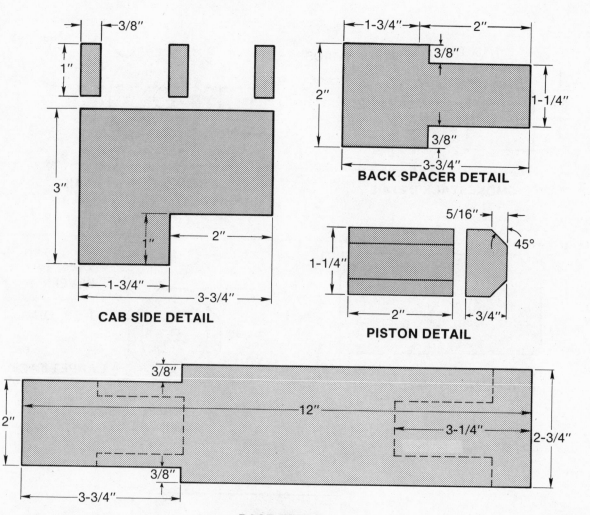

CAB SIDE DETAIL

BACK SPACER DETAIL

PISTON DETAIL

BASE DETAIL

PROCEDURE

1. BASE

To make the locomotive base (A), on a 3/4" × 2-3/4" × 12" piece of stock, mark the locations of the notches on the back of the piece where the sides will go. Using a scroll saw or bandsaw, cut out the wheel notches. Then resaw the stock to form two 3/8"-thick pieces. Save the extra base for another engine.

2. COWCATCHER

Prepare the stock for the back spacer (B) and the cowcatcher top (C). Lay out the notches in these parts as indicated; then cut out the profiles. Make the cowcatcher (D) by gluing and clamping together two pieces of 3/4" × 2-3/4" × 1-1/2" stock. After the glue has dried, sand the edges flush, and glue and clamp the cowcatcher to the cowcatcher top.

Next, using a power sander or a rasp, round the front corners of the cowcatcher.

Glue and clamp the back spacer and the cowcatcher to the base, then set the assembly aside.

3. AXLE BLOCK

Either glue up stock for the axle block (E), or cut the block from 2 × 4 stock. Once you've gotten the block to size, locate and drill all the axle holes where shown. Sand the block; then glue and clamp the part to the base assembly.

4. BOILER

To make the boiler (F), glue up three pieces of 3/4" × 2-1/4" × 17" stock. The extra length of the glued-up block serves a dual purpose: First, it makes the stock safer to handle than an 8" piece; second, you'll have enough boiler stock for a second engine.

After the glue dries, sand the block square. Set a bandsaw, scroll saw, or table saw to cut a 45° bevel. Make some test cuts on scrap wood until you're satisfied with the cut. When the saw is set, cut the bevels on the boiler.

Once the stock is beveled, cut the boiler(s) to length. Prepare a 3/4" × 5/8" × 1-5/8" block of stock for the smokestack (G), and drill the holes in it as shown. After the holes are drilled, use a power sander to form the contour of the smokestack and to round the front corners. Glue and clamp the smokestack to the boiler according to the plans.

Next, make the steam domes (H). Using a 1-7/8"-diameter hole saw, make a 3/4"-thick, 1-3/4"-diameter blank for both. Sand the blank; then cut the two domes even with the pilot hole. Glue and clamp the domes to the top of the boiler.

Make the boiler front (I) with a 1-3/4"-diameter hole saw. Cut the part out of 1/4"-thick stock; then glue and clamp the part to the boiler. Use an upholstery tack to cover the pilot hole.

Finally, complete the boiler by making the side shields (J). Take a 3/4" × 2" × 4" piece of stock and miter the corners as shown. Resaw the block into two 3/8"-thick pieces, sand them smooth, then set aside.

Glue and clamp the boiler assembly to the base assembly, making sure the boiler front (I) is flush with the front of the base (A). Next, glue and clamp the shields (J) to the boiler; be sure they are flush with the front of the base. Set the engine assembly aside.

5. CAB

The cab is made of several parts. Glue together three pieces of 3/4" × 2" × 3-3/4" stock to form the core of the cab (K).

Next, cut the stock for the six window frames (M) to size. Glue and clamp the window frames to the cab block flush with the top of the block.

Resaw stock for the cab roof (N) and cab roof vent (O). Cut these parts to proper length and width; then glue and clamp them to the cab block (K). Make sure the front of the roof is flush with the front of the cab block. After the glue dries, use a power sander or rasp to round the front edge of the roof. Next, power-sand the front and rear of the cab assembly flush; then glue the entire cab assembly to the base. The cab should fit up against the boiler and remain flush with the back edge of the base.

Complete assembly by taking a 3/4" × 3" × 3-3/4" block and transferring the outline of the cab sides (L) to it. Cut the contours of the sides using a scroll saw or bandsaw. Resaw the block into two 3/8"-thick pieces. Do not glue and clamp these pieces to the main engine assembly yet; wait until the wheels are in place.

6. WHEELS

The wheels (R, S) are made by the hole saw method. Prepare enough 3/8"-thick stock for all of the wheels. Create the 1/8"-deep rims for the main drive wheels (R) with a 2"-diameter hole saw. After forming the rims, use a 2-1/2"-diameter hole saw to cut out the 2-3/8"-diameter wheels. Sand the wheels and set aside. Next, make the truck wheels (S) using the same procedure but with a 1"-diameter hole saw for the rim and a 1-1/2"-diameter hole saw for the wheels. Sand all the wheels smooth.

Take 1/4"-diameter dowel stock and cut the five axles (T) to length. Attach the wheels and axles to the axle block.

The sides cover up part of the rear wheels. Since the wheels are in place, glue and clamp the sides into place.

7. PISTONS

Cut out the stock for the piston mounts (P); then glue and clamp these mounts in place. Form the pistons from a 3/4" ×

1-1/4″ × 12″ piece of stock. (The extra long stock here is for safe handling while machining.) Chamfer the edges of the stock as indicated; then cut the pistons to 2″ lengths. Glue and clamp the pistons to the piston mounts.

The modern steam locomotive is complete. Drill a 3/32″-diameter hole in the rear of the locomotive for a screw eye so you'll be able to hook up the tender when it's done.

Decorations for the locomotive can be made from contact paper. When you finish the tender, you can decorate both toys as a final step.

MATERIALS

Part	Description	Pieces	Dimensions
			(finished dimensions in inches)
A	Base	1	3/8 × 2-3/4 × 12
B	Back spacer	1	3/4 × 2 × 3-3/4
C	Cowcatcher top	1	3/4 × 2-3/4 × 5
D	Cowcatcher	1	1-1/2 × 2-3/4 × 1-1/2
E	Axle block	1	1-1/4 × 1-1/4 × 12
F	Boiler	1	2-1/4 × 2-1/4 × 8
G	Smokestack	1	3/4 × 1 × 2
H	Steam domes	2	3/4 × 5/8 × 1-5/8
I	Boiler front	1	1-5/8 dia. × 1/4
J	Boiler side shields	2	3/8 × 2 × 4
K	Cab	1	2-1/4 × 2 × 3-3/4
L	Cab sides	2	3/8 × 3 × 3-3/4
M	Cab window frames	6	3/8 × 3/8 × 1
N	Cab roof	1	3/8 × 2 × 4
O	Cab roof vent	1	1/8 × 3/4 × 3
P	Piston mounts	2	1/2 × 3/4 × 1
Q	Pistons	2	3/4 × 1-1/4 × 2
R	Main drive wheels	6	2-3/8 dia. × 3/8
S	Truck wheels	4	1-3/8 dia. × 38
T	Axles	5	1/4 dia. × 2

MISCELLANEOUS
1-1/8″ screw eye
Nickel-plated upholstery tack

TENDER

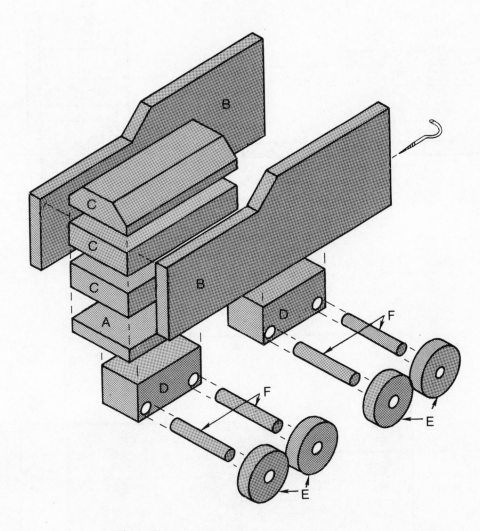

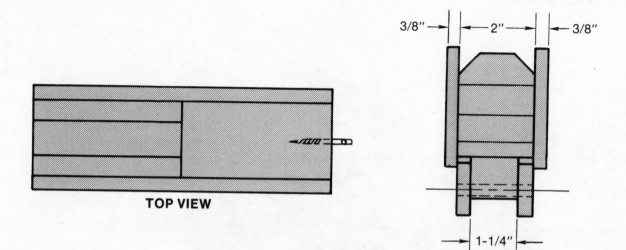

TOP VIEW

END VIEW

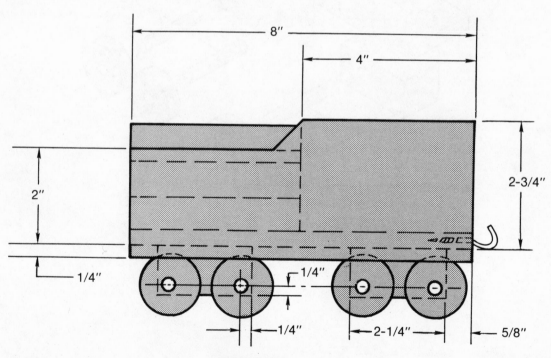

SIDE VIEW

PROCEDURE

1. BASE/AXLE HOLDERS

Cut 3/4" stock to length and width for the base (A). Resaw the base stock to 3/8" thick and set the part aside.

Next, glue up and resaw stock to get the two blocks for the axle holders (D). Locate and drill the 5/16" holes for the axles; then glue and clamp the holders to the base. Set the assembly aside.

2. TANK

Glue up three 3/4"-thick pieces of stock to form a 2-1/4" × 2" × 10" block. (The extra length is to permit safe handling while machining.) Chamfer the two top edges; then cut the tank (C) to length. Cut another 4" tank in case you want to make another tender. Glue and clamp the tank to the base assembly; then sand the sides flush.

3. WHEELS

The wheels (E) are made the same as for the locomotive. Prepare 3/8"-thick stock; then use a 1"-diameter hole saw to make the 1/8"-deep rim kerfs for the eight wheels. Cut out the wheels using a 1-1/2"-diameter hole saw and sand them smooth. Cut the axles (F) to length, and glue the wheels and axles to the axle blocks.

4. SIDES

Prepare a 3/4" × 3" × 8" block of stock for the sides (B).

Transfer the profile from the plans to the stock. Cut the profile using a bandsaw or scroll saw. Resaw the stock into two 3/8"-thick pieces. Sand; then glue and clamp them to the tender body.

Finally, drill 3/32"-diameter holes in the front and rear of the base. Install the screw hook in the front and the screw eye in the rear of the tender.

The locomotive and tender can be stained, painted, or just left natural. Or you can use various colors of contact paper to put stripes or a design on the toy.

MATERIALS

Part	Description	Pieces	Dimensions
			(finished dimensions in inches)
A	Base	1	3/8 × 2 × 8
B	Sides	2	3/8 × 3 × 8
C	Tank	1	2-1/4 × 2 × 4
D	Axle holders	2	1-1/8 × 1-1/4 × 2-1/4
E	Wheels	8	1-3/8 × 3/8
F	Axles	4	1/4 dia. × 2

MISCELLANEOUS
1-5/8" screw hook
1-1/8" screw eye

GREATEST SHOW ON EARTH

The animal train has been the most popular train among toddlers. As a train, there are six designs here for different animals. But don't stop at just these designs; you can make more patterns for other animals.

Pine or a suitable hardwood is best for the animals. If the toys are for a child under 2 years old, eliminate the ears, tails, and horns—these parts could be bitten off and swallowed.

Leave the stock for these toys natural or paint it with bright colors. If applying paint, make sure you prime the wood first; then use a nontoxic paint to finish.

To make a really fun toy out of this project, double the size of the animals. It's not necessary to make all of them, but the ones you do make will be big and fun. Use 1-1/2"-thick stock for all the parts.

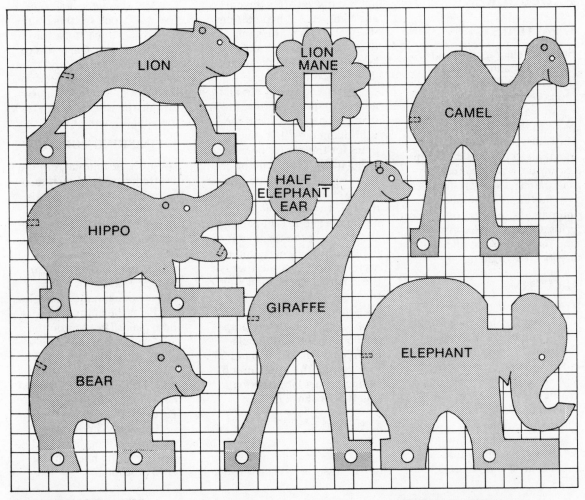

ONE SQUARE = 1/2"

ANIMAL AND WHEEL PATTERNS

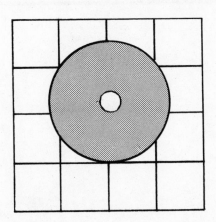

PROCEDURE

1. PATTERNS

Start by making patterns for the various animals. Draw 1/2" grids onto stiff cardboard or tempered hardboard; then transfer the patterns from the plans to the grids. The elephant ear is just a half pattern. You can make a full pattern for the ear or just trace around the half pattern twice on the stock.

For larger or smaller animals, draw larger or smaller grids. Cut out the templates and make sure that all holes are located on them.

2. CUTTING

Transfer the patterns to the stock making sure the grain direction on all the animals is horizontal (except for the giraffe, which is vertical). If you've laid out all the animals on the same stock, cut the stock into blocks for easy handling. Cut out the pieces using a scroll saw or bandsaw. (A scroll saw is really the better tool because almost no sand-ing is required after the cuts are complete.) When cutting the shapes, form the smiles on these animals with a saw kerf—just cut into the area; then back out the blade.

After you've cut out all the animal shapes, drill the 5/16"-diameter axle holes and the 1/8"-diameter × 1/4"-deep holes for the giraffe horns and hippo teeth. Then drill the holes for all the ears and tails. The eyes are formed by using the 1/8" twist drill bit and drilling a hole about 1/8" deep on either side of the toy. Locations of the tails, ears, and eyes aren't critical; just put them in the general area as indicated in the plans.

Once all the holes have been drilled, glue and clamp the lion's mane and the elephant ears into place. Sand all the edges of the toys smooth, paying particular attention to splinters or sharp edges.

3. WHEELS

The 1-1/4"-diameter wheels for this train are formed using a 1-3/8"-diameter hole saw. Use 3/4" stock for this train and 1-1/2"-thick stock for one double the size. Once you've cut out the wheels, sand them smooth. When completed, cut the axles to length; then assemble the wheels and axles to the animals with glue.

4. FINISHING TOUCHES

To finish the animals, cut the giraffe horns and hippo teeth to length and sand the ends. Glue them into the 1/8"-diameter holes drilled earlier.

The ears for the animals are made from brown felt. Cut out the ears and glue them into the 1/8"-diameter ear holes with aliphatic resin glue.

Paint the animals or leave them plain. The eyes on the animals can be painted in with a felt-tipped marker.

Finally, drill 3/32"-diameter holes in each end of the animals and insert the screw hooks and eyes.

Crimp the hooks so the eyes barely fit in them, and be sure to put the hooks in the *down* position.

MATERIALS

Part	Description	Pieces	Dimensions
			(finished dimensions in inches)
A	Lion	1	3/4 × 3-3/4 × 6
B	Lion's mane	1	3/4 × 2-3/4 × 2-3/4
C	Hippo	1	3/4 × 2-3/4 × 6
D	Hippo teeth (not shown)	2	1/8 dia. × 1/2
E	Giraffe	1	3/4 × 5 × 8
F	Giraffe horns (not shown)	2	1/8 dia. × 1/2
G	Bear	1	3/4 × 3-3/4 × 4-3/4
H	Camel	1	3/4 × 4-1/4 × 5-3/4
I	Elephant	1	3/4 × 5 × 5-3/4
J	Elephant ears	1	3/4 × 2 × 3-1/2
K	Wheels	24	1-1/4 dia. × 3/4
L	Axles (not shown)	12	1/4 dia. × 2-3/8

MISCELLANEOUS
1-1/8" screw eyes (6)
1-5/8" screw hooks (6)
Felt (for ears)
Yarn or string (for tails)

BASIC PULL-ALONG TRAIN

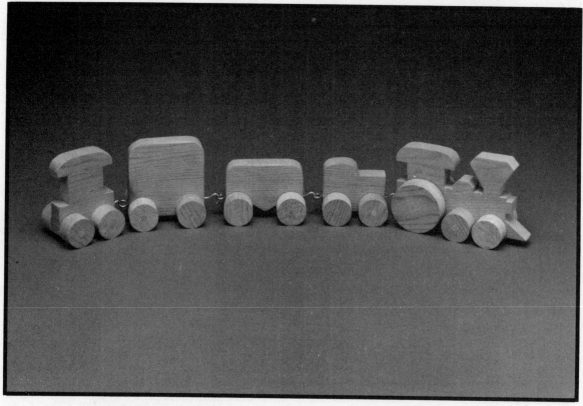

Toy trains are always a favorite of children. Here's a plan for a very simple toy pull-along train that's sure to delight the little ones. This train is so simple to make that building extra ones for needy children at Christmastime is an easy way to bring joy into a lot of little lives.

As with all of the toys, make sure you use good stock and sand all edges smooth so there's no chance of splintering.

This project can be made entirely on a scroll saw or bandsaw. Be sure to read through the instructions for more details on how to make this train.

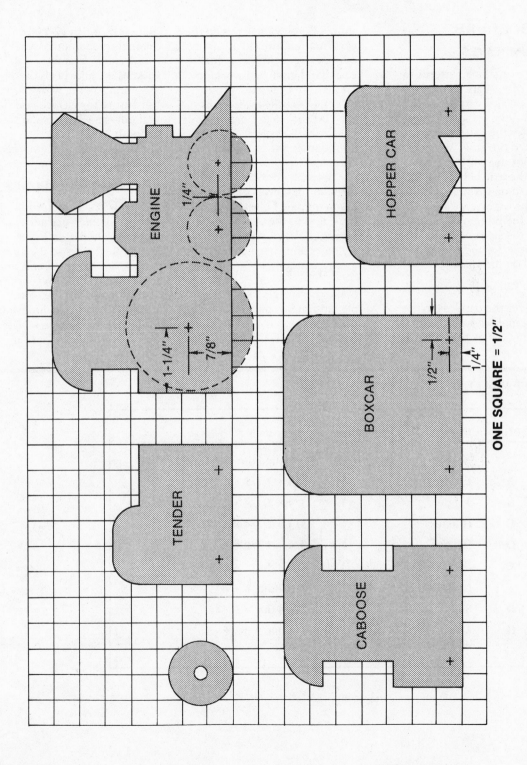

ENGINE

1/4"

HOPPER CAR

1-1/4"

7/8"

TENDER

BOXCAR

1/2"

1/4"

CABOOSE

ONE SQUARE = 1/2"

PROCEDURE

1. TEMPLATES

Start by making patterns for the various cars. Draw 1/2" grids on stiff cardboard or tempered hardboard; then transfer the patterns from the plans to the grids. When cutting out the patterns, make sure the axle hole locations are marked on them. Axle hole locations for all cars are 1/4" from the bottom edge and 1/2" from the side edge. The hole locations for the engine are noted on the plans.

2. CUTTING

Transfer the patterns to the stock, making sure the grain direction on all the cars is horizontal. If you've laid out all the cars on the same stock, cut it into manageable blocks for easy handling when working on the scroll saw. Cut out the pieces. (A scroll saw is really the best tool to use here because almost no sanding is required after the cuts have been complete.)

When all the cars have been cut out, drill the 5/16"-diameter axle holes. Sand all the edges of the cars smooth, paying particular attention to splinters and sharp edges.

3. WHEELS

Make the wheels for this simple old-time train using a hole saw. For the 1-1/4"-diameter wheels, use a 1-3/8"-diameter hole saw; for the 2-1/4"-diameter locomotive wheels, use a 2-3/8"-diameter hole saw. Make all wheels out of 3/4" stock along with extras for future toys. Once you've cut out the wheels, sand them smooth.

Cut axles to length; then glue the wheels to the axles.

4. FINISHING TOUCHES

Drill a 3/32"-diameter hole in the end of each car and insert the screw hooks and eyes. Crimp the hooks so the eyes barely fit onto them and turn the hook to the *down* position for safety. Leave the wood natural or paint it with primer and nontoxic paints.

MATERIALS

Part	Description	Pieces	Dimensions
			(finished dimensions in inches)
A	Engine	1	3/4 × 3-1/2 × 6
B	Tender	1	3/4 × 2-1/4 × 2-3/4
C	Hopper Car	1	3/4 × 2-1/4 × 3-1/2
D	Boxcar	1	3/4 × 3-1/2 × 3-1/2
E	Caboose	1	3/4 × 3-1/2 × 2-3/4
F	Large wheels	2	2-1/4 dia. × 3/4
G	Small wheels	20	1-1/4 dia. × 3/4
H	Axles (not shown)	11	1/4 dia. × 2-3/8

FANCY PULL-ALONG TRAIN

This version of a pull-along train is fancier than the previous train and provides more interest for the older toddler. This project requires only a 4'-long piece of 1 × 4 stock, is simple to build, and goes together fast. Be sure to read through all the instructions before making any cuts.

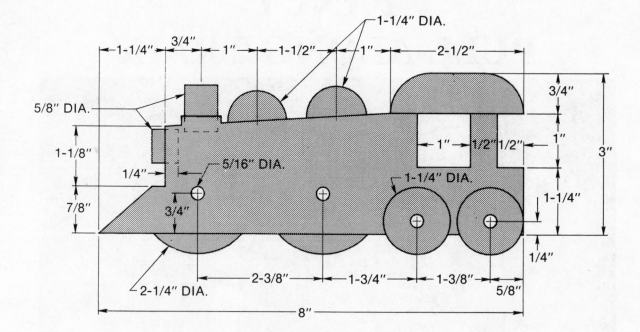

ENGINE DETAIL

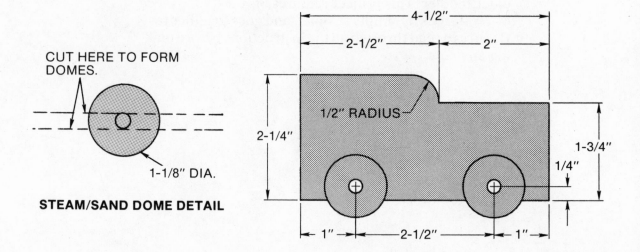

STEAM/SAND DOME DETAIL

TENDER DETAIL

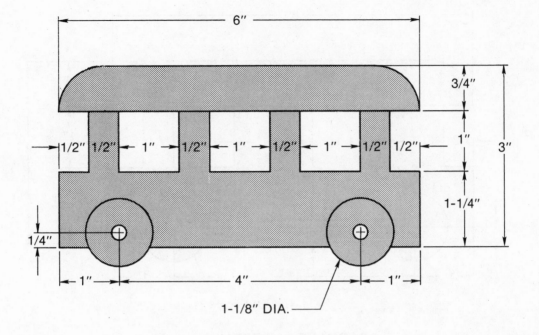

PASSENGER CAR DETAIL

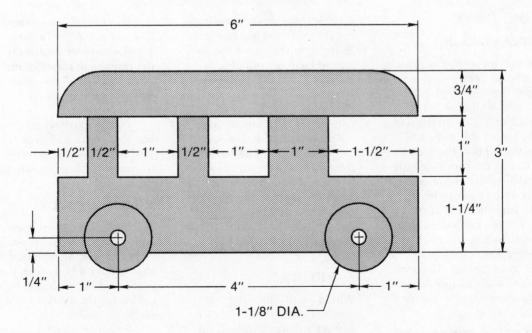

OBSERVATION CAR DETAIL

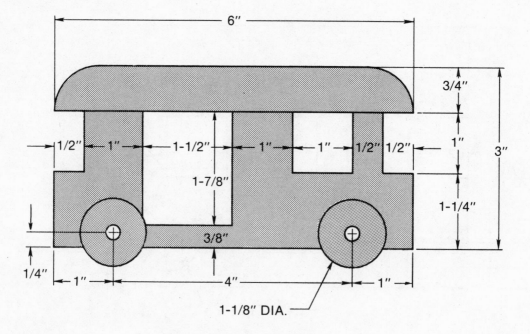

BAGGAGE CAR DETAIL

PROCEDURE

1. PREPARATION

Although these train cars look complicated, construction is simple. Rip a 3/4″ × 3-1/2″ × 32″ piece of stock to 3-1/4″ width. Cut 3/4″ from the width of the board; this piece will form the roofs of the cars.

Cut all the cars to length as specified under Materials; then cut the roofs to length. Make sure the roofs correspond to the car bodies. (It's possible to crosscut all the cars to length first, then rip-cut the roofs from the cars. However, if you're using a table saw, the cars are too small to handle safely when cutting.)

2. CUTTING THE SHAPES

Making cardboard templates for this train means constructing future trains will be easier. Refer to the plans for the required location and dimensions of the doors, windows, and roof profiles of the various cars. Also, don't forget to locate the 5/16″-diameter axle holes on each of the cars.

Once you've laid out all the profiles, use a scroll saw or bandsaw to cut out the shapes. Sand the shapes; drill the axle holes; then drill the 1/4″-deep holes for the headlamp (D) and the smokestack (C) in the locomotive.

3. WHEELS

With a 2-3/8″-diameter hole saw, cut out the four 2-1/4″-diameter drive wheels (I) for the locomotive. Sand the wheels and set aside.

Use a 1-3/8″-diameter hole saw to cut out the twenty 1-1/4″-diameter wheels (J) for the remaining cars. Cut out one extra 1-1/4″-diameter wheel for the steam/sand domes (B).

On the extra wheel draw a line just above and below the 1/4″ pilot hole. Use a scroll saw to cut along these lines to form the two domes.

4. LOCOMOTIVE

The locomotive is the most complicated car, but it's still rather simple. At this point you should have a body with the profile cut out on it and holes drilled for the axles, smokestack, and headlamp.

Finish construction by gluing and clamping the steam and sand domes to the top edge of the boiler. Next, cut the smokestack and headlamp to length and glue them into place. Finally, cut the axles to length and assemble the wheels and axles with glue.

5. ASSEMBLY
Assemble the rest of the cars by gluing and clamping the roofs to the profiled car bodies. After the glue dries, power-sand the sides of each car flush and knock off all sharp edges. Assemble the wheels and axles to the cars.

Finish the cars by drilling a 3/32"-diameter hole in the end of each car. Install the screw hooks and eyes. After mounting the screw hooks, turn them facing down; then crimp them so the screw eyes barely slip in and out.

If you like, you can paint the train—first with a coat of primer, then with a coat of nontoxic paint.

Your old-time pull-along train is complete and ready to serve the needs of an eager child...all aboooard!

MATERIALS

Part	Description	Pieces	Dimensions
			(finished dimensions in inches)
A	Locomotive	1	3/4 × 3-1/8 × 8
B	Steam/sand domes	2	3/4 × 1/2 × 1-1/8
C	Smokestack	1	5/8 dia. × 1
D	Headlamp	1	5/8 dia. × 1/2
E	Tender	1	3/4 × 2-1/4 × 4-1/2
F	Baggage car	1	3/4 × 3-1/8 × 6
G	Passenger car	1	3/4 × 3-1/8 × 6
H	Observation car	1	3/4 × 3-1/8 × 6
I	Large wheels	4	2-1/4 dia. × 3/4
J	Small wheels	20	1-1/4 dia. × 3/4
K	Axles	12	1/4 dia. × 2-3/8

MISCELLANEOUS
1-1/8" screw eyes (4)
1-5/8" screw hooks (4)

CONSTRUCTION NOTES
1. Dimensions of the cars include roof dimensions.

2. Steam/sand domes are made from a 1-1/4"-diameter wheel blank.